The Genesis+ Experiment

How Genesis 1:1 – Exodus 19:2
can help you know God better

by
Andrew Page

VTR
Publications

ISBN 978-3-95776-174-3

Author photo on the back cover:
(c) Roger Eldridge Photography, www.eldridgephotos.com

Cover design: Chris Allcock / VTR Publications

Contents

Acknowledgements

I am grateful to Chris Allcock for his willingness, once again, to do the drawings and the cover design, and especially to Thomas Mayer for agreeing to publish this book.

A number of people read the manuscript and gave me their comments and suggestions, so I am glad to thank them here: Graham Ball, Beth Devonish, Gerhild Haitchi, Callom Harkrader, Biddy Taylor and Wolfgang Widmann.

I owe a huge debt to friends, many of them (but not all) in Above Bar Church Southampton, who pray for me and encourage me. I would be a lesser person without my church family.

As I have learnt to meditate my way through Genesis 1:1 – Exodus 19:2, my love for God has grown, along with my desire to tell others about him. I pray that many people will make the same discovery.

To God be the glory!

Andrew Page
andrew@themarkdrama.com

My Introduction: Invitation to an Experiment

This is a book about two things at once.

First, it's about learning Genesis+ (which is what I call Genesis 1:1 – Exodus 19:2). I don't think this material was written to be read but to be listened to: few, if any, in the ancient world could own a copy for themselves. It was written so people could memorize it. Not word for word, but chunk by chunk – so they could get to know God better and share the story with one another.

So, second, this is a book about loving God more. You may already know the book of Genesis and the first eighteen chapters of Exodus very well, or you may just be starting out: but as we spend time together in this material the aim will be that as a result we will love and enjoy God more. If that's what you want, you're in the right place.

So that's what the experiment is about: learning Genesis+ so that our love for God will grow. I hope you will try it out for yourself.

Please take time to read the rest of this introduction. It won't take you long, but it will help you get the maximum out of *The Genesis+ Experiment*.

The Structure of Genesis+

There are many suggested structures for the books of Genesis and Exodus. But I have only found one that is *learnable*, so that it's possible to learn the order of the events from Genesis 1:1 to Exodus 19:2.

The first books of our Old Testament were not originally individual books: the division into Genesis, Exodus, Leviticus etc was made later.

In his book *The Literary Structure of the Old Testament*, Dr David Dorsey suggests that the first major block of material is Genesis 1:1 – Exodus 19:2. What I find particularly persuasive about this is that Genesis+ is *learnable*.

(For more on the structure of Genesis+ and details about Dorsey's book, go to Appendix 1.)

Dorsey identifies seven main sections in Genesis+. The headings are mine, but the sections themselves are Dorsey's:

Section A	Primeval History	Genesis 1:1 – 11:32
Section B	*The Abraham Story*	Genesis 12:1 – 21:7
Section C	The Isaac Story	Genesis 21:8 – 28:4
Section D	*The Jacob Story*	Genesis 28:5 – 37:1
Section C'	The Joseph Story	Genesis 37:2 – 50:26
Section B'	*The Exodus Story*	Exodus 1:1 – 13:16
Section A'	Wilderness Journey	Exodus 13:17 – 19:2

Each of the sections is constructed in such a way that it's easy to get an overview of the whole.

Look, for example, at Section B. Here is the structure:

Section B: The Abraham Story / Genesis 12:1 – 21:7

a. Introduction: the promise of descendants (12:1-9)
b. *Abram lies about Sarai in Egypt* (12:10-20)
c. Lot settles in Sodom (13:1-18)
d. *Abram intercedes for Lot and Sodom militarily* (14:1-24)
e. Promise of a son: from Abram himself (15:1-21)
f. *Ishmael: his birth* (16:1-16)
g. **CENTRE: God's covenant with Abram/Abraham** (17:1-21)
f'. *Ishmael: his circumcision* (17:22-27)
e'. Promise of a son: from Sarah herself (18:1-15)
d'. *Abraham intercedes for Lot and Sodom in prayer* (18:16-33)
c'. Lot flees Sodom, which God destroys (19:1-38)
b'. *Abraham lies about Sarah in Gerar* (20:1-18)
a'. Conclusion: the birth of Isaac (21:1-7)

There are five things to notice about this structure:

1. The section contains mirror links

You will see that incident a and incident a' have something in common, and b and b', and c and c' etc. This makes learning the order of the events surprisingly simple.

And the structure of every one of the seven sections involves mirror links in some way.

2. The section has a main topic

In Section B it's the story of Abraham, all the way from God promising him descendants to the birth of Isaac.

As we noted above, Section A's topic is primeval history, from creation to the tower of Babel, while the following four sections focus in turn on Abraham, Isaac, Jacob and Joseph.

The final two sections are about the Exodus of God's people from Egypt, and their wilderness journey to Mount Sinai.

(For the complete outline of this structure of Genesis+, see Appendix 4.)

3. The section has a symbol which serves as a visual aid

This symbol points to the central message of the section. In Section B it's the altar. As Abraham encounters God this moves him to worship, so he builds an altar. This is a visual aid for what's happening in his heart: he's getting to know God.

Each section, apart from Sections A and A', has its own symbol.

4. The section has a mirror link with another section

This means that *Section B: The Abraham story* is mirror-linked with *Section B': The Exodus story* (Exodus 1:1 – 13:16). The two sections have a number of things in common.

Section A and Section A' are mirror-linked too, as are Sections C and C'. Section D, however, doesn't have a mirror link with another section because it forms the centre of Genesis+.

(For more on the mirror links between the sections, see Appendix 2.)

5. The section can easily be learnt by heart

This is not about learning every word, but simply the order of the events in the section. I have tested this: most people can do this in 15 minutes, especially if they have read through the whole section in their Bible first, so that they know the stories.

And this is true of all the sections.

But why should I learn Genesis+ by heart?

That's a great question. But there are some very good reasons:

I.   Because the Bible is the word of God it has remarkable power. We often forget this. In Psalm 119:11 David says to God: *I have hidden your word in my heart that I might not sin against you.*

II.   Because the material is structured as it is. If you read *The Genesis+ Experiment* you will notice how easy it is to learn the order of the events. My guess is that the Holy Spirit arranged this because he wants us to have his word in our hearts.

III.   Because learning scripture in this way makes it possible to do Bible study in the shower without getting your Bible wet! Of course I normally have my Bible with me when I'm doing Bible study, but sometimes it's brilliant to meditate on the Bible just using your memory. So as you are walking down the road you can tell yourself the Genesis+ events and begin talking to God about what you're remembering.

IV.   Because I would love you to experience what I have experienced. Since my student days Genesis has been my favourite Old Testament book, but only in the last few years have I been able to meditate my way through the material (with the first eighteen chapters of Exodus thrown in). The Holy Spirit has used this to help my love for God to grow. And this makes me want to share this with others.

How to use this book

This book is one you can read through instead of just using for reference. As we look at the seven main sections of Genesis+ there'll be an introduction called *Enjoying the View*: this provides the structure, the main theme of the section and the symbol which points to it.

Next comes *Unpacking the Content*. Here I look at each part of the section in turn, explaining the message and showing us the greatness of God.

Then I make some suggestions as to how you can memorize the section (this is called *Learning Genesis+*). Most people aren't used to learning by heart, but it really is worth it. And remember we're not talking about learning every word but the order of events in the section. As I mentioned above, most people can do this in 15 minutes.

One good way of getting the learning done is to team up with a friend. You agree to both read through, say, Section A and learn the order of events. Then you meet up to go for a walk or have a coffee, and re-tell the section together (see My Conclusion, point 3, page 214, for more details). Doing this with a friend will help you to do the learning rather than just skip it!

The last part is called *Meeting God*. This is a reminder of the reason we are doing all this: we want to rediscover the greatness of God. As you talk to him about what you have been reading you will start knowing, admiring and loving God more.

Please don't read *The Genesis+ Experiment* too quickly. You might want to take at least a week over each of the seven sections, so that you have time to let what you are reading sink in. You might want to meet up with a friend once a week who is also trying the experiment, to tell one another the stories and talk about the greatness of God.

Or you might just want to choose one of the seven sections and focus on that for a few weeks. If one section intrigues you more than the others, start there.

Thank you for reading my introduction. Now it's time to turn to Section A of Genesis+.

I am praying that everyone who reads this book will enjoy Genesis+ and enjoy getting to know God better. The Genesis+ experiment starts here…

Section A
Primeval History (Genesis 1:1 – 11:32)

The opening could not be bolder: *In the beginning God...* We all want to know where we came from, even if that's just discovering information about our great-grandparents. But Genesis+ takes us back to the very start, to God's decision to create. In Section A we will learn about Creation, the Fall, the flood and the tower of Babel. And through it all we will see God's righteousness and God's grace.

When the dove returned to him in the evening,
there in its beak was a freshly plucked olive leaf!
Then Noah knew
that the water had receded from the earth.

Genesis 8:11

Enjoying the View

a. Creation (1:1 – 2:3)
b. *Degeneration* (2:4 – 4:26)
c. Ten generations from Adam to Noah (5:1 – 6:8)

a'. The flood (6:9 – 9:29)
b'. *Degeneration* (10:1 – 11:9)
c'. Ten generations from Shem to Abram (11:10-26)

d. Conclusion: Introducing Abram (11:27-32)

Section A covers a long period of time in eleven chapters. Six times we read the words *This is the account...* (see chapter 2:4; 5:1; 6:9; 10:1; 11:10; 11:27): it looks like the phrase marks a new beginning. The result is that the material is divided into seven parts.

In parts a, b and c we see that after God's act of creation, humanity begins to turn away from his authority: everything goes downhill. And we learn that there was a descendant of Adam called Noah.

In parts a', b' and c' there is a similar pattern. God judges humanity's rebellion by sending a flood, but there is almost a new act of creation as everything starts again with Noah. But, once again, things fall apart: men and women continue to disobey God.

So, at the end of Section A, we are introduced to a descendant of Noah called Abram. What God will do with this man will be the focus of Section B.

It would be good to read through the first eleven chapters of the book of Genesis before reading on in *The Genesis+ Experiment*. Take the opportunity to talk to God about what you're reading: he is always inviting us to *meet* him.

Unpacking the Content

a. – Creation (1:1 – 2:3)

It's the title for the whole chapter: *In the beginning God created the heavens and the earth* (1). Everything that exists finds its origin in him.

Christians have different views as to how literally we should take this passage. Did God create everything in six literal days, or did he use an evolutionary process to make the world and the universe?

You could argue that the structure of the chapter is intended to be logical rather than chronological. But what all Christians agree on is that God created everything. *How* he did it is less important than *that* he did it.

And that is unmistakeably the message of this chapter.

As God begins the work of creation, there is *darkness* [...] *over the surface of the deep* (2). And *the Spirit of God was hovering over the waters* (2b).

Three things about God are worth noting before we look at the six days one by one.

We see **God's power**. He speaks, and then we read *And it was so* (7b, 9b, 11b, 15b, 24b and 30b). When *we* create, we are using what already exists, but when God creates he creates out of nothing.

And he does it by speaking words.

We also see **God's joy**. On Day One God creates light and *saw that the light was good* (4). And that becomes pretty much a refrain throughout the chapter (see 10b, 12b, 18b, 21b and 25b). He is satisfied with his handiwork.

And when creation is finished, *God saw all that he had made, and it was very good* (31a).

And there is **God's plan**, too. When he has just begun the work of creation *the earth was formless and empty* (2a). During the first three days God creates form, or spaces, so that the earth is no longer *formless*; during the next three days he fills those spaces, so that the earth is no longer *empty*.

1. God makes spaces (1:3-13). It's like creating rooms in a house, but this is spaces in the universe. The enormity of this should fill us with awe.

+ On Day One, God creates light and dark (see 3-5). And he calls *the light 'day', and the darkness he called 'night'* (5).

+ On Day Two, God creates sea and sky (see 6-8). He makes a *vault and separated the water under the vault from the water above it* (7).

+ On Day Three, God creates fertile earth (see 9-13). He says *Let the water under the sky be gathered to one place, and let dry ground appear* (9). But he is not finished yet. God says *Let the land produce vegetation* (11a): now there are plants and trees.

God has created these spaces, so the earth is no longer *formless.* But it is still *empty.*

Which brings us to the next three days.

2. God fills the spaces (1:14-25). It's worth noticing that the paragraphs for the fifth and sixth days are longer, as God's creative activity unleashes a huge diversity of life.

+ **On Day Four**, God creates the sun and the moon (see 14-19). He speaks into existence *lights in the vault of the sky to separate the day from the night* (14). And we read that God *also made the stars* (16b).

+ **On Day Five**, God creates creatures of the water and of the air (see 20-23). He makes *every living thing with which the water teems and that moves about in it* and *every winged bird* (21). And then God speaks again, telling these animals to *be fruitful and increase in number and fill the water in the seas, and let the birds increase on the earth* (22).

+ **On Day Six**, God creates creatures of the land (see 24-30). He speaks into existence *the wild animals according to their kinds, the livestock according to their kinds, and all the creatures that move along the ground according to their kinds* (25).

But now comes something that will take our breath away. God does something else on Day Six.

3. God creates humankind (1:26 – 2:3). As he does this, God says *Let us make mankind in our image, in our likeness* (26a). This is the first time he has said *Let us*: it's like this is a divine pronouncement to the heavenly court.

So important is this that the writer tells us again what God did, and underlines it by using poetry: *So God created mankind in his own image, in the image of God he created them* (27a).

On the one hand human beings are in the same category as the land animals, created on the same day as them. But on the other hand we are God-like, made in his *likeness* and *image.* You can't say that about any other part of creation.

This is probably not two things about human beings, but rather two ways of stating one thing: we are made in God's image, we are *like God.*

Whatever this means it applies to all humankind. The writer ends his poetic summary by telling us this: *Male and female he created them* (27b).

But what *does* it mean? What do human beings do that animals don't?

Only to human beings does God give the command to *rule* over all the animals (26 and 28b). They are to *be fruitful and increase in number; fill the earth and subdue it* (28a).

Which doesn't mean *ransack* or *subjugate* (although sometimes we've behaved as if it did). It means *take charge* and *cultivate*.

So God is calling humankind to look after his world. This is surely part of what it means that we are made in his image.

But there is more about this in chapter 2 of Genesis.

Now God promises to provide humankind and all the animals with food (see 29-30). And Day Six ends with a reminder of God's joy and satisfaction as he looks at his creation: he *saw all that he had made, and it was very good* (31a).

God's creation work is done: *the heavens and the earth were completed in all their vast array* (2:1). And so we learn that *on the seventh day he rested from all his work* (2:2).

Because of that God *blessed the seventh day and made it holy* (2:3).

b. – Degeneration (2:4 – 4:26)

This is the account… signals the beginning of a new part of the narrative (2:4). We return to the time when *the LORD God made the earth and the heavens* (2:4b).

But now we are invited to focus on humankind: three descriptions show us the downhill path of degeneration.

But the starting point for humankind is entirely positive.

1. Made in God's image (2:5-25). We've seen this already (see chapter 1:27), but now this is fleshed out for us. After a brief summary of creation (see 5-6), we're reminded that *the LORD God formed a man from the dust of the ground and breathed into his nostrils the breath of life* (7).

The result is that *the man became a living being* (7b).

But what does it mean that the man is made in God's image? What does the man do that animals don't? In what ways is he like God?

It's worth noticing five things.

+ He enjoys beauty (8-14). God has put the man in *a garden in the east, in Eden* (8a). In this garden are four rivers to ensure that the plants God has made will flourish (see 10-14).

But the spotlight is on the trees, which are *pleasing to the eye and good for food* (9b). Whose eye are we talking about? This must be about the man: he sees the trees not only as a source of food, but also as good to look at.

In other words, he is appreciating beauty. As far as we know, animals don't do that. But the God who appreciates beauty (see chapter 1:31a) has made humankind in his image.

So we enjoy beauty too.

Because of what we will read later, it's important that we learn that two of the trees have names: *the tree of life and the tree of the knowledge of good and evil* (9b).

But there's a second thing the man does.

+ He digs his garden (15). There's a reason God has put the man in the Garden of Eden: *to work it and take care of it* (15b).

We've already been told that God is a worker: *By the seventh day God had finished the work he had been doing* (2a). Now we're seeing that, because humankind is made in God's image, the man is a worker too.

When human beings work, that is an expression of our being made in God's image. But there is more to come.

+ He practises self-control (16-17). God is unbelievably generous: he tells the man that he may *eat from any tree in the garden* (16).

But there is one exception: the man *must not eat from the tree of the knowledge of good and evil* (17a).

This is God treating the man as someone who can practise self-control. He isn't a robot, but a person: made in God's image.

And he's warned of the consequences of disobedience: God tells him that *when you eat from it you will certainly die* (17b).

But there is more we can say about this man made in God's image.

+ He is creative (18-20). God recognises that *it is not good for the man to be alone* (18a): so he decides to *make a helper suitable for him* (18b).

God brings all the animals he's made to the man: will any of them be the helper he needs? But God also wants to see *what he would name them* (19b).

So this is God inviting the man to be creative, and taking his decisions seriously: *whatever the man called each living creature, that was its name* (19b).

Creativity is part of what it means for us to be made in God's image.

However, none of these animals is the solution to the man's aloneness: *for Adam no suitable helper was found* (20b).

So God creates the solution, which the man rejoices in.

+ He embraces the woman (21-25). Using one of the man's ribs (see 21), God *made a woman* (22) and *brought her to the man* (22b).

The man is so delighted that he launches into poetry: *This is now bone of my bones and flesh of my flesh* (23a).

God is love: the Father loves the Son and the Spirit; the Son loves the Father and the Spirit; the Spirit loves the Father and the Son.

And so relationship is part of what makes us like God. And this is the origin of marriage: *That is why a man leaves his father and mother and is united to his wife, and they become one flesh* (24).

So humankind, the pinnacle of creation, is made in God's image.

But now the degeneration begins: we see human beings turning away from God.

2. Disobedient to God's command (3:1-24). This chapter tells us about humankind's rebellion against God, known as the Fall.

It's important to see that the Fall is a historical event. Christians differ as to whether the tree, the fruit and the snake are to be taken literally, but there must have been a moment of human rebellion against God's rule: if there wasn't, that means that God created a spoilt world. Which would make sin his fault and not ours.

Genesis chapter 3 explains the meaning of the Fall.

+ Seduction (1-7). The snake is a representation of Satan, an evil personality who hates human beings because he hates God.

He draws the woman into conversation with his question *Did God really say..?* (1b). Her reply mentions God's generosity about the trees made available to them (see 2), but also God's prohibition about the tree of the knowledge of good and evil: *You must not eat* and *you must not touch it* (3).

And she remembers the penalty for disobedience, too: God has warned them that they *will die* (3b).

Now the seduction grows. Satan flatly contradicts what God has said: *You will not certainly die* (4). When the man and the woman eat the fruit of that tree they *will be like God, knowing good and evil* (5b).

This is like saying that they will become like little gods, able to live independently of the God who made them.

And so it happens. The woman likes what she sees (see 6a): the fruit is *desirable for gaining wisdom,* so *she took some and ate it* (6b). And *she also gave some to her husband, who was with her, and he ate it* (6c).

The man and the woman realise that *they were naked* (7); they have rejected God's authority. The seduction is complete.

And now we learn about the first results of the Fall.

+ Alienation (8-13). Put simply, sin separates, and in two respects.

There is vertical alienation. When Adam and his wife hear God coming, *they hid from the LORD God among the trees of the garden* (8b). And when God asks Adam *Where are you?* (9), he replies *I was afraid because I was naked; so I hid* (10).

The relationship between humans and God is broken: sin has separated the man and the woman from their Creator.

But there is horizontal alienation too. When God asks Adam *Have you eaten from the tree…?* he tries to shift the blame on to his wife: *The woman you put here with me – she gave me some fruit from the tree, and I ate it* (12).

And the blame game continues. When God asks the woman *What is this you have done?* she replies that she is not the one who is at fault: *The snake deceived me, and I ate* (13b).

Sin separates: it causes vertical and horizontal alienation. But there is another result too.

+ Judgment (14-20). The snake, representing Satan, is the first to hear words of judgment from God: *Cursed are you…* (14a).

Satan has seduced the woman, but one day one of her descendants will destroy Satan. God tells Satan that *I will put enmity between you and the woman, and between your offspring and hers* (15a).

A human being will come, says God, who will *crush your head* (15b): this is talking about God's judgment on Satan.

But in the process this human figure will himself suffer: Satan will *strike his heel* (15b).

This is astonishing. God's judgment on Satan will mean grace and rescue for humanity. This is the first good news in Genesis after the disaster of the Fall: a human being will one day destroy Satan and his works.

And the rest of the Bible will tell us the fulfilment of that promise as it points us to Jesus and his cross (and see Rom 16:20).

And now God speaks words of judgment to the woman. She will have pain in childbirth (see 16a), and her relationship with Adam will be damaged: *Your desire will be for your husband, and he will rule over you* (16b).

This doesn't sound like marriage characterised by loving and cherishing, but rather by desiring and dominating.

There are words of judgment for Adam, too. Not only is his relationship with his wife damaged; his relationship with nature is damaged, too: *Cursed is the ground because of you* (17b).

There will be *thorns and thistles* (18a), and getting food from *the plants of the field* (18b) will involve *painful toil* (17b).

Adam named his wife Eve (20a): she will be *the mother of all the living* (20b; *Eve* probably means *living*).

It's been a bleak picture. God's judgment falls on human disobedience. But, after seduction, alienation and judgment, there is something else too.

+ Grace (21-24). We've already seen this in the first promise of good news, as Satan received his judgment from God (see 15).

But now there is more grace at the end of the chapter.

God makes *garments of skin for Adam and his wife* (21). And now comes something which sounds like judgment but is actually grace. God takes Adam and *banished him from the Garden of Eden* (23): *he drove the man out* (24a).

But why does God do this? He has decided that Adam *must not be allowed to reach out his hand and take also from the tree of life, and live for ever* (22b).

If Adam were to do this, he would be a sinner for ever, under God's judgment for ever, spiritually dead for ever.

God is being gracious. He positions *cherubim and a flaming sword flashing back and forth to guard the way to the tree of life* (24b).

This is amazing grace. Adam and Eve are banished from the garden: God is barring the way to their eating from the tree of life and becoming sinners for ever.

And one day a Saviour will come (see 15).

So far we have seen human beings *made in God's image* and then *disobedient to God's command.*

And now the results of God's judgment are spelt out for us even more clearly. As we discover something else about humanity, we see that the degeneration continues.

3. Excluded from God's presence (4:1-24). As we begin to look at Adam's family there is clear evidence that things are deteriorating further. Chapter 4 develops in five stages.

+ Murder (1-8). Adam and Eve have two sons: Cain and Abel. Eve recognises that this is *with the help of the LORD* (1).

Now we're told the background for what is about to happen: *Abel kept flocks, and Cain worked the soil* (2b). Apparently without being prompted, they both want to bring *an offering to the LORD* (3). God looks *with favour on Abel and his offering, but on Cain and his offering he did not look with favour* (4b-5a).

Why is this?

The answer the text gives us is that, while Abel offers fat portions *from some of the firstborn of his flock* (4a), Cain simply brings *some of the fruits of the soil* (3). Cain brings *some* of what he has, while Abel brings *the best* of what he has.

God reasons with Cain, asking him why he's angry (see 6), and warning him that *if you do not do what is right, sin is crouching at your door* (7b). God is teaching him about the dangers of sin: *it desires to have you, but you must rule over it* (7b).

Cain makes his decision. While they are in the fields, *Cain attacked his brother Abel and killed him* (8).

This is desperately sad: the first murder has taken place. So it is clear what comes next.

+ Judgment (9-16). When asked by God where his brother is, Cain is evasive: *Am I my brother's keeper?* (9b). There is no trace of regret or repentance.

God's judgment comes because *your brother's blood cries out to me* (10): everything done in secret is seen by him.

Now Cain is *under a curse* (11a): when he works the ground *it will no longer yield its crops for you* (12a). And, even worse, Cain will be *a restless wanderer on the earth* (12b).

Cain cries out to God that *my punishment is more than I can bear* (13). He is in fear of his life (see 14b) and, worst of all, *I will be hidden from your presence* (14a).

God reassures him that he will not be killed and *puts a mark on Cain so that no one… would kill him* (15b).

But the judgment is clear. Cain is excluded from fellowship with God, and so *went out from the LORD's presence* (16).

+ Culture (17-22). A descendant of Cain is called Lamech (see 17-18): he has two wives, which was not God's original intention (see chapter 2:24).

But it is not all bad news.

Lamech's three sons start doing things which are the beginnings of human culture. Jabal is *the father of those who live in tents and raise livestock* (20); Jubal is *the father of all who play stringed instruments and pipes* (21); Tubal-Cain *forged all kinds of tools out of bronze and iron* (22).

The family may, like Lamech, be godless, but the three brothers are all made in God's image: their music and their technology demonstrate a creativity that mirrors God's.

And now we get a further glimpse of Lamech's godlessness.

+ Revenge (23-24). Lamech boasts to his wives that he has *killed a man for wounding me* (23). The punishment is greater than the crime.

Lamech will stop at nothing in his desire for revenge: *If Cain is avenged seven times, then Lamech seventy-seven times* (24). This short poem (see 23-24) may suggest that Lamech is in the habit of repeating his commitment to violence.

Culture may be developing, but humanity's moral sense is deteriorating. This is another reminder that the degeneration which began at the Fall is continuing.

However, there is good news at the end of chapter 4.

+ Grace (25-26). Adam and Eve have another son: his name is Seth. Eve sees God's hand in this: he has *granted me another child instead of Abel* (25 and see 1; *Seth* probably means *granted*).

Adam and Eve may have disobeyed God's command, but he is still being kind to them. And Seth has a son, which Abel never had the chance to do.

And now we're told something which should make us catch our breath again: *At that time people began to call on the name of the LORD* (26b).

Despite the degeneration, people are beginning to cry out to God for a relationship with him. Not everyone, but it's happening.

This is God's grace at work: he's not giving up on humankind.

c. – Ten generations from Adam to Noah (5:1 – 6:8)

Chapter 5 of Genesis marks a new beginning with the refrain *This is the written account...* (1a; see also chapter 2:4). This is reinforced by the reminder that humankind was created *in the likeness of God* and *male and female* (1b-2a; and see chapter 1:26-27).

This chapter counts down the generations through Adam and Eve's third son, Seth (see 3-4). Abel is dead, and Cain's line godless, so the focus is on Adam's descendants through Seth.

A glance at the list reveals that these people lived very long lives: Adam died at 930, Seth at 912 and Enosh at 905. I think there is every reason to believe that these numbers are meant literally: I have no difficulty in believing that before the flood people's life-span was much greater.

But what unites nearly everyone in Genesis chapter 5 is that they died. Since Adam and Eve's rebellion in the Garden of Eden, human life comes to an end: we die.

But not everyone.

The seventh position in *Cain's* genealogy was occupied by bloodthirsty Lamech (see chapter 4:18, 23-24), but the seventh place in *Seth's* belongs to godly Enoch (18). The contrast could hardly be greater.

And Enoch escapes death.

We're told twice that he *walked faithfully with God* (22 and 24). This man is in relationship with God: his whole life centres on this. The expression suggests a daily, intimate friendship.

Did God tell Enoch that he was going to send a flood and destroy human-kind? Did he tell him that this flood would come only after his son Methuselah had died? The account doesn't teach this, but some simple addition shows that the flood came in the year Methuselah died (see chapter 5:25, 27-28 and chapter 7:6).

And the letter of Jude in the New Testament tells us that Enoch prophesied about God's coming judgment (see Jude 14 and 15).

But in any case, in Genesis chapter 5 we suddenly find ourselves reading that Enoch *was no more, because God took him away* (24).

Enoch is a sign of hope. Death does not always have the last word.

And Noah occupies the tenth position in the genealogy (see 29). God is going to do something extraordinary through him.

The next time the refrain *This is the account...* occurs isn't till chapter 6 verse 9. So, after reading about the ten generations from Adam to Noah, there are two crucial things we need to learn.

1. The degeneration continues (6:1-4). However we understand this paragraph, a new stage is being reached in the progress of evil.

Is *the sons of God* (2) a reference to angels? Are we intended to see *the Nephilim* as the result of these angelic beings having sex with *the daughters of humans* (4 and 2)?

These are questions we cannot answer. But clearly this development is seen as negative. It results in God making a decision: *their days will be a hundred and twenty years* (3).

But he makes another decision too.

2. The judgment comes (6:5-8). This last paragraph tells us three things about God.

+ First, what he sees (5). God sees *how great the wickedness of the human race had become.* But there's more: *every inclination of the thoughts of the human heart was only evil all the time* (5). God's diagnosis couldn't be bleaker.

+ Second, what he feels (6). These words are shocking: *The LORD regretted that he had made human beings* (6a); *his heart was deeply troubled* (6b). God is sorry that he had ever decided to create humankind.

So the last thing we read about God is inevitable.

+ Third, what he decides (7). God decides to *wipe from the face of the earth the human race I have created,* as well as every other living thing

(7). And he repeats the reason for this judgment: it's because *I regret that I have made them* (7b).

So judgment and destruction are coming.

But now, right at the end of the paragraph, as we have seen before, there is a note of grace and hope (see chapter 3:22, 4:26b).

Noah, we are told, *found favour in the eyes of the Lord* (8). This is a surprise: after what we have just read it would be easy to believe that there was no room for grace.

But Noah found God's grace.

And the best way of understanding that is to read it the other way round: God's grace found Noah.

a'. – The flood (6:9 – 9:29)

In the centre of this account, we read that *God remembered Noah* (chapter 8:1a).

Before that key phrase we see God's judgment as he floods the earth and destroys nearly every living being. *After* the key phrase we see God's grace at work as the world recovers from the flood: it's an act of re-creation.

So one way of looking at this account is to see it in six stages, with the key phrase *God remembered Noah* halfway through.

1. God's command to build the ark (6:9-22). The account reminds us of two things. First, that Noah is *a righteous man, blameless among the people of his time* (9). And, like Enoch, he *walked faithfully with God* (9b, and see chapter 5:24).

The second reminder is that the earth is *corrupt* and *full of violence* (11).

And so God tells Noah that he is going to *put an end to all people* (13). But there is grace here too: Noah is to build *an ark of cypress wood* (14).

The instructions are detailed (see 14-16). The ark is huge, but of course it won't need to be launched: it's a chest rather than a boat.

And God spells out what he is going to do. First, there's judgment: *I am going to bring floodwaters on the earth* (17a); *everything on earth will perish* (17b).

But there's also grace: *I will establish my covenant with you, and you will enter the ark* (18a). And Noah and his family are to *bring into the ark two of all living creatures, male and female, to keep them alive with you* (19).

In other words, this is not simply judgment on creation: there is going to be a re-creation, as Noah and his family, and all these animals, are *kept alive* (20b).

So God commands Noah to build the ark. And, crucially, *Noah did everything just as God commanded him* (22).

2. God's command to board the ark (7:1-5). Noah is to *go into the ark,* because God has found him *righteous in this generation* (1).

He is to take his *whole family* with him (1), as well as *seven pairs of every kind of clean animal.., one pair of every kind of unclean animal* (2) and *seven pairs of every kind of bird* (3a).

The aim of all this, says God, is to *keep their various kinds alive throughout the earth* (3b).

So God commands Noah to board the ark, with his family and the animals. And, once again, *Noah did all that the LORD commanded him* (5).

3. The flood arrives (7:6-24). Noah, we read, *was six hundred years old when the floodwaters came on the earth* (6).

He doesn't need to go looking for the animals: the pairs *came to Noah and entered the ark* (9).

And then it happens: *the springs of the great deep burst forth, and the floodgates of the heavens were opened* (11b): *and the rain fell on the earth for forty days and forty nights* (12).

But Noah, his family and the animals are safe: God has *shut him in* (16b).

During the forty days the flood *kept coming on the earth* (17a), and *as the waters increased they lifted the ark high above the earth* (17b). Even *the high mountains... were covered* (19).

The judgment is complete: *every living thing that moved on land perished... and all mankind* (21), because *the waters flooded the earth for a hundred and fifty days* (24).

But we're reminded of God's grace, too: *Only Noah was left, and those with him in the ark* (23b).

+ *But God remembered Noah* (chapter 8:1a). The first three stages of the flood account are finished, and God remembers Noah: he hasn't forgotten his promise.

And so we arrive at the last three stages of the account: they point to a re-creation.

4. The flood recedes (8:1-22). Now that the rain has stopped, *the water receded steadily from the earth* (3a). Seven months after the end of the flood *the ark came to rest on the mountains of Ararat* (4).

And three months after that, *the tops of the mountains became visible* (5b).

So Noah wants to find out how much the waters have receded. First, he sends out a raven, because it's an unclean bird: it's no use for food or for sacrifice. The raven *kept flying back and forth until the water had dried up from the earth* (7).

Three times Noah sends out a dove: it's white and clean and can be used for sacrifice (see 20).

The first time, the dove *could find nowhere to perch* (9a), so it returns to the ark. The second time (seven days later) the dove returns, but this time *there in its beak was a freshly plucked olive leaf!* (11).

So, seven days later, Noah sends the dove out for a third time, *but this time it did not return to him* (12).

When Noah removes the covering from the ark he sees that *the surface of the ground was dry* (13).

And now God speaks directly to Noah: he and his family are to *come out of the ark* (15a). And they are to *bring out every kind of living creature that is with you* (17a), *so they can multiply on the earth and be fruitful and increase in number on it* (17b).

This is re-creation happening.

After everyone and everything has left the ark, Noah's instinct is to worship: he *built an altar to the LORD and... sacrificed burnt offerings on it* (20). And God *smelled the pleasing aroma* (21a).

And now God makes a decision: *Never again will I curse the ground because of humans* (21a). He still recognises that *every inclination of the human heart is evil*, but his mind is made up: *Never again will I destroy all living creatures* (21b).

God is promising to maintain the regularity that sustains life on earth. It's expressed in poetry: *As long as the earth endures,* the seasons and day and night *will never cease* (22).

After his devastating act of judgment, God's grace is clearly heard. And we're still experiencing the blessing of that today.

5. God's covenant with Noah (9:1-17). At the end of chapter 8, God is speaking *in his heart* (chapter 8:21). Now, in the first half of chapter 9, he speaks to *Noah and his sons* (1, 8).

+ What Noah and his descendants are to do (1-7). This is like a re-creation: Noah and his sons are called to *be fruitful and increase in number and fill the earth* (1, and see chapter 1:28).

There are two changes. All the animals are still *given into your hands* (2b), but now *the fear and dread of you will fall* on them (2a). And now humankind is to be permitted to eat meat: God tells Noah that *everything that lives and moves about will be food for you* (3).

But God takes the blood of animals and of humans seriously: *You must not eat meat that has its lifeblood still in it* (4). And, what's more, the killing of every human being is to be punished, whether the killer is an animal (see 5) or a fellow-human (see 5b).

The importance of the latter is underlined by God speaking a poetic stanza: *Whoever sheds human blood, by humans shall their blood be shed* (6a). And this is because *in the image of God has God made mankind* (6b).

This is what Noah and his descendants are to do. But now God explains his covenant with humankind.

+ What God will do for Noah and his descendants (8-17). God commits to something for *every living creature on earth* (10b). *I establish my covenant with you,* says God (11a): *never again will all life be destroyed by the waters of a flood* (11).

And the covenant has a sign, as a reminder of what God is committing himself to *for all generations to come* (12b): *I have set my rainbow in the clouds* (13).

The Hebrew simply has *I have set my bow in the clouds*: it's like God is saying that he is hanging up his weapon of war and will no longer use it against humankind.

In any case: God promises that *whenever the rainbow appears in the clouds, I will see it and remember the everlasting covenant between God and all living creatures* (16).

It's not that God needs the reminder; but whenever men and women see a rainbow we are being reminded of God's covenant promise.

There is one last stage in the Genesis flood account.

6. Prophecies about Noah's sons (9:18-29). The scene is set: Noah's sons are called *Shem, Ham and Japheth* (18). At the end of the story, Noah will prophesy about his sons and their descendants.

But first we see that this righteous and blameless man who walked with God (see chapter 6:9) is still a sinner.

+ Noah sins (20-21). This happens some years after the flood: it takes time for a vineyard to bring fruit, and it sounds like Noah already has grandsons at this point. So there is no reason to think that what is described here happened the first time Noah drank wine produced from his vineyard.

But one day, *when he drank some of its wine, he became drunk and lay uncovered inside his tent* (21). This helpless drunk has stripped himself naked and passed out.

+ His sons respond (22-23). Ham *saw his father naked and told his two brothers outside* (22).

It's worth noticing that Noah is described here as *his father*: Ham is doing something here that shows that he is failing to honour his parent. When he accidentally catches sight of Noah, he could have covered him up and kept quiet about what he'd seen; but instead he goes out of the tent and tells his brothers.

Maybe he's joking about it; he's certainly gossiping. Ham is *uncovering* his drunken father's nakedness.

Shem and Japheth, on the other hand, honour their father: they *took a garment and laid it across their shoulders; then they walked in backwards and covered their father's naked body* (23a).

The account makes it clear that Shem and Japheth are doing the right thing: *their faces were turned the other way so that they would not see their father naked* (23b).

+ Noah prophesies (24-27). This is the first and only time we hear Noah speaking. He prophesies curse and blessing.

First, there is curse: *Cursed be Canaan! The lowest of slaves will he be to his brothers* (25).

Why does Noah's curse focus on Ham's fourth son (see chapter 10:6), and not on Ham himself? Perhaps Canaan was in some way involved in his father's sinful behaviour.

And maybe God is giving Noah a sense of what will happen one day through the descendants of Canaan. God will warn his people not to live like the Canaanites (see Leviticus 18:3) because of their abuse of sexuality (the Hebrew expression *uncover nakedness* is used to refer to sexual sin in Leviticus chapter 18).

But there is also blessing. Noah's heart is full of thanksgiving: he calls out *Praise be to the LORD, the God of Shem!* (26a). Canaan will be *the slave of Shem* (26b) and *the slave of Japheth* (27).

And Shem is clearly the senior partner of the two brothers: Noah prays that Japheth may *live in the tents of Shem* (27).

Why is this blessing directed to Shem? Shem is the ancestor of Israel: Noah's prophecy is paving the way for Abram, a descendant of Shem, to be the father of the people of God.

The flood story is complete. As it ends we're told that *Noah lived a total of 950 years, and then he died* (29).

b'. – Degeneration (10:1 – 11:9)

This part of the primeval history has two ingredients.

1. The table of nations (10:1-32). *This is the account...* (1a, see also chapter 2:4, 5:1 and 6:9): this is a new beginning. And we start with an explanation of what is coming: *This is the account of Shem, Ham and Japheth, Noah's sons, who themselves had sons after the flood* (1).

The purpose of the table is to explain the spreading out of people (see verses 5, 18 and 32) and is only concerned with nations in and around the Ancient Near East that might come into contact with those who receive God's promise, starting with Abraham.

The table of nations is carefully structured. There are groups of seven (the fact that Noah has seven grandsons is only one example) and the entire list includes seventy nations that descended from Noah's three sons (fourteen from Japheth, thirty from Ham and twenty-six from Shem).

There is not the space here to look at the individual people and nations: for the details please see the commentaries. But it's worth mentioning that the names of some of these descendants came to signify the lands where they settled.

Japheth's and Ham's descendants are introduced to us first, because they are not so central to the fulfilment of God purposes for the world. The climax of the table of nations is Shem and his descendants.

+ Japheth (2-5). This is the shortest list, perhaps because the nations mentioned here are on the outer fringes of the known world, and furthest from the land of Canaan.

The maritime peoples (5) probably refers to all the descendants of Japheth. They seem to have lived around the Mediterranean, and around the Black Sea.

+ Ham (6-20). The nations referred to here are southwards from Canaan, including some African peoples.

Nimrod is singled out for special mention. He's *a mighty hunter before the LORD* (9): in other words God sees his skill. But it's ironic that the first part of his kingdom is *Babylon* (10), when we consider the tower of Babel (see chapter 11) and Babylon's history through the Bible story, culminating in Revelation chapter 18.

When we reach the Canaanites we get the most detail (see verses 15-19). This is probably because of the promise of the land of Canaan given to Abraham, Isaac and Jacob later in the book of Genesis.

And the summary verse tells us four ways in which the list of Ham's descendants is organised: *clans and languages* [...], *territories and nations* (20; see also verse 31).

+ Shem (21-31). This family line is the one on which God's promise is focused: it goes from Shem to Arphaxad, Shelah, Eber and Peleg (see 22-25). This will be repeated in chapter 11:10-26, but continued through to Abram.

But the introduction to this genealogy calls Shem *the ancestor of all the sons of Eber* (21). The name *Eber* is significant because the labelling of his decendants as Hebrews is derived from his name (see chapter 14:13; 39:14 and 17; 41:12).

One of Eber's sons is Peleg, *because in his time the earth was divided* (25; Peleg means *division*). This may mean that the scattering of the peoples and the confusion of languages happened during his lifetime.

Once again, we're told that this line of descent is organised according to *clans and languages* [...], *territories and nations* (31; and see verse 20).

The summary verse for the whole of chapter 10 reminds us that we have been looking at the descendants of Noah's sons (see 32a). The final sentence links the table of nations with what is to come in chapter 11: *From these the nations spread out over the earth after the flood* (32b).

Which brings us to the second ingredient of the degeneration.

2. The tower of Babel (11:1-9). This event actually happened *before* the spreading out of the nations in chapter 10, because the peoples who come into being from the descendants of Noah have their own languages (see chapter 10:5, 20, 31).

But at the beginning of chapter 11 we learn that *the whole world had one language and a common speech* (1).

Perhaps this account is where it is because it serves as a climax to the degeneration after the flood.

+ Human rebellion (3-4). People start saying *Come, let us make bricks* (3) and *Come, let us build ourselves a city, with a tower that reaches to the heavens* (4a).

The aim seems to be protection from enemies: they don't want to be *scattered over the face of the whole earth* (4b).

But the root of it all is that they want to *make a name for ourselves* (4b). This is all without reference to God and in defiance of God, who had told Noah after the flood that his descendants were to *fill the earth* (chapter 9:1).

So they start to build their city and their tower.

+ Divine judgment (5-8). While the building project is going on, God *came down to see the city and the tower* (5).

He sees the rebellion behind what's happening and decides to step in. One reason they can defy God in this way is that they're all *speaking the same language* (6a): communication is easy. If God doesn't intervene, he says, *nothing they plan to do will be impossible for them* (6b).

So the divine decision is made: *Come, let us go down and confuse their language so they will not understand each other* (7).

And that's what God does: *the LORD scattered them from there over all the earth* (8a). And the confusion of languages reinforces that. In any event, *they stopped building the city* (8b).

The account ends with an explanation as to why the city and the tower were called Babel: it's because *there the LORD confused the language of the whole world* (9a; *Babel* sounds like the Hebrew for *confused*).

The message is clear. The flood event has not solved the problem of human fallenness: it's still true that *every inclination of the human heart is evil from childhood* (see chapter 8:21).

Humankind is still looking for ways to *make a name for ourselves* (see chapter 11:4b). The degeneration continues.

And the world is going to need a Saviour.

c'. – Ten generations from Shem to Abram (11:10-26)

This is another new beginning: *This is the account of Shem's family line* (10a).

Just as part c (5:1 – 6:8) gave us ten generations from Adam to Noah, so part c' presents us with ten generations from Shem to Abram. This connects the primeval history to the narratives about the patriarchs.

This table of descent differs somewhat from the earlier one. First, people are not living as long as they did before the flood. Second, the age of becoming a parent has dropped. And third, we no longer read about each person on the list *And he died.*

They did all die, of course. But now, instead of being reminded of the inevitability of death we are looking forward to what is to come: God has a plan for human history, and it will be realised through the line of Shem.

When the table of descent reaches Eber we are told that he *became the father of Peleg* (16). In chapter 10:25 another son was mentioned too: Joktan. But here in chapter 11 he is nowhere to be found.

The reason is not hard to find. Joktan's line leads to the disaster at Babel, while Peleg's leads to the great man Abram, through whom God is going to save the nations.

And so we read that *after Terah had lived 70 years, he became the father of Abram, Nahor and Haran* (26).

d. – Conclusion: Introducing Abram (11:27-32)

The name of Abram's wife was Sarai (29): she is actually his half-sister, but that won't be spelt out for us until chapter 20.

Abram's brother Haran *became the father of Lot* (27b), something which is going to be important when we read on in the book of Genesis.

Abram, on the other hand, has no children: *Sarai was childless because she was not able to conceive* (30).

The foundation is being laid for Section B: The Abraham story (chapter 12:1 – 21:7).

But there is something else we need to know about Abram. Terah's family are living in *Ur of the Chaldeans* (28), which is the leading centre of lunar religion. Abram, with the rest of his family, is a moon-worshipper.

Joshua gives us a hint of this. One day he will tell all the tribes of Israel that *your ancestors, including Terah the father of Abraham and Nahor, lived beyond the River Euphrates and worshipped other gods* (Joshua 24:2).

This introduction to Abram tells us that *Terah took his son Abram, his grandson Lot son of Haran, and his daughter-in-law Sarai, the wife of his son Abram* (31a). And *they set out from Ur of the Chaldeans to go to Canaan* (31b). But they settle in a place called Harran (see 31b).

The bridge has been built between the primeval history and the story of Abraham. Which makes us want to read on in the book of Genesis.

But first, let's look back on Section A.

Learning Genesis+

Section A is easy to learn because it only contains seven elements.

First, learn the main heading: *Primeval history.* Then repeat the first three headings (a, b and c) several times: doing this aloud makes it all the easier.

Now do the same thing with the second half of the section (parts a', b', c' and d).

You will enjoy this more if you've arranged with a friend to meet up after you've both learnt Section A.

This is not difficult, but it is so worthwhile.

Section A: Primeval History

a. Creation
b. *Degeneration*
c. Ten generations from Adam to Noah

a'. The flood
b'. *Degeneration*
c'. Ten generations from Shem to Abram

d. Conclusion: Introducing Abram

Meeting God

As you run through Section A in your mind you'll find that you remember some of the details of each incident. So, as you do (on your own, or with a friend), please take time to thank God for what he is doing.

You might like to use the study questions on Section A (see Appendix 3): you could do this on your own, or discuss them with a friend.

This material is in the Bible not only so that we can learn information, but also so that we'll meet the God we are reading about. So let's be talking to God about what we're remembering: and we will begin to love him more.

The Genesis+ Experiment is an invitation to do just this.

How to help your memory

1. **Make learning visual** by remembering where the events are on the page of your Bible.
2. **Make learning audible** by learning out loud.
3. **Make learning practical** by doing a little every day.
4. **Make learning enjoyable** by using the experiment to help you pray and worship.

Section B
The Abraham Story (Genesis 12:1 – 21:7)

To this point the recounting of human history has proceeded at a relatively rapid pace, but with Genesis chapter 12 the progression of history slows almost to a halt. Section B traces events that occurred during a twenty-five-year period in the life of a single individual. Abraham will be the father of what will become God's people, and through one of his descendants the whole world will be blessed.

God took Abram outside and said
Look up at the sky and count the stars
– if indeed you can count them.
Then he said to him,
So shall your offspring be.

Genesis 15:5

Enjoying the View

a. Introduction: the promise of descendants (12:1-9)
b. *Abram lies about Sarai in Egypt* (12:10-20)
c. Lot settles in Sodom (13:1-18)
d. *Abram intercedes for Lot and Sodom militarily* (14:1-24)
e. Promise of a son: from Abram himself (15:1-21)
f. *Ishmael: his birth* (16:1-16)
g. CENTRE: God's covenant with Abram/Abraham (17:1-22)
f'. *Ishmael: his circumcision* (17:23-27)
e'. Promise of a son: from Sarah herself (18:1-15)
d'. *Abraham intercedes for Lot and Sodom in prayer* (18:16-33)
c'. Lot flees Sodom, which God destroys (19:1-38)
b'. *Abraham lies about Sarah in Gerar* (20:1-18)
a'. Conclusion: the birth of Isaac (21:1-7)

Section A is organised with mirror links (a/a', b/b' etc), which has two results. First, it means that the order of the events is easily learnt. And second, it makes it easy to see God's plan being worked out.

A couple of examples will make that clear. The section begins with God promising childless Abram that he will have descendants, and ends with the birth of Isaac. And, right in the middle of the section, the focus is on the covenant: Abram becomes Abraham, Sarai becomes Sarah, the covenant sign of circumcision is given, and the promise of descendants is spelt out more clearly than previously.

Everything begins with God making astonishing promises to Abram. As the section progresses, he learns what it means to trust those promises. Step by step, he's getting to know God better: he's becoming more and more a man of faith. As this happens, he's moved to worship.

The visible evidence of this is the building of altars. Several times we read of Abram building an altar: he's learning to trust the promises and the God who made them. The altar is the symbol for Section B.

Before reading further it would be good to read through Genesis 12:1 – 21:7. Watch Abram building his altars and learning to trust God. As you read you may find yourself talking to God and worshipping him.

Unpacking the Content

a. – Introduction: the promise of descendants (12:1-9)

1. God calls Abram (1-3). This call has two ingredients.

+ Command (1). God tells Abram to leave *your country, your people and your father's household*: he is to leave what he is most attached to. Abram isn't told what country he's aiming for: rather he is to travel *to the land I will show you.*

+ Promise (2-3). There are seven promises of divine blessing here. God's promise that *I will make you into a great nation* (2a) is huge: Abram is childless and his wife Sarai is barren (see chapter 11:30).

God promises, too, that *I will make your name great* (2b, and contrast chapter 11:4): this won't be Abram's achievement, but a gift from God.

And there is blessing. God tells Abram that *I will bless you* (2a) and that *you will be a blessing* (2b). So special is Abram going to be that *I will bless those who bless you, and whoever curses you I will curse* (3a).

And this is not just referring to Abram's family and others close to him: God promises that *all peoples on earth will be blessed through you* (3b).

This is immense. What God is doing here is laying the foundation for his plan to bless the whole world.

How will Abram respond to God's call?

2. Abram obeys God (4-9). The report is matter of fact: *So Abram went, as the LORD had told him* (4a). He seems to have needed no time to consider things: rather he takes *his wife Sarai* (5a) and *set out for the land of Canaan* (5b).

There are two mentions of Abram's nephew Lot going with him (see 4 and 5); they take *all the possessions they had accumulated and the people they had acquired in Harran* (5).

So Abram is in Canaan (see 5b), as a foreigner: *at that time the Canaanites were in the land* (6b).

And now Abram has another encounter with God. This time he sees something, as well as hearing words: *the LORD appeared to Abram* (7a).

And the message is clear: God promises Abram that *to your offspring I will give this land* (7b). Canaan will belong to the people that are Abram's descendants.

This time Abram responds not with obedience (there has been no command), but with worship: *he built an altar there to the LORD, who had appeared to him* (7c). It looks like this is Abram's instinctive reaction to his encounter with God.

This is the first appearance of Section B's symbol.

There's more: Abram travels twenty miles further on (see 8a) and *there he built an altar to the Lord* (8b). But now he does something new: he *called on the name of the LORD* (8b, and see chapter 4:26b).

Abram has obeyed God's command and trusted God's purposes. He's already in relationship with God: obeying him, worshipping him and crying out to him. And building altars as an expression of that.

And he's remembering that God has promised to give him descendants (see 2a and 7a).

b. – Abram lies about Sarai in Egypt (12:10-20)

1. What Abram does (10-16). There's a famine in Canaan, so *Abram went down to Egypt to live there for a while* (10). There's no indication that he asks God for guidance: he just gets on and does what makes sense to him, without reference to God.

And Abram resorts to subterfuge.

He explains to Sarai that the Egyptians, having seen her beauty, will *kill me but will let you live* (12). So his solution is simple: he tells Sarai to *say you are my sister* (13).

This is half-true: Sarai is Abram's half-sister (though we don't know that at this point in the story). But he wants Sarai to go along with his deceit. And this is all for his sake: then *I will be treated well for your sake and my life will be spared because of you* (13).

Abram must know that there is a risk of Sarai being co-opted into Pharaoh's harem, but it doesn't look like that concerns him.

But the scheme works. Sarai's beauty does indeed lead to her being recommended to Pharaoh and *taken into his palace* (15). And the lying pays off: Pharaoh *treated Abram well for her sake* (16a) and showers him with gifts (see 16b).

2. What God does (17-20). So there is a divine intervention: *the LORD inflicted serious diseases on Pharaoh and his household* (17).

And Pharaoh gets the message. He asks Abram three questions: *What have you done to me?* (18), *Why didn't you tell me she was your wife?* (18), and *Why did you say 'She is my sister,' so that I took her to be my wife?* (19).

So Sarai has been having sex with Pharaoh in order to save Abram's skin.

And Abram doesn't answer any of the questions. How does he think Sarai feels about what's been happening? And surely he knows that he's doing wrong: he's *using* his wife, rather than honouring her as someone made in God's image.

So Pharaoh's people take Abram and *sent him on his way, with his wife and everything he had* (20).

Despite Abram's faithlessness, God remains faithful to him: his commitment to his promise overrides human weakness.

There is one more thing to note before we move on to incident c. The seven major sections of Genesis+ are themselves structured with mirror links. This means that Section B (the Abraham story) is linked with Section B' (the Exodus story).

The Exodus story (Section B') tells us about the plagues that God sent on the Egyptians. But here in Section B, when Abram has lied about Sarai in Egypt, God inflicted *great plagues* on Pharaoh (chapter 12:17, literal translation). (For more on this, see Appendix 2.)

God is working out his purposes.

c. – Lot settles in Sodom (13:1-18)

So Abram went up from Egypt to the Negev (1a): it looks like an opportunity for a new start. Has he learnt his lesson?

Having forgotten God's promise by going to Egypt, Abram is back in the land of Canaan. And he seems to have turned over a new leaf.

1. Abram remembers God's promise (1-4). He comes back to *the place between Bethel and Ai... where he had first built an altar* (3b-4a, and see chapter 12:8).

So Abram isn't just coming back from Egypt. He's coming back to God: *there Abram called on the name of the LORD* (4b). It looks like he's remembering God's promise.

But there's more.

2. Abram trusts God's promise (5-13). Lot, Abram's nephew, is travelling with his uncle (see 1 and 5). But there's a problem: *their possessions were so great that they were not able to stay together* (6b), and their herdsmen are quarrelling with each other (see 7).

So Abram invites Lot to choose in which direction he takes his flocks, his herds and his people: *If you go to the left, I'll go to the right; if you go to the right, I'll go to the left* (9b).

Abram could have made this decision himself: after all, he's the senior partner in this relationship. But he's trusting God's promise: he believes that everything God has told him at his call is going to happen (see chapter 12:2-3, 7).

Lot's decision is not a wise one: he looks around *and sees that the whole plain of the Jordan towards Zoar was well watered, like the garden of the LORD* (10). So we read that he *chose for himself the whole plain of the Jordan* (11).

The upshot is that Lot sets out towards the east *and pitched his tents near Sodom* (12b). It's a dangerous move: *the people of Sodom were wicked and were sinning greatly against the LORD* (13).

We don't know whether Lot knew Sodom's reputation, but we do know that his decision to travel east was an unwise one.

But the other thing we know is that Abram's offer to Lot shows that he's trusting that God's promises to him will be fulfilled.

And he does something else too.

3. Abram embraces God's promise (14-18). In the light of Abram's renewed trust, God repeats the promises. And he makes it easier for Abram to believe them.

He makes it visual: *All the land that you see I will give to you and your offspring for ever* (15, and see 14 too). Here it comes again: God is promising Abram descendants and a land.

He's telling him to *look* (14) and to *see* (15).

And Abram embraces the promise. What does he do when he's travelled to Hebron and *pitched his tents* (18a)? The answer doesn't surprise us: *he built an altar to the LORD* (18b).

Abram is already a man of faith: he's in relationship with his Creator. And the relationship is growing: he's embracing God's promises.

d. – Abram intercedes for Lot and Sodom militarily (14:1-24)

In the previous chapter Lot had *pitched his tents <u>near</u> Sodom* (chapter 13:12). By the time the events of this chapter take place he's *living <u>in</u> Sodom* (12).

And Abram is going to decide to rescue him.

The background is clear. Four kings, including *Kedorlaomer king of Elam* (1), have been forcing five kings, including *Bera king of Sodom* (2), to pay them tribute: it's an ancient version of demanding protection money.

But now the five kings decide to say No: *For twelve years they had been subject to Kedorlaomer, but in the thirteenth year they rebelled* (4).

So *Kedorlaomer and the kings allied with him* (5a) go on the rampage: they subdue a number of peoples throughout the Transjordan before turning to the five rebel kings. It's *four kings against five* (9b).

Kedorlaomer's gang of four seize victory: among others defeated, *the kings of Sodom and Gomorrah fled* (10). The four kings now have *all the goods of Sodom and Gomorrah* (11).

And now comes the sentence that this has all been leading up to: *They also carried off Abram's nephew Lot and his possessions* (12).

At this point Abram steps onto the stage again: we learn three things about him.

1. Abram: rescuing Lot (13-16). The news reaches *Abram the Hebrew* (13a). He could have said that it wasn't his problem: after all, it was Lot's decision to move to Sodom.

But instead, with some of his local allies (see 13b), *he called out the 318 trained men born in his household and went in pursuit* (14).

It's almost certain that they are outnumbered, but Abram *divided his men to attack them and he routed them* (15a). This is a huge victory: he *brought back his relative Lot and his possessions, together with the women and the other people* (16).

This is Abram interceding for Lot militarily, rescuing his nephew so completely that all his people and his possessions are restored to him too.

So what happens now?

2. Abram: rewarded by God (17-20). Now two kings come out to meet Abram: *the king of Sodom* (17) and *Melchizedek king of Salem* (18). From the way these encounters are interwoven (see 17-21), it looks like they happen pretty much at the same time.

As well as being *king of Salem* (which almost certainly refers to Jerusalem), Melchizedek is *priest of God Most High* (18): he's a Canaanite who acknowledges the same God as Abram. And he brings a celebration meal for Abram: he *brought out bread and wine* (18).

First, he blesses Abram with the words *Blessed be Abram by God Most High, Creator of heaven and earth* (19). Melchizedek is calling down a blessing from God on victorious Abram.

And second, he blesses God with the words *Praise be to God Most High, who delivered your enemies into your hand* (20a). Melchizedek isn't congratulating Abram for his victory, but praising God who gave it.

This is God using Melchizedek to reward Abram. And Abram recognises that Melchizedek is speaking in God's name: he *gave him a tenth of everything* (20b).

But there's a third thing we see about Abram.

3. Abram: trusting God (21-24). The king of Sodom hasn't come with blessing but with a demand: he wants Abram to *give me the people and keep the goods for yourself* (21).

He shows no gratitude for what Abram has done. Abram is entitled to keep everything he's rescued: people and property. The king of Sodom is willing to lose the property, but not the people.

But Abram has no intention of keeping any of the spoils, *not even a thread or the strap of a sandal, so that you will never be able to say, 'I made Abram rich.'* (23).

And he tells the king of Sodom that he is making this decision in God's presence: *With raised hand I have sworn an oath to the LORD, God Most High, Creator of heaven and earth* (22).

Abram's trust in God is growing. He has not done what he has done because of what he can get out of it; rather he has done it all for the glory of *God Most High* (22).

Before we move on to incident e, it's worth noting that Melchizedek never reappears in the book of Genesis.

Melchizedek appears from nowhere: we know nothing about his parentage. The New Testament letter to the Hebrews sees in him a foreshadowing of Jesus Christ, the king-priest (see Hebrews 5:6-10; 7:1-17).

In any case, Abram seems conscious of the fact that, in his encounter with Melchizedek, God is at work.

e. – Promise of a son: from Abram himself (15:1-21)

This chapter is one of the most important in Section B.

1. God's promise to Abram (1-6). Following on from the events of chapter 14, Abram may be in need of reassurance.

+ God's promise (1). So *the word of the LORD came to Abram in a vision* (1a). God addresses him by name: *Do not be afraid, Abram* (1b).

And now comes the promise: *I am your shield, your very great reward* (1b). It's like God is wrapping up all his previous promises to Abram in this word *reward*.

+ Abram's question (2-3). God's promise means that Abram is bold enough to voice his doubts: *Sovereign LORD, what can you give me since I remain childless..?* (2). If Abram has no descendants, his servant *Eliezer of Damascus* (2b) will inherit everything.

So how can God's promises be fulfilled? Abram spells it out: *You have given me no children* (3). It's like he has no hope.

+ God's promise (4-5). So God replies to Abram's doubt. Eliezer is not going to inherit everything, but *a son who is your own flesh and blood will be your heir* (4).

And now, once again, God gives Abram a visual aid: he takes him outside and tells him to *look up at the sky and count the stars – if indeed you can count them* (5a).

And then, as Abram gazes up at the stars, he hears God say the words *So shall your offspring be* (5b).

This is a moment that changes Abram. And it changes history too.

+ Abram's faith (6). *Abram believed the LORD, and he credited it to him as righteousness* (6).

The New Testament helps us to understand these words. The apostle Paul quotes them (see Romans 4:9 and 22; Galatians 3:6), explaining that this is justification by faith. Abram received a righteous status before God because he *believed.*

Abram has believed God's repeated promise of a son, and believed, too, that this son will be his *own flesh and blood* (4).

2. God's covenant with Abram (7-21). The divine promise is going to be made all the more certain: God will make a covenant with Abram. This is his commitment to keep his promises.

+ God's promise (7). He tells Abram *I am the LORD, who brought you out of Ur of the Chaldeans* (7a). He has kept his promises thus far.

And God's purpose is *to give you this land to take possession of it* (7b).

+ Abram's question (8). Once again, Abram addresses God as *Sovereign LORD* (8, see also 2). And, once again, he is expressing his doubts: he asks God *How can I know that I shall gain possession of it?* (8b).

+ God's promise (9-16). This is God preparing the way to make a covenant with Abram. He tells him to *bring me a heifer, a goat and a ram, each three years old, along with a dove and a young pigeon* (9).

Abram obeys: he brings the animals, *cut them in two and arranged the halves opposite each other* (10a).

What is this about?

This was a common way to make a covenant in the ancient world, so much so that people talked of *cutting* a covenant: animals were divided in two, thus creating a corridor between them. When the two parties cutting the covenant walked through the corridor, it's like they were both saying *If I don't keep my promises, may it be done to me as we have done to these animals.*

Now God prepares to make a solemn promise to Abram about his descendants: *As the sun was setting, Abram fell into a deep sleep, and a thick and dreadful darkness came over him* (12). He is still conscious, but nothing will distract him as he hears God's words.

God tells Abram what is going to happen: *For four hundred years your descendants will be strangers in a country not their own; […] they will be enslaved and ill-treated there* (13). Those who have read the whole of Genesis+ know that this is about God's people living as slaves in Egypt (see Section B').

God continues the story: *I will punish the nation they serve as slaves* (14a). The Egyptians will experience God's judgment, but God's people *will come out with great possessions* (14b).

Abram himself will have died (see 15). But *in the fourth generation your descendants will come back here* (16a): the nation will return to the land of Canaan. Israel's later conquest of the land was not only a fulfilment of the promise to Abram: it was also God moving in judgment against the pagan inhabitants of Canaan.

This is what God is promising Abram (see verses 13-16). So it is clear what comes next.

+ God's covenant (17-21). On that day *the LORD made a covenant with Abram* (18a, literal translation: <u>cut</u> *a covenant*).

He promises Abram two things: *To your descendants I give this land* (18). God is giving Abram descendants and he will give those descendants the land of Canaan.

It's worth reading all of this: *When the sun had set and darkness had fallen, a smoking brazier with a blazing torch appeared and passed between the pieces* (17).

And where is Abram? Why is he not also walking through the animal corridor? He is still in *a deep sleep* (12): God has made sure that Abram is unable to move.

By being the only one walking between the animal pieces, God is saying this: *When Abram's descendants fail to keep their side of the covenant, I will take the consequences upon myself.*

This idea that God takes on himself the consequences of human sin finds its fulfilment at the cross of Jesus: *he* died for *our* sins.

In incident e we have seen Abram being justified by faith (see 6). But it's worth underlining that the *sign* of the covenant – circumcision – is not introduced until incident g (see chapter 17:1-22).

That's fourteen years later.

The apostle Paul makes much of this. He asks the Christians in Rome *when* Abraham was justified by faith: *Was it after he was circumcised, or before? It was not after, but before!* (Romans 4:10; see, too, Genesis 15:6 and 17:24).

This means that being circumcised doesn't contribute to justification or salvation in any way. And the Genesis account makes that crystal clear.

This is a good opportunity to thank God that justification is by faith alone. And that that's all possible because of the death of Jesus.

f. – Ishmael: his birth (16:1-16)

1. Sarai and Hagar (1-6). Ten years have passed since we first met Abram and Sarai at the end of Section A (see chapter 11:27-32). She is now seventy-five years old, and it's still true that she had *borne him no children* (1a).

+ Sarai suggests Hagar (1-4a). Hagar is Sarai's *Egyptian slave* (1b), and Sarai suggests that Abram takes her as his second wife (see 2). So *Sarai his wife took her Egyptian slave Hagar and gave her to her husband to be his wife* (3).

And it happens: *he slept with Hagar, and she conceived* (4a).

+ Sarai ill-treats Hagar (4b-6). Hagar begins to look down on Sarai: knowing she's pregnant leads her to *despise her mistress* (4b, see also 5b).

Abram is not willing to take responsibility: he tells Sarai to *do with her whatever you think best* (6a). So *Sarai ill-treated Hagar* (6b): we don't know the details, but that's all we need to know.

And so Hagar does what you'd expect: *she fled from her* (6b).

2. The angel of the LORD and Hagar (7-16). Hagar is in the desert on *the road to Shur* (7b), which means she's on her way to Egypt.

+ What the angel of the LORD says (7-12). When *the angel of the LORD* finds her (7a), he reminds her that she is Sarai's slave and asks where she's going (see 8).

Hagar doesn't answer the question: is she embarrassed to be making for Egypt? But she doesn't hide her relationship with Sarai: she tells the angel that she's *running away from my mistress Sarai* (8b).

The angel of the LORD tells Hagar to *go back to your mistress and submit to her* (9). And what the angel says next is important: *I will increase your descendants so much that they will be too numerous to count* (10).

There are three things to note here. First, Hagar will have many descendants: she is not *the* fulfilment of the promise to Abram, but she will be *a* fulfilment.

Second, the angel reveals that he represents God himself: he says that *I will increase your descendants...* (10).

And third, the angel gives a name to the son she will give birth to: *Ishmael,* which means *God hears* (11). He explains: *...for the LORD has heard your misery* (11b).

Ishmael will be *a wild donkey of a man* (12a), a survivor, able to cope with those who oppose him.

+ How Hagar responds (13-14). After her encounter with God in the desert Hagar, in turn, gives a name to God: she calls him *the God who sees me* (13). He has not ignored her plight.

The chapter is rounded off with a reminder of what we've learnt: *So Hagar bore Abram a son, and Abram gave the name Ishmael to the son she had borne* (15).

If God's promises are not to be fulfilled through Ishmael, there needs to be another birth before too long. At the end of the chapter Abram is *eighty-six years old* (16).

The clock is ticking.

g. – CENTRE: God's covenant with Abram/Abraham (17:1-22)

There is a gap of thirteen years between chapter 16 and chapter 17: everything in this new chapter happens *when Abram was ninety-nine years old* (1a).

Now God will spell out the details of the covenant initiated in chapter 15. This is not going to be a bargain struck between equals; rather it's God telling Abram what is to happen.

I am God Almighty (1b). This is the first time God has introduced himself in this way: does he do this because of the impossibility, humanly speaking, of his promises to Abram becoming reality?

And now God tells Abram that he is to *walk before me faithfully and be blameless* (1b). This is not a demand for sinlessness, but a call to total commitment: Abram is to give everything to live in covenant relationship with the LORD.

The reaction is immediate: *Abram fell face down* (3). He is worshipping.

1. God's covenant (4-16). What God has to say to Abram is in three main parts, each introduced with the phrase *As for...* (4, 9, 15).

+ *As for me...* (4-8). This is God committing himself to keep his promises. He starts with the matter of descendants by telling Abram that he will be *the father of many nations* (4).

So certain is this that *Abram* (meaning *exalted father*) will now be called *Abraham* (meaning *father of many*). God underlines this by speaking about it in the past tense: *I have made you a father of many nations* (5b, and see 6).

God promises that this covenant will be *an everlasting covenant between me and you and you and your descendants after you for the generations to come* (7).

And God Almighty is promising the land too: *the whole land of Canaan, where you now reside as a foreigner, I will give as an everlasting possession to you and your descendants after you* (8).

And he adds *I will be their God* (8b).

These are extraordinary promises. And whenever someone calls Abraham by his new name he's going to be reminded of them.

But there is more to come.

+ *As for you...* **(9-14).** Now God tells Abraham that he *must keep my covenant* (9), and explains what that is going to involve for Abraham and for his descendants.

Abraham is to *undergo circumcision,* which will be *the sign of the covenant between me and you* (11). Male circumcision was widely practised at the time, but for Abraham and his descendants it now *means* something.

So from now on *every male among you who is eight days old must be circumcised* (12): this is to apply to those *born in your household or bought with your money* (13a).

God calls this *my covenant in your flesh* and tells Abraham that this is to be *an everlasting covenant* (13b).

The circumcision command is not all, of course. This is all in the context of the commands which introduced the covenant: *Walk before me faithfully and be blameless* (1b).

Abraham may well be thinking that his new name will become reality through Ishmael: it would be surprising if he weren't.

Which underlines the importance of what God will tell him now.

+ *As for Sarai* **(15-16).** Abraham's wife is to have a new name, too: *her name will be Sarah* (15).

And now comes a staggering statement: God will *bless her and will surely give you a son by her* (16a). Sarah will be *the mother of nations* (16b).

God's covenant promises focus on descendants for Abraham and the land of Canaan for them to live in. But now here is God spelling out Sarah's role in all this: *I... will surely give you a son by her* (16a).

So how is Abraham reacting to what God has just told him?

2. Abraham's response (17-18). He *fell face down* again (17a, and see 3a). But this time he does this not because he's worshipping, but in order to hide his laughter (see 17a).

Abraham's asking himself two questions: *Will a son be born to a man a hundred years old? Will Sarah bear a child at the age of ninety?* (17b).

It just doesn't seem possible to believe what God has just promised him. And so Abraham cries out to God with the words *If only Ishmael might live under your blessing!* (18).

3. God's plan (19-22). Now Abraham hears God repeat the promise, but this time the son he will have is given a name: *Your wife Sarah will bear you a son, and you will call him Isaac* (19a), which means *he laughs.* Whenever Abraham uses that name, he will remember God's promise and his own scepticism.

And God underlines his commitment to this course of action: of Isaac he says *I will establish my covenant with him as an everlasting covenant for his descendants after him* (19b).

And what about Ishmael? *I have heard you,* says God: *I will surely bless him* (20a). This blessing will involve Ishmael becoming *the father of twelve rulers* (20b): God will *make him into a great nation* (20b).

So God will bless Ishmael. But he is very clear that he won't establish his covenant with him: *My covenant I will establish with Isaac, whom Sarah will bear to you by this time next year* (21).

So this is the covenant, with its sign of circumcision. Abram has become Abraham, Sarai has become Sarah, and God has, once again, promised to give the land of Canaan to Abraham's descendants.

And the first of those descendants within this everlasting covenant will be Isaac, whose mother will be Sarah.

The encounter is over: *When he had finished speaking with Abraham, God went up from him* (22).

But it's clear what must happen next.

f'. – Ishmael: his circumcision (17:23-27)

Abraham takes *his son Ishmael and all those born in his household or bought with his money, every male in his household* and circumcises them (23).

There is no delay: he does it *on that very day... as God told him* (23). This is unquestioning obedience.

So *Abraham and his son Ishmael were both circumcised on that very day* (26): Abraham is ninety-nine years old and Ishmael thirteen (see 24-25).

Ishmael's circumcision forms a mirror link with his birth (see incident f, chapter 16:1-16). God's plan is being fulfilled.

e'. – Promise of a son: from Sarah herself (18:1-15)

This incident forms a mirror link with *Promise of a son: from Abram himself* (incident e, chapter 15:1-21).

Abraham already knows that Sarah is going to give birth to his son (see chapter 17:15-16, 19). Has he not told his wife about the events of chapter 17? Or has he told her but failed to convince her that this is really going to happen?

1. A visitor for Abraham (1-2). Abraham looks up and sees *three men standing nearby* (2a). We know that two of them are angels (see chapter 18:22 and 19:1), and we know that one is God himself: chapter 18 begins with the words *The LORD appeared to Abraham* (1a).

But Abraham doesn't know any of this, though he may be surprised that the three men seem simply to have materialised (see 2a).

When he sees the three visitors Abraham *hurried from the entrance of his tent to meet them and bowed low to the ground* (2b): these are the basics of middle-eastern hospitality.

2. A meal for his guests (3-8). Abraham insists on offering his visitors a meal. He calls the one he sees as their leader *my lord* (3), which may mean no more than the English word *sir.*

After they have washed their feet (see 4), they eat a meal: Abraham gets Sarah to bake bread (see 6) and a servant to prepare *a choice, tender calf* (7). He brings *some curds and milk and the calf that had been prepared, and set these before them* (8a).

And Abraham is ready to see to all his visitors' needs: *While they ate, he stood near them under a tree* (8b).

But now comes the conversation that all this has been leading up to.

3. A message for Sarah (9-15). It's like the visitors want to be sure that Abraham's wife is within earshot: they ask him *Where is your wife Sarah?* (9).

Learning that she is nearby (*in the tent,* 9b), *one of them* has something to say (10a). The speaker is presumably God himself, and not one of the angels.

So here it comes: *I will surely return to you about this time next year, and Sarah your wife will have a son* (10a).

Now Sarah was listening (10b): the focus is on her reaction to this message. The account reminds us that *Abraham and Sarah were already very old, and Sarah was past the age of childbearing* (11): she is ninety and post-menopausal.

So *Sarah laughed to herself* (12a), as Abraham had when he had first heard this news (see chapter 17:17). And she asks herself *After I am worn out and my lord is old, will I now have this pleasure?* (12b).

Now the account tells us straight out who the leading visitor is: we're told what *the LORD said to Abraham* (13a). God asks *Why did Sarah laugh..?* (13).

And he poses the question *Is anything too hard for the LORD?* (14a): Abraham and Sarah need to learn that the answer to that question is *No.*

But she's not there yet: she lies and says *I did not laugh* (15).

Sarah does this, despite having heard God saying, once again, that *I will return to you at the appointed time next year, and Sarah will have a son* (14b).

The message could not be clearer: God is promising that Abraham's wife Sarah will bear him a son.

d'. – Abraham intercedes for Lot and Sodom in prayer (18:16-33)

When God first called Abraham, he told him *I will bless you* and *you will be a blessing* (see chapter 12:2). He has already been a blessing in interceding for Lot and Sodom militarily (see chapter 14:1-24); now, in the second part of the mirror link, he intercedes for Lot and Sodom in prayer.

As Abraham's visitors get up to leave, *they looked down towards Sodom* (16). It looks like they're thinking about what God is going to do.

1. What God tells Abraham (17-22). God doesn't speak to Abraham until verse 20, but before that we learn what motivates him. We're being allowed to hear God's thoughts.

He asks himself *Shall I hide from Abraham what I am about to do?* (17). God remembers that *I have chosen him* (19a): because of this, Abraham will *become a great and powerful nation, and all nations on earth will be blessed through him* (18).

Because of all this, God tells Abraham what is on his mind: *The outcry against Sodom and Gomorrah is so great and their sin so grievous* (20). It's like their sin is calling out to God, asking that justice be done.

So, says God in human terms that Abraham will be able to understand, *I will go down and see if what they have done is as bad as the outcry that has reached me* (21).

With that, the two *men turned away* (22a): they are on their way to Sodom (see chapter 19:1). But it looks as if Abraham has something on his mind: he *remained standing before the LORD* (22).

2. What Abraham asks God (23-32). This is Abraham interceding for Sodom and for Lot. He asks God *Will you sweep away the righteous with the wicked?* (23). Surely he isn't going to sweep the city away if there are fifty righteous people there not deserving of judgment?

He argues his point: *Far be it from you to do such a thing – to kill the righteous with the wicked, treating the righteous and the wicked alike* (25a). Abraham ends with a question, as he began: *Will not the Judge of all the earth do right?* (25b).

Abraham knows that God is just, so it seems to him impossible that God will destroy the city of Sodom if there are fifty righteous people living there.

God responds by telling Abraham *If I find fifty righteous people in the city of Sodom, I will spare the whole place for their sake* (26).

Abraham's faith is growing: what about if there are forty-five righteous people? Or forty?

Each time, God repeats his decision not to destroy Sodom if there are righteous people there.

Abraham is fearful: *May the Lord not be angry* (30), and asks what God will do if there are thirty righteous people there. Or twenty. Or ten.

God's final answer is that *For the sake of ten, I will not destroy it* (32b).

This is an extraordinary encounter. God is treating Abraham as his friend, telling him his plans and allowing him to ask him questions.

Why does Abraham not go any lower than ten? Before that last question he asks God to *let me speak just once more* (32a). It's probably because he's thinking of Lot and his family.

In any case the conversation is over: *the LORD had finished speaking with Abraham* (33a). So *he left, and Abraham returned home,* back to his tents near the great trees of Mamre (33b, and see chapter 18:1).

Abraham has been interceding for Lot and for Sodom: he is being a blessing. And he has been getting to know God better.

c'. – Lot flees Sodom, which God destroys (19:1-38)

Now we are going to see God's justice at work as he destroys Sodom. But there is mercy too.

1. Sodom's wickedness (1-5). When *the two angels arrived at Sodom in the evening, […] Lot was sitting in the gateway of the city* (1a): it looks like he is well known, and may even be considered a leader.

Lot welcomes the visitors with a show of middle-eastern hospitality (see 2 and 3b). He insists that they stay in his house rather than outside in the square (see 2b-3a): is this because he knows they will be in danger from the men of Sodom?

The account is clear. *All the men from every part of the city of Sodom* surround the house, *both young and old* (4). They call out to Lot *Where are the men who came to you tonight? Bring them out to us so that we can have sex with them* (5).

This is going to be homosexual gang rape. Even ancient cultures who permitted homosexual activity between consenting adults would have seen this as degrading and disgraceful, but the men of Sodom have no such inhibitions.

It's worth mentioning that the Bible doesn't say that same-sex *attraction* is sinful: sin happens when that becomes same-sex *activity*.

So this is Sodom's wickedness. It's blatant, bestial and unashamed.

2. God's mercy (6-22). One way of looking at what happens now is to look at these verses in four episodes. And in each of them we see God's mercy at work.

+ Episode One (6-11). Lot goes outside *and shut the door behind him* (6), and tells the men of Sodom not to do *this wicked thing* (7). Astonishingly, and appallingly, he offers them his two virgin daughters: *you can do what you like with them* (8). What kind of man *is* this?

But the wickedness continues: *they kept bringing pressure on Lot and moved forward to break down the door* (9b).

And now we see God's mercy. The men inside (ie the angels) *reached out and pulled Lot back into the house and shut the door* (10). Then *they struck the men who were at the door of the house… with blindness so that they could not find the door* (11).

The word *blindness* probably refers to a temporary blinding, rather than something permanent.

+ Episode Two (12-14). The two men ask Lot if he has family *or anyone else in the city who belongs to you* (12). They tell him to *get them out of here, because we are going to destroy this place* (12b-13a). They make it clear that this is God's justice at work: *The outcry to the LORD against its people is so great that he has sent us to destroy it* (13).

This is mercy again.

Lot pleads with his family to get out of Sodom, *but his sons-in-law thought he was joking* (14b). Which means that they're going to stay in Sodom.

+ Episode Three (15-16). The angels urge Lot to *take your wife and your two daughters… or you will be swept away when the city is punished* (15).

When Lot hesitates, *the men grasped his hand and the hands of his wife and of his two daughters and led them safely out of the city* (16). And we're to understand why they do this: it's because *the LORD was merciful to them* (16b).

+ Episode Four (17-22). One of the angels tells Lot and the three women to *flee to the mountains or you will be swept away!* (17b). But Lot, once again, prevaricates: he says that he *can't flee to the mountains* (19). He asks, instead, to be allowed to escape to *a town near enough to run to* (20).

Extraordinarily, the angels grant Lot's request: one of them promises that *I will not overthrow the town you speak of* (21).

This is mercy again. Lot is being so half-hearted about being saved, but God is clearly utterly committed to rescuing him.

And so we come to the end of Sodom.

3. Sodom's destruction (23-29). As soon as Lot is in safety, *the LORD rained down burning sulphur on Sodom and Gomorrah* (24). In doing this he is *destroying all those living in the cities – and also the vegetation in the land* (25b).

The destruction is complete. This is God's just judgment in action.

But Lot's wife becomes one of those destroyed: she ignores the angel's instructions not to look back (see 17) and *became a pillar of salt* (26). Perhaps she was from Sodom herself and is hankering after her old life in a city she felt comfortable in.

In any case, Jesus uses her as a warning example to his disciples (see Luke 17:31-33).

Now we see Abraham witnessing what God has done. He *looked down towards Sodom and Gomorrah, towards all the land of the plain* (28a), as the two angels had earlier (see chapter 18:16a).

Abraham sees *dense smoke rising from the land, like smoke from a furnace* (28b). And he's reminded that Lot has been rescued because God *remembered Abraham* (29).

But the chapter is not finished. First, we get a snapshot of Lot's life after Sodom.

4. Lot's degradation (30-38). We've already seen how Lot dragged his feet when the angels were wanting to get him out of Sodom: it looks like he has been influenced by the sins of the city.

Now *Lot and his two daughters left Zoar and settled in the mountains, for he was afraid to stay in Zoar* (30). He's lost all his great wealth and is now living *in a cave* (30b).

His elder daughter comes up with a plan to get children. Because *there is no man round here to give us children* (31), she suggests to her sister that they get their father drunk and then have sex with him (see 32).

Which is what happens, over two nights. Lot is *not aware of* what's happening (33b and 35b), but he's still responsible. He had been willing for his daughters to be sexually abused in Sodom (see 8); now they are taking sexual advantage of their own father.

And yet, despite Lot's behaviour in the book of Genesis, the New Testament describes him as righteous (three times in 2 Peter 2:7-8, and see Genesis 18:23ff). God has graciously allowed Lot to be in relationship with him.

But he is compromised. Sinful ways can get ingrained in the lives of those who trust God: Lot is a warning to us. We need not only to remember Lot's wife; we need to remember Lot too.

Both of the daughters *became pregnant by their father* (36). Two sons are born. And it looks like neither of the daughters is ashamed of her actions.

What comes next will seem familiar to us.

b'. – Abraham lies about Sarah in Gerar (20:1-18)

1. Abraham's sin (1-2). When settled in Gerar for a while, Abraham says *of his wife Sarah, 'She is my sister'* (2a).

It's the same old sin (see incident b, chapter 12:10-20). Later in chapter 20 Abraham even claims that when God had first called him he had told Sarah *Everywhere we go, say of me 'He is my brother'* (13b).

It looks like he's unable to trust God to look after him.

In any event, *Abimelek king of Gerar sent for Sarah and took her* (2b).

2. Abimelek's dream (3-7). God tells Abimelek that Sarah is married, so he's about to commit adultery: he adds that because of this the king is *as good as dead* (3).

Abimelek, rightly, defends himself. Before telling God that Abraham and Sarah had both deceived him, the account tells us that *Abimelek had not gone near her* (4a). God is in this: he is making sure that when Sarah becomes pregnant there will be no doubt as to who the father is.

So Abimelck adds that *I have done this with a clear conscience and with clean hands* (5b).

God acknowledges that Abimelek is right, adding that *I did not let you touch her* (6b). The king is to give Sarah back to Abraham, who will *pray for you and you will live*, because *he is a prophet* (7a).

This is the only time Abraham is so described. But a prophet he most certainly is: he's in relationship with God and has prayed for Lot and Sodom (see chapter 18:16-33). Soon he will pray for Abimelek too.

3. Abraham's excuse (8-13). Abimelek's officials are *very much afraid* (8b): they clearly believe in the reality of a God of justice. The king asks Abraham why he has *brought such guilt on me and my kingdom* (9).

Abraham's excuse is to say that *there is surely no fear of God in this place, and they will kill me because of my wife* (11). But he's wrong about that: Abimelek clearly does fear God (see 4-5 and 8).

Then Abraham argues that what he had said wasn't really a lie at all, because Sarah is his half-sister, *the daughter of my father though not of my mother* (12).

This doesn't sound like a man of God at all. He's committing this sin, knowingly and repeatedly (see 13).

Abraham even admits how he had persuaded Sarah to join him in his lie in the first place: he had said to her *This is how you can show your love to me* (13b).

In other words: You can show your love to me by telling this lie and probably having sex with other men as a result.

4. Abimelek's response (14-16). The king gives gifts to Abraham (see 14): is this his way of reassuring him that he has really not slept with Sarah?

And he tells Abraham *My land is before you; live wherever you like* (15). Perhaps he thinks it will be an advantage to have a prophet of God living nearby.

Abimelek tells Sarah about the *thousand shekels of silver* he is giving to Abraham (16a): this, he says, is *to cover the offence against you* (16).

5. God's grace (17-18). Because of what Abraham and Sarah had done, *the LORD had kept all the women in Abimelek's household from conceiving* (18).

Then *Abraham prayed to God* (17a) and God answered his prayer: he *healed Abimelek, his wife and his female slaves, so they could have children again* (17b). We don't know if Abraham also asked God for forgiveness for his repeated, wilful sin.

God's grace is astonishing. Despite Abraham's behaviour he is still *a prophet* (7) and God still answers his prayers.

And, by making sure that Abimelek never got as far as sleeping with Sarah, God has done two things: he's rescued Sarah from this horrific situation, and he's prevented there being any confusion as to who the father of her baby will be.

God Almighty (chapter 17:1) is making sure that all his promises to Abraham will be fulfilled.

And so now we see his grace in action again.

a'. – Conclusion: the birth of Isaac (21:1-7)

1. What God does (1-2). *The LORD was gracious to Sarah as he had said* (1a), but this is so important that it needs repeating: *the LORD did for Sarah what he had promised* (1b).

And now we're reminded of what that means in practice. Sarah *became pregnant and bore a son to Abraham in his old age* (2): and this all happened *at the very time God had promised him* (2b).

2. What Abraham does (3-5). He names the boy Isaac (which means *he laughs,* and see chapter 17:19), and eight days after the birth *Abraham circumcised him* (4). And he does this *as God commanded him* (4b).

Abraham is getting back into the habit of obeying God.

Surely he must also be full of awe and gratitude? He is, after all, *a hundred years old when his son Isaac was born to him* (5).

3. What Sarah does (6-7). It looks like faith is growing here: she asks *Who would have said to Abraham that Sarah would nurse children?* (7).

And she has laughter on her mind. In giving her Isaac, *God has brought me laughter* (6), a very different laughter this time. Her initial laughter, when told she would have a son, was a laughter of unbelief (see chapter 18:12).

But this is a laughter of joy and of faith. And a laughter Sarah invites us to share: *Everyone who hears about this will laugh with me* (6b).

Isaac has been born. The mirror link with incident a (*Promise of descendants*, chapter 12:1-9) points us clearly to God's astonishing grace.

Learning Genesis+

You will find it easier to learn Section B if you count on your fingers as you say the incidents out loud; when you reach incident g, do a finger-count back to the beginning.

First, say the titles of incidents a, b and c (using your fingers as you do). When you can do that without looking at *The Genesis+ Experiment*, do the same with incidents d, e and f. When you've got those in your memory, say all six incidents aloud several times.

Now say *God's covenant with Abram/Abraham* (incident g) until you can say it by heart.

Now say incidents f', e' and d' out loud until you can do that without looking at this book. This will be easier because of the mirror links with the first half of the section (and using your fingers will be a help, too).

Then do the same with incidents c', b' and a'. Remember that this is much easier if you do it aloud.

When you're ready, try to say the whole of Section B. Within fifteen minutes you'll know the order of the incidents by heart.

Section B: The Abraham Story

a.   Introduction: the promise of descendants
b.   *Abram lies about Sarai in Egypt*
c.   Lot settles in Sodom
d.   *Abram intercedes for Lot and Sodom militarily*
e.   Promise of a son: from Abram himself
f.   *Ishmael: his birth*
g.   CENTRE: God's covenant with Abram/Abraham
f'. *Ishmael: his circumcision*
e'. Promise of a son: from Sarah herself
d'. *Abraham intercedes for Lot and Sodom in prayer*
c'. Lot flees Sodom, which God destroys
b'. *Abraham lies about Sarah in Gerar*
a'. Conclusion: the birth of Isaac

Meeting God

Once you have committed the structure to memory, start to tell the events of the section to yourself, or to a friend, including as many details as you remember. As you do this, the Holy Spirit will be using the Abraham story in your life.

You might like to use the study questions about the Abraham story: you'll find them in Appendix 3.

And you might like to think about Abraham's altars. I'm not suggesting you build one, but can you think of an object which would be a visible reminder to you that you're in relationship with God?

Take time to thank God for his promises; and for his faithfulness, despite Abraham's mistakes, in fulfilling them. Thank God for his justice, and for his grace to Abraham.

And thank him, too, that *you* are experiencing the blessing of those promises, because you trust in Jesus.

This is the Genesis+ experiment: as you re-tell the Abraham story you will meet God and worship him.

Section C
The Isaac Story (Genesis 21:8 – 28:4)

Although Section B is over, there is still more for us to learn about Abraham. But the focus in Section C is on the son of the promise: Isaac. At the start of the section he is an infant, while at its end he is so old that he can no longer see. During Section C we will watch Isaac being sacrificed by his father Abraham, see his marriage to Rebekah, and meet their sons Esau and Jacob. And, in it all, God remains faithful to his promises.

Abraham looked up and there in a thicket
he saw a ram caught by its horns.
He went over and took the ram
and sacrificed it as a burnt offering
instead of his son.

Genesis 22:13

Enjoying the View

a. God chooses the younger son: Isaac (21:8-19)
b. *Marriage of nonchosen older son: Ishmael* (21:20-21)
c. Strife with Abimelek of Gerar over Abraham's wells (21:22-34)
d. *Abraham's sacrifice of Isaac* (22:1-19)
e. Nonchosen genealogy: the family of Nahor (22:20-24)
f. *The death of Sarah* (23:1-20)
g. CENTRE: God chooses Rebekah as Isaac's wife (24:1-67)
f'. *The death of Abraham* (25:1-11)
e'. Nonchosen genealogy: the family of Ishmael (25:12-18)
d'. *Esau's sacrifice of his birthright* (25:19-34)
c'. Strife with Abimelek of Gerar over Abraham's wells (26:1-33)
b'. *Marriage of nonchosen older son: Esau* (26:34-35)
a'. God chooses the younger son: Jacob (27:1 – 28:4)

Once again, the section is written with mirror links, making it easy to commit to memory.

In the centre of the section is God's choice of Rebekah to be Isaac's wife and the matriarch of God's people. While God clearly blesses Ishmael and then Esau (see b and b'), his covenant is with Isaac and then Jacob (see incidents a and a').

In the best-known incident in the section we see Abraham's faith in action: he is determined to trust God and to obey him whatever happens (see incident d). Esau, on the other hand, shows scant regard for the most important things (see incident d'). But, through all of this, we see the next stages of God's plan being fulfilled.

Isaac is thirsty. Of course he and his household need water, but there's another kind of thirst, for meaning and purpose. What can quench *this* thirst? Ultimately the answer is that the promised seed and blessing-bringer of Genesis 3:15 will come.

The pointer to Isaac's thirst is the digging of wells. It's God's gift that the diggers find water, just as it's true that he is the one who quenches our thirst for meaning and purpose. The wells are Section C's symbol.

It would be good to read through Genesis 21:8 – 28:4 before going on. Look out for the wells: they're a reminder that our deepest thirst can only finally be quenched by God.

Be ready to meet him: it's only a short step from reading to worship.

Unpacking the Content

a. – God chooses the younger son (21:8-19)

This is not new information: we already know this. But the first incident of Section C reminds us of two promises that God has made.

1. God repeats the Isaac promise (8-13). Abraham holds *a great feast* to celebrate Isaac being weaned (8): in an age before modern medicine there was a high infant mortality rate, so this is a huge event.

But Sarah sees Ishmael *mocking* Isaac (9b), which means he is mistreating him in some way. So she tells Abraham to *get rid of that slave woman and her son* (10a): she wants there to be no doubt that Isaac is the only heir of Abraham's fortune (see 10b).

Because Ishmael is *his son* (11b), *the matter distressed Abraham greatly* (11a). But God assures him that he can send Hagar and Ishmael away, because he *will make the son of the slave into a nation also, because he is your offspring* (13).

And God repeats the Isaac promise: it is *through Isaac that your offspring will be reckoned* (12b, and see chapter 17:19).

So *early the next morning*, Abraham gives food and water to Hagar and *sent her off with the boy* (14).

2. God repeats the Ishmael promise (14-19). God has already done this for Abraham in verse 13, but Hagar needs to hear the promise again, too.

Wandering in the desert, the time comes when Hagar has no more water. So she places her son *under one of the bushes* (15) and leaves him there, because she *cannot watch the boy die* (16).

Then *she began to sob* (16b).

When God hears Ishmael crying, *the angel of God called to Hagar from heaven* (17a). He reassures her that Ishmael is not going to die: God will *make him into a great nation* (18).

Before Ishmael had even been born, God had already told Hagar that he would *increase your descendants so much that they will be too numerous to count* (chapter 16:10): but now God is repeating the promise.

Hagar suddenly sees *a well of water* (19a). She gives *the boy a drink,* and doubtless herself drinks as much as she needs. This is the first mention of Section C's symbol.

God is looking after Ishmael and his mother. He will make a great nation of Ishmael, but Isaac is the heir of the promise. The goal of that promise is blessing for all nations.

Including the nation that will come from Ishmael.

b. – Marriage of nonchosen older son: Ishmael (21:20-21)

This is a brief summary of the rest of Ishmael's life. As he grows up, *God was with the boy* (20a). He lives *in the Desert of Paran* (21) and *became an archer* (20b).

And *his mother got a wife for him from Egypt* (21b): as an Egyptian herself, it's the obvious place to look.

c. – Strife with Abimelek of Gerar over Abraham's wells (21:22-34)

This incident brings us back to King Abimelek of Gerar again (see chapter 20). It begins with the king approaching Abraham: he brings *Phicol the commander of his forces* with him (22).

1. A pact gets agreed (22-24). Abimelek tells Abraham that he recognises that *God is with you in everything you do* (22). He knows too that Abraham is powerful. So he asks him to *swear to me here before God that you will not deal falsely with me or my children or my descendants* (23).

Abimelek reminds Abraham of his status as a resident alien: *Show to me and the country where you now reside as a foreigner the same kindness that I have shown to you* (23).

It's like he's asking for a non-aggression pact. And Abraham, happy to comply, replies *I swear it* (24).

2. A treaty gets made (25-31). Now Abraham *complained to Abimelek about a well of water that Abimelek's servants had seized* (25): presumably this means that the well is no longer available to Abraham. Abimelek is hearing about this for the first time (see 26).

So Abraham takes the initiative. After he brings *sheep and cattle* for Abimelek, *the two men made a treaty* (27).

There is an odd aspect to this. Abraham *set apart seven ewe lambs from the flock* (28). What's this about?

Which is exactly what Abimelek asks: *What is the meaning of these seven ewe lambs?* (29). Abraham replies that in accepting these valuable animals Abimelek will be acknowledging *that I dug this well* (30).

This matters. Abraham had not seized a water resource from others; rather he had made one of his own.

So then *the treaty had been made* (32): *the two men swore an oath* at the place, which they called *Beersheba* (31).

There is a play on words here. *Beersheba* can mean *well of the oath* or *well of the seven*, and seven is the number of completion.

In other words, this treaty is important. This well at Beersheba is a foretaste of what is to come, as God's promises become reality: one day the whole land will belong to Abraham's descendants.

3. A tree gets planted (32-34). After *Abimelek and Phicol the commander of his forces* have left (32), *Abraham planted a tamarisk tree in Beersheba* (33a). This may be his way of claiming the well and the land around Beersheba as his own.

But after planting the tree, Abraham *called on the name of the LORD, the Eternal God* (33b). By addressing God in this way, he is acknowledging two things. First, God is eternally unchanging.

And second, the promises of God about descendants and the land have enduring character.

And Abraham is already experiencing the beginning of their fulfilment.

d. – Abraham's sacrifice of Isaac (22:1-19)

Although we are in a section called *The Isaac Story*, Isaac himself was nowhere to be seen in incident c.

Now we see him centre stage. But in a largely passive role.

In verse 14 of the chapter Abraham calls God *the LORD will provide*, which suggests a way of looking at the whole passage.

1. The God who tests (1-2). God tells Abraham *Take your son, your only son, whom you love – Isaac* (2a). He is to go to Moriah and *sacrifice him there as a burnt offering* (2b).

We can scarcely imagine the shock. Isaac is the son of the promise, and God has specifically named Isaac as part of that promise (see chapter 17:19 and 21). And yet now he is to kill his son, whom he loves, and offer him to God.

The account tells us what God is doing: he *tested* Abraham (1a). So how will Abraham react?

2. The God who watches (3-10). Abraham gets ready to leave for Moriah, and takes with him *two of his servants and his son Isaac* (3a). And he does this *early the next morning* (3a).

He sets out after *he had cut enough wood for the burnt offering* (3b): Abraham clearly plans to obey God and sacrifice Isaac.

Abraham is a man of faith. On the third day he tells his servants that Isaac and he will go on alone. He adds that *we will worship and then <u>we</u> will come back to you* (5b).

He is expecting to return with his son alive. Indeed, the letter to the Hebrews in the New Testament tells us that *Abraham reasoned that God could even raise the dead* (Heb 11:19a).

This is extraordinary. Abraham has never had a Bible to read, but he believes that if he kills his son God will bring him back to life.

Abraham and Isaac finish the journey together. Abraham is carrying the fire and the knife, but he takes *the wood for the burnt offering and placed it on his son Isaac* (6).

As they walk on, Isaac asks his father *Where is the lamb for the burnt offering?* (7b).

Abraham replies that *God himself will provide the lamb* (8a). As we watch Abraham's obedient faith, God is watching too.

When they reach the spot, Abraham *built an altar there and arranged the wood on it* (9a). Then *he bound his son Isaac and laid him on the altar* (9b).

There is no mention of a struggle: does Isaac share Abraham's faith? In any case: Abraham *took the knife to slay his son* (10).

We are seeing Abraham's faith and Abraham's obedience. And God is watching.

3. The God who provides (11-14). And now the focus is on what God does: *the angel of the LORD called out to him* (11) and tells him *Do not lay a hand on the boy* (12a).

Through the angel God tells Abraham *Now I know that you fear God, because you have not withheld from me your son, your only son* (12b).

Abraham looks up and *there in a thicket he saw a ram caught by its horns* (13a). Understanding what he is to do, he *took the ram and and sacrificed it as a burnt offering instead of his son* (13b). There's substitution here: the ram dies *instead of* Isaac.

And so Abraham calls the place *The LORD will provide* (14a).

Abraham had never read the New Testament, but we have. And it's impossible to read Genesis chapter 22 without thinking of God sacrificing his Son Jesus as a substitute for sinners: he provided a sacrifice so that we could be forgiven.

And that happened on the cross.

Isaac carries the wood to Moriah for the sacrifice (see 6a), just as Jesus carried his cross to Golgotha (see John 19:17). And Mount Moriah is in Jerusalem (see 2 Chronicles 3:1).

And although the focus in this chapter is on Abraham, Isaac demonstrates God's pattern for the chosen seed: to be a servant sacrificed. Jesus, a descendant of Isaac, will one day come *not to be served but to serve, and to give his life as a ransom for many* (Mark 10:45).

This is a good opportunity to lift our hearts and to worship God.

But the angel of the LORD speaks again.

4. The God who promises (15-19). God's words here are the only divine oath in the book of Genesis. *I swear by myself,* he says (16a), because there is no higher authority by which he could do it (see Hebrews 6:13).

God tells Abraham *why* he's swearing the oath: it's *because you have done this and have not withheld your son, your only son* (16b) or, in other words, *because you have obeyed me* (18b).

The oath promises three things.

+ First, Abraham will have many descendants, *as numerous as the stars in the sky and as the sand on the seashore* (17a).

+ Second, one of Abraham's descendants *will take possession of the cities of his enemies* (17b; the verb is singular and in the Hebrew the word is *his*, not *their*).

+ And third, through this descendant *all nations on earth* will consider themselves blessed (18a).

Those last two promises are messianic: they will find their fulfilment in Jesus.

As Abraham and Isaac return *to his servants* (19), their minds and hearts are full. One of their descendants will be a Saviour: through him all nations will find blessing.

e. – Nonchosen genealogy: the family of Nahor (22:20-24)

Abraham gets news of his brother Nahor.

He has twelve sons, eight by his wife Milkah (see 20-22) and four by his concubine (see 24).

In the context of God's promises being fulfilled, the most important son is the eighth born to Milkah: his name is *Bethuel* (22b). And here's why: *Bethuel became the father of Rebekah* (23a).

Soon we will read that Rebekah will become Isaac's wife and the mother of the nation.

But Abraham only receives news of Nahor's sons, and not of his grandchildren (apart from Aram, see 21b). So before sending his servant to find a wife for Isaac (see chapter 24), it looks like Abraham knows nothing of Rebekah.

The account is preparing us for what we will soon read about. God is working out his purposes.

f. – The death of Sarah (23:1-20)

At the beginning of this incident Abraham is a resident alien in Canaan. But he ends up as the owner of a piece of land there.

Introduction: the death of Sarah (1-2). Sarah dies when she is *a hundred and twenty-seven years old* (1). She dies in Canaan, and *Abraham went to mourn for Sarah and to weep over her* (2).

The two of them have been through so much together. There have been highs and lows, but the greatest joy has been the birth of Isaac, the son God had promised them.

Abraham has no intention of taking Sarah's body back to his country of origin to bury her there. Of course not: because he believes God's promise she must be buried in Canaan.

One way of looking at the chapter is to see three things Abraham wants. Each one is introduced by him showing respect to the Hittites.

1. Abraham wants a permanent tomb (3-6). *Then Abraham rose from beside his dead wife* (3). He admits that he is *a foreigner and stranger among you* (4a), and asks the Hittites to *sell me some property for a burial site here* (4b).

The Hittites are respectful to Abraham, acknowledging him as *a mighty prince among us* (6a). The offer is generous: Abraham may *bury your dead in the choicest of our tombs* (6).

But they seem to be trying to prevent Abraham from buying any property.

2. Abraham wants Ephron's cave (7-11). *Then Abraham rose and bowed down before the people of the land* (7): his show of respect is designed to coax them into listening to him.

He has set his heart on *buying* a burial plot. And he has one in mind: he asks them to *intercede with Ephron son of Zohar on my behalf* (8), with the aim that *he will sell me the cave of Machpelah* (9a). Abraham wants to buy it *for the full price as a burial site* (9b).

Ephron makes as if he is not interested in selling. He tells Abraham *I give you the field and I give you the cave that is in it* (11).

On the surface, it looks like Abraham may not be able to buy the cave. But, on the other hand, Ephron has a buyer here who is very motivated.

3. Abraham wants to buy the field with its cave (12-16). Once again *Abraham bowed down before the people of the land* (12). He is quietly insistent: he tells Ephron *I will pay the price of the field* (13).

Now Ephron names his price: *The land is worth four hundred shekels of silver* (15). This is extortionate: but Ephron is hoping that Abraham will close the deal anyway.

So, without trying to negotiate a fairer price, Abraham *agreed to Ephron's terms* (16a): he *weighed out for him the price he had named* (16a).

Conclusion: the deal is done (17-20). So the whole property (the field and the cave) is *legally made over to Abraham* (17b-18a). There's a deed of sale.

This is so important that it's repeated: *the field and the cave in it were legally made over to Abraham by the Hittites as a burial site* (20).

Why does this matter so much? Why is most of chapter 23 about Abraham buying this property?

The answer is clear: the whole country is destined to belong to Abraham's descendants, and this is the first piece of it that he actually owns. The fact that he buys a tomb for Sarah in the heart of the promised land is a declaration of his faith in God's promise.

By owning a part of the land it's like Abraham's prophesying the ultimate ownership of the whole land.

So the story ends: *Abraham buried his wife Sarah in the cave in the field of Machpelah... in the land of Canaan* (19).

g. – CENTRE: God chooses Rebekah as Isaac's wife (24:1-67)

This is the longest single narrative in Genesis: it is clearly very important. If the promises to Abraham are going to be fulfilled, Isaac needs to have a son.

It's helpful to look at the account in five stages.

1. Abraham commissions his servant (1-9). Abraham knows that it's time to act: he is *now very old* (1a). He recognises that *God had blessed him in every way* (1b).

So he calls *the senior servant in his household* (2a): he's going to ask him to swear an oath. Abraham underlines the seriousness of this by telling his servant to *put your hand under my thigh* (2b): the nearness to Abraham's genitals demonstrates what a big deal this is.

The servant is to *swear by the LORD, the God of heaven and the God of earth* (3a) that he will get *a wife for my son* (3b).

But she is not to be *from the daughters of the Canaanites* (3b), but rather from *my country and my own relatives* (4). In other words, the servant is to go back to Harran in Mesopotamia, where God had first called Abraham (see chapter 12:4).

When the servant wonders if it might be necessary for Isaac to go with him (see 5), Abraham is insistent: *Make sure that you do not take my son back there* (6).

And he explains the reason to his servant: God had told him *To your offspring I will give this land* (7). So Abraham is sure that there is no need for Isaac to leave Canaan, because God will *send his angel before you so that you can get a wife for my son* (7b).

So success is guaranteed.

In the unlikely event of Isaac's prospective wife being *unwilling to come back with you, then you will be released from this oath of mine* (8).

Abraham has commissioned his servant, and his servant has sworn the oath.

2. The servant meets Rebekah (10-27). The servant leaves with ten camels and *all kinds of good things from his master* (10a): there is going to be a bride-price to pay. He makes for the region of *Aram Naharaim* (10b) and goes to *the town of Nahor,* which is Harran (10b).

Now the servant prays. He shares his master's faith and is a circumcised member of his household (see chapter 17:27).

Standing near the well, he asks God to *make me successful today* (12). His request is simple. He will ask a young woman for a drink. If she replies *Drink, and I'll water your camels too* (14), he will know that she is *the one you have chosen for your servant Isaac* (14b).

There is no delay: *Before he had finished praying, Rebekah came out with her jar* (15a). The account reminds us that she is *the daughter of Bethuel son of Milkah, who was the wife of Abraham's brother Nahor* (15b).

And Rebekah's described for us, too: she is *very beautiful, a virgin* (16a).

After Rebekah has filled her jar, the servant asks her for a drink: and as he drinks he's waiting for what she will say next. Here it comes: *I'll draw water for your camels too* (19).

As Rebekah does this, the servant *watched her closely* (21): he is seeing the answer to his prayer.

So he takes out *a gold nose ring... and two gold bracelets* (22) and asks if Rebekah's family can offer him hospitality. And in answer to his question *Whose daughter are you?* (23), she tells him what the account has already reminded us of in verse 15 (see 24).

My guess is that the servant is overwhelmed. He *bowed down and worshipped the LORD* (26), who *has not abandoned his kindness and faithfulness to my master* (27a).

There is no doubt in this man's mind: this is God at work. Blessing has come to him at the well. Here's Section C's symbol again.

3. Rebekah's family make their decision (28-54a). When Rebekah runs home and tells the family what has happened, her brother Laban *hurried out to the man at the spring* (29). It looks like his enthusiasm is first and foremost because he has *seen the nose ring, and the bracelets on his sister's arms* (30a).

So Laban brings the servant, his men and the camels to the house: *straw and fodder were brought for the camels* (32), as well as water *for him and his men to wash their feet* (32b).

But when food is offered him, the servant shows that he has another priority: *I will not eat until I have told you what I have to say* (33).

So the servant tells his story. He is Abraham's servant, whose wife Sarah has borne him a son (see 34-36); he has sworn an oath to find a wife for Abraham's son from his father's family and clan (see 37-38); and Abraham has assured him that God will make his journey a success (see 40).

The servant tells Laban and his father Bethuel about his prayer, asking God that a young woman he asked for a drink would volunteer to draw water for the camels too (see 42-44). And he explains that this is exactly what had happened with Rebekah (see 45-47).

The servant is sure that God has *led me on the right road to get the granddaughter of my master's brother for his son* (48b).

And so he waits for the family's decision.

Laban and his father Bethuel are convinced that *this is from the LORD* (50): so they say *Here is Rebekah; take her and go* (51a).

Now the servant worships again (see 52). He gives jewellery and clothing to Rebekah, and *costly gifts to her brother and to her mother* (53b): this looks like the bride-price, which it would be the custom to pay.

Now at last the meal can take place: the servant *and the men who were with him ate and drank* (54a).

The family have made their decision.

4. Rebekah leaves her home and her family (54b-61). The following morning, Laban and his mother, understandably, want to delay her departure. But the servant wants to leave immediately.

So the family call Rebekah and ask her *Will you go with this man?* (58). Her reply is simple: she says *I will go* (58b).

So the group are sent on their way: Rebekah, *along with her nurse, Abraham's servant and his men* (59).

And the family send Rebekah off with a blessing: *May you increase to thousands upon thousands; may your offspring possess the cities of their enemies* (60, and compare chapter 22:17b). God is at work here, even prompting the content of their blessing prayer.

And so *the servant took Rebekah and left* (61b).

5. Isaac marries Rebekah (62-67). Now the focus shifts abruptly to Isaac: *he went out to the field one evening to meditate* (63a).

Isaac *saw camels approaching* (63b), while Rebekah sees Isaac, gets off her camel and asks the servant *Who is that man in the field coming to meet us?* (65a).

His reply is striking: *He is my master* (65b).

This is the first time the servant describes Isaac as his master: it's like he senses that the central figure in the story he's part of is shifting from Abraham to Isaac.

So Rebekah does what decorum dictates. *She took her veil and covered herself* (65b): it was common practice for a woman to wear a veil in the presence of her fiancé.

The servant tells Isaac *all he had done* (66), and, doubtless, all God has done too.

The narrative rushes to its conclusion: Isaac marries Rebekah by bringing her *into the tent* (67a). In this way *she became his wife* (67).

The account closes by telling us one more thing about Isaac and Rebekah: *he loved her* (67b).

Abraham's last significant act has been to make sure that Isaac gets the right wife: the promises of God can continue to be fulfilled.

And the marriage of Isaac and Rebekah signals a turning point in the book of Genesis: Rebekah is taking Sarah's place, and Isaac is taking Abraham's.

And God continues to work out his purposes for this family and for his world.

f'. – The death of Abraham (25:1-11)

Abraham's death is related before the birth of Esau and Jacob, even though they were born fifteen years before he died (see chapter 21:5; 25:7 and 26b).

One reason for the change in chronology is to make the structure of Section C work.

1. Life after Sarah (1-6). *Abraham had taken another wife, whose name was Keturah* (1): actually, we don't know if this happened before Sarah's death or after it.

In any case, she bears Abraham six sons (see 2) and becomes a grandmother too (see 3-4): *All these were descendants of Keturah* (4b).

The account tells us that *Abraham left everything he owned to Isaac* (5). The *sons of his concubines* (6) are the sons of Hagar and Keturah and would not have expected to inherit anything. But Abraham *gave gifts to them* before he died (6), and then *sent them away from his son Isaac* (6b): is this so that he is not in any danger from them?

2. Blessing after Abraham (7-11). Abraham lived *a hundred and seventy-five years* (7): this means that he had lived for a century since first coming to Canaan (see chapter 12:4).

Abraham's death is described as a good one: he *breathed his last and died at a good old age* (8a), he was *an old man and full of years* (8), and *he was gathered to his people* (8b).

And *his sons Isaac and Ishmael buried him* (9): this is the only verse which places Isaac and Ishmael together as adults. Despite the tensions there will inevitably have been between them, they reunite to bury their father.

We already know the burial place: it's *the cave of Machpelah near Mamre* (9) and its full description underlines its importance. This site belongs to Abraham and to his descendants.

And so to Isaac too. Already part of the promised land of Canaan belongs to him.

But God's blessing has not died with Abraham: we read that *after Abraham's death, God blessed his son Isaac* (11).

e'. – Nonchosen genealogy: the family of Ishmael (25:12-18)

This, we are told, is *the account of the family line of Abraham\s son Ishmael* (12a). There's a mirror link here with the genealogy of the family of Nahor (see chapter 22:20-24). But before we go further, we're reminded that Ishmael was not the son of the promise: he's the boy *Sarah's slave, Hagar the Egyptian, bore to Abraham* (1b).

But there is blessing here. Ishmael has twelve sons (see 13-15), who are *twelve tribal rulers according to their settlements and camps* (16b).

And now we are told of Ishmael's death: it's described in a similar way to Abraham's (see 8). He lived *a hundred and thirty-seven years*; he *breathed his last and died*; and *he was gathered to his people* (17).

That last phrase suggests that Ishmael, though not in the line of promise, is a circumcised son of Abraham (see chapter 17:23) and also a believer in Yahweh.

Ishmael's descendants settle *in the area from Havilah to Shur, near the eastern border of Egypt* (18), which is northwest Arabia. And *they lived in hostility towards all the tribes related to them* (18b).

This account of Ishmael's family line reminds us that Yahweh is not only the God of Abraham and Isaac, but also the One who wants to bless all the nations.

d'. – Esau's sacrifice of his birthright (25:19-34)

The incident of Esau selling his birthright to his brother Jacob is the climax of this passage. There's a mirror link here with Abraham's sacrifice of Isaac.

But first we get some vital background.

1. Listening to Yahweh (19-26). Isaac *prayed to the LORD on behalf of his wife, because she was childless* (21a). And God answers his prayer.

But Rebekah's pregnancy is difficult: *the babies jostled each other within her* (22a, the Hebrew is *struggled with each other*). In her desperation she asks *Why is this happening to me?* (22b, the Hebrew is *Why this I?*).

So Rebekah asks God. We don't know how she did this, but she may have asked her husband, who is described as a prophet in Psalm 105 (verses 8-15).

In any event, Yahweh speaks to her. The message is not simply that there are nonidentical twins in her womb: it's *two nations* (23a). They *will be separated* (23a): they are incompatible.

One people, says God, *will be stronger than the other* (23b), and the stronger one will be the younger son whom the elder will serve.

This is strong stuff.

God's choice of the younger son demonstrates that he acts in grace: his favour is not earned by human effort or human position.

When Rebekah gives birth, *the first to come out was red... like a hairy garment; so they named him Esau* (25). Then *his brother came out, with his hand grasping Esau's heel* (26a).

The younger son is given the name *Jacob* (26a), which in Hebrew has the same consonants as the word for *heel.* The name can mean *May he be protected,* but it can also mean *cheat* or *deceiver.*

But we've listened to what God has said about these two boys, and Isaac and Rebekah have listened too. This sets the scene for what will follow.

2. Meeting the family (27-28). Now we're introduced to Esau and Jacob as adults. Esau is *a skilful hunter* (27a), an outdoorsman, while Jacob is *content* and lives *among the tents* (27b). The Hebrew uses the word *quiet,* which probably means *thoughtful* and perhaps even *calculating.*

And their parents take sides. Isaac *loved Esau* because he has *a taste for wild game*; but *Rebekah loved Jacob* (28).

Isaac and Rebekah's favouritism will only increase the conflict between Esau and Jacob.

3. Despising the birthright (29-34). At this stage we are only told about one incident to do with Esau and Jacob's relationship.

One day, Jacob is *cooking some stew* (29), when Esau comes in from the fields: he's *famished* (29). Esau says to his brother *Quick, let me have some of that red stew!* (30).

Jacob's reply is brusque and calculating: he sees an opportunity here. He tells Esau to *sell me your birthright* (31).

The birthright is the privileged status of the firstborn son: it means he will one day be the head of the family.

But Esau isn't interested in his birthright, because he's hungry: he asks *What good is the birthright to me?* (32). He claims that he's *about to die* (32a).

So Esau is going along with Jacob's plan. But Jacob wants to be sure that his brother will stick to his side of the bargain, so he tells Esau to *swear to me first* (33). Which Esau does.

Now Esau gets *some bread and some lentil stew* (34a). And then we're told that after eating and drinking, he *got up and left* (34a).

Apparently unbothered. Esau has got what he wants. He's a slave of his appetites; he doesn't believe in delayed gratification; he views the birth-right as something trivial.

And so we read that *Esau despised his birthright* (34b, and see Hebrews 12:16).

The account criticises Esau, and not Jacob. Jacob is devious and calculat-ing: he takes advantage of his brother's weakness to get the birthright for himself. He is a schemer who will do anything to get what he wants.

But he believes the promise. Sure, he doesn't think it will be his without his sinful manipulation of Esau, but he believes.

The account doesn't praise Jacob for his actions. But it does show that God works through imperfect humans to accomplish his purposes.

c'. – Strife with Abimelek of Gerar over Abraham's wells (26:1-33)

This passage is full of God's blessing on Isaac's life. Once again, wells are centre-stage here: they're a crucial factor.

This passage forms a mirror link with Genesis 21:22-34.

1. Yahweh's blessing and an old sin (1-11). There's another famine, and *Isaac went to Abimelek king of the Philistines in Gerar* (1b). It looks like Abimelek was a popular name in this dynasty.

+ Yahweh's blessing (1-6). Yahweh *appeared to Isaac* (2a), so this is a really important moment. He tells him to *not go down to Egypt; live in the land where I tell you to live* (2b).

On the face of it, this is a course of action that could lead to catastrophe. So this requires faith from Isaac.

God encourages him by telling him of all the blessings that will flow his way: *To you and your descendants I will give all these lands* (3), *I will make your descendants as numerous as the stars in the sky* (4), and *through your offspring all nations on earth will be blessed* (4).

This will all happen *because Abraham obeyed me* (5).

So, risky though it is, why wouldn't Isaac decide to trust God? Which is what he does: *Isaac stayed in Gerar* (6).

+ An old sin (7-11). When asked about Rebekah, Isaac replies that *she is my sister* (7a): he's afraid that the men here *might kill me on account of Rebekah* (7b).

This is sadly familiar. Isaac learned from his father how easy it is to use deception instead of trusting God to be faithful to his promises: trickery is almost becoming a family trait.

After *Isaac had been there a long time* (8a), Abimelek sees Isaac behaving towards Rebekah in a way that is inappropriate between brother and sister (NIV2011 has that he was *caressing* her).

So Isaac has been rumbled. Abimelek tells him that *one of the men might well have slept with your wife* (10), which *would have brought guilt upon us* (10b).

Isaac has deliberately set out to deceive. Which is a reminder that God's favour is being given to such people *despite* their misbehaviour. There is chronic weakness in God's chosen material.

2. Yahweh's blessing and Abraham's wells (12-22). Once again we read of Isaac that *the LORD blessed him* (12). But this blessing brings tensions with it.

+ Yahweh's blessing (12-15). Isaac's crops *reaped a hundredfold* (12): he *became rich* and *very wealthy* (13).

So much so, that *the Philistines envied him* (14). As a result they resort to vandalism: all the wells that Abraham's men had dug *the Philistines stopped up, filling them with earth* (15b).

+ Abraham's wells (16-22). The wells are vital. The Negev area is close to being desert, but there is water underground. So wells need to be dug, which requires huge amounts of manpower. And they're a reminder, too, that it's God who can quench our thirst for meaning and purpose.

Anyway, Isaac has so many flocks and herds that Abimelek tells him to *move away from us* (16). In *the valley of Gerar* (17), he *reopened the wells that had been dug in the time of his father Abraham* (18a). In giving them *the same names his father had given them* (18b), Isaac is reasserting ownership.

They're *his* wells now.

Isaac's servants are busy: they dig a new well, but the herdsmen in Gerar maintain *The water is ours!* (20). So Isaac calls the well *Esek* (which means *Argument,* 20b).

They dig another well, but there's a quarrel about that one too, so Isaac *named it Sitnah* (which means *Hostility,* 21).

When one more well is dug there is no dispute this time, so Isaac calls it *Rehoboth* (which means *Open Spaces,* 22).

The astonishing thing in all of this is that in a time of famine Isaac keeps on finding water. God is blessing him. Once again, wells are linked with the blessing of God: that's why they are Section C's symbol.

3. Yahweh's blessing and a pact with Abimelek (23-33). Isaac, still on the move for more open spaces, finally reaches *Beersheba* (23).

And *that night the LORD appeared to him* again (24a).

+ Yahweh's blessing (23-25). God repeats his promise of blessing, beginning with the reminder that he is *the God of your father Abraham* (24a).

He promises Isaac that *I am with you* (24): *I will bless you and will increase the number of your descendants* (24b). And he will do this *for the sake of my servant Abraham* (24b).

The promises of blessing for Isaac keep coming.

And Isaac keeps believing: he *built an altar there and called on the name of the LORD* (25). And *there his servants dug a well* (25).

+ A pact with Abimelek (26-33). Now Abimelek arrives, bringing with him *Phicol the commander of his forces* (26): this is another link with incident c (see chapter 21:22).

In answer to a question from Isaac, they reply that *We saw clearly that the LORD was with you* (28a). So they want to *make a treaty with you that you will do us no harm* (28b-29a).

Isaac agrees to this. A feast in the evening seals the deal, and in the morning *the men swore an oath to each other* (31). Isaac is able to make peace with honour.

And confirmation of God's blessing comes on the day Abimelek leaves: Isaac's servants have dug another well and tell him *We've found water!* (32).

Isaac calls the well *Shibah* (33), which means *oath*. But it also means *seven*. Is this the seventh well? Does Isaac feel that the job is done and the blessing is complete? Does the water remind him that God has been pouring out blessing on to him?

The account ends by telling us that *to this day the name of the town has been Beersheba* (33, and see my comments on chapter 21:31).

b'. – Marriage of nonchosen older son: Esau (26:34-35)

The message is short but clear: *When Esau was forty years old, he married* two Canaanite women (34). He's not bothered about being married to people who don't share his faith.

And this marriage, and these wives, were *a source of grief to Isaac and Rebekah* (35). Doubtless Esau is going to adopt Canaanite religious practices: he's not being true to the covenant promises.

Isaac and Rebekah are united at least in this: they both want to maintain the family's faith in the God of Abraham.

a'. – God chooses the younger son: Jacob (27:1 – 28:4)

Jacob has already got the birthright that should have been Esau's (see chapter 25:19-34); now he will steal the blessing from him, too.

The blessing means that prosperity and dominion will be part of that son's life.

We don't know how Yahweh would have fulfilled his will for Jacob, as revealed in the promise at the time of the twins' birth. But we do know that Rebekah and Jacob decide to use deceit to get all these things to happen.

We'll look at this incident in five stages.

1. Isaac sends Esau to hunt game (1-4). Isaac's eyes are *so weak that he could no longer see* (1a), and he knows that he is *now an old man* (2a).

So he decides that he wants to give Esau *my blessing before I die* (4b).

Isaac wants to make an occasion of it: he sends Esau to *hunt some wild game for me* (3b). Then Esau is to *prepare me the kind of tasty food I like and bring it to me to eat* (4a).

Isaac's favouritism for Esau has blinded his spiritual sight. He knows that it's God's purpose to bless Jacob and not Esau, but he's not having that.

Esau must have the blessing.

2. Rebekah sends Jacob to Isaac (5-17). Rebekah has been *listening as Isaac spoke to his son Esau* (5a). So, as soon as Esau has left the tents to hunt his game, she sets to work.

Rebekah has the opportunity to trust God to fulfil his promise at the birth of the twins; but instead she decides to work against her husband's plans through deception.

So she tells Jacob about Isaac's conversation with Esau, and sends him to get *two choice young goats, so I can prepare some tasty food for your father, just the way he likes it* (9).

Then she explains the plan: Jacob will *take it to your father to eat, so that he may give you his blessing before he dies* (10).

But Jacob has identified a problem. His brother Esau *is a hairy man while I have smooth skin* (11): so if Isaac touches him, Jacob would *bring down a curse on myself rather than a blessing* (12).

But Rebekah has thought of that. If Isaac were to spot the deception, *let the curse fall on me* (13).

So Jacob gets the goats from the flock and Rebekah cooks the meal. Then she takes *the best clothes of her elder son Esau ... and put them on her younger son Jacob* (15). More: she puts goatskins on Jacob's hands and on the back of his neck.

She's thought of everything: she's leaving nothing to chance.

So she *handed to her son Jacob the tasty food and the bread she had made* (17).

3. Jacob deceives Isaac and receives the blessing (18-29). Jacob, apparently quite unashamedly, lies to his father: he says *I am Esau your firstborn* (19).

And then he resorts to blasphemy. When Isaac asks how he's managed to get the game so quickly, Jacob replies that *the LORD your God gave me success* (20).

Isaac wants to be sure: it doesn't *sound* like Esau. After touching him, he says *The voice is the voice of Jacob, but the hands are the hands of Esau* (22). So, we read, *he proceeded to bless him* (23b).

But not before he asks his question one more time: *Are you really my son Esau?* (24). And Jacob replies *I am* (24b).

After enjoying the meal, Isaac says he is to kiss him, and that's when he catches the smell of Esau's clothes. And that seals it: this really is Esau.

And so Isaac, without realising what he is doing, blesses Jacob. He blesses him with agricultural prosperity: *heaven's dew and earth's richness – an abundance of grain and new wine* (28).

And he blesses his son with the promise first given to Abraham: *May nations serve you and peoples bow down to you. [...] May those who curse you be cursed and those who bless you be blessed* (29).

It's done. Jacob has received the blessing.

4. Esau discovers Jacob's deception and begs for the blessing (30-40). Esau comes home from hunting, prepares a meal and brings it to his father. When Isaac asks who it is, Esau replies *I am your son,... your firstborn, Esau* (32).

Isaac knows that voice. He *trembled violently* (33a), because he now knows what's happened. He asks who it was who came before, but he knows the answer. And Esau knows too.

It was Jacob who had brought the meal: Isaac *ate it just before you came and I blessed him – and indeed he will be blessed!* (33b).

Isaac knows that the blessing is now Jacob's, and he knows, too, that he has been fighting against God. So when Esau begs Isaac, *with a loud and bitter cry,* to *bless me – me too!* (34), Isaac can only reply that that's impossible: *Your brother came deceitfully and took your blessing* (35).

So the blessing has gone.

Esau is angry with his brother: *Isn't he rightly named Jacob?* (36a). He adds that Jacob *has taken advantage of me* (36): you could almost translate that *he's jacobed me.* And this is the second time: *He took my birthright, and now he's taken my blessing!* (36).

So Esau's begging now: *Haven't you reserved any blessing for me?* (36), and *Do you have only one blessing, my father?* (38a).

He's desperate: because Jacob has received the blessing, Isaac tells Esau that *I have made him lord over you* (37a). So Esau cries out in anguish *Bless me too, my father!* (38).

But all Isaac has for his favourite son is an anti-blessing: Esau will live unblessed (see 39) and untamed (see 40).

There is one more part to this extraordinary story.

5. The results of Jacob's deceit (27:41 – 28:4). Esau decides to murder his brother, but he decides to wait until his father has died: he *held a grudge against Jacob* (41).

Rebekah gets wind of this, so she tells Jacob to *flee at once to my brother Laban in Harran* (43): she thinks he will only need to *stay with him for a while* (44). But Jacob will stay there for twenty years.

And she will never see him again.

But Rebekah is crafty. She knows that it will be much better if it's Isaac who sends Jacob away. So she tells her husband *if Jacob takes a wife from among the women of this land, from Hittite women like these, my life will not be worth living* (46).

Having two Canaanite daughters-in-law is bad enough; to have three would be too much for her.

Rebekah's strategy works. Isaac calls Jacob and tells him *Do not marry a Canaanite woman* (chapter 28:1). He is to go to Paddan Aram, *to the house of your mother's father Bethuel* (2): Jacob should *take a wife for yourself there* (2).

And now Isaac blesses Jacob again: *May God Almighty bless you and make you fruitful and increase your numbers* (3); *May he give you and your descendants the blessing given to Abraham, so that you may take possession of the land where you now reside as a foreigner, the land God gave to Abraham* (4).

It was always God's will that Jacob receive the blessing, but that doesn't excuse the behaviour of him and his mother: God never asked for their help.

Everyone in this story behaves badly.

Isaac wants to give God's blessing to Esau, despite God having revealed that it's Jacob who should be blessed (see chapter 25:23). Esau plans to murder his brother. Rebekah uses her position to deceive her husband and involves her younger son in this.

And Jacob deceives his father, and even resorts to blasphemy (see 20). He's a cheat and a schemer. He doesn't deserve the blessing, but God doesn't operate on the basis of merit.

The covenant promises are being entrusted to Jacob. How secure will they be in his hands?

But God is not finished with this man yet.

Learning Genesis+

Begin by saying the titles of incidents a, b and c aloud several times, until you can say them without looking at *The Genesis+ Experiment*. Then do the same with incidents d, e and f, before saying all six incident titles. And remember that using your fingers will help.

Now say the title of incident g several times: *God chooses Rebekah as Isaac's wife.*

Then do the same with the second half of the section: this will be easier because the mirror links will help you. First learn incidents f', e' and d'; and then incidents c', b' and a'.

It will help you to do this if you do it with a friend: it's fun and you can support each other.

As more and more of the content of the section gets into your memory, it will *change* you. There is power in the word of God!

Section C: The Isaac Story

a   God chooses the younger son: Isaac
b.   *Marriage of nonchosen older son: Ishmael*
c.   Strife with Abimelek of Gerar over Abraham's wells
d.   *Abraham's sacrifice of Isaac*
e.   Nonchosen genealogy: the family of Nahor
f.   *The death of Sarah*
g.   CENTRE: God chooses Rebekah as Isaac's wife
f'. *The death of Abraham*
e'. Nonchosen genealogy: the family of Ishmael
d'. *Esau's sacrifice of his birthright*
c'. Strife with Abimelek of Gerar over Abraham's wells
b'. *Marriage of nonchosen older son: Esau*
a'. God chooses the younger son: Jacob

Meeting God

As you move through the ingredients of Section C in your mind, tell yourself the story (with as many details as you can remember), or do this with a friend.

You might find it helpful to look at the study questions in Appendix 3, either alone or with someone else.

And you might like to think about Section C's symbol: the wells. You could talk to God about the way his love for you satisfies your thirst for meaning and purpose.

Praise God for his good plan to bless the nations, and thank him that you share in that blessing. Worship God as you see his patience with the men and women he has chosen, and his determination that his kingdom will be built.

One of the main reasons God has given us the book of Genesis is so that we can encounter God. He is waiting to meet you.

Section D
The Jacob Story and the Birth of the Nation (Genesis 28:5 – 37:1)

As a result of what happened at the end of Section C, Jacob has to flee for his life. His father Isaac sends him to Paddan Aram, to the region where his grandfather Abraham had lived before coming to Canaan: this will mean that he will find a wife from among his own people. Jacob will have twelve sons: the twelve tribes that will result from this will be the birth of a nation. In all of this we see God at work to accomplish his purposes.

Jacob had a dream
in which he saw a stairway resting on the earth,
with its top reaching to heaven,
and the angels of God were ascending and descending on it.
There above it stood the LORD…

Genesis 28:12-13a

Enjoying the View

a. Jacob's exile begins (28:5)
b. *Esau's family* (28:6-9)
c. Stop at Bethel (28:10-22)
d. *Departure from Canaan and arrival in Paddan Aram* (29:1-30)
e. Jacob's family becomes large (29:31 – 30:24)
f. *Jacob keeps scheming* (30:25-43)
g. CENTRE: Jacob escapes and departs for home (31:1-55)
f'. *Jacob stops scheming* (32:1-32)
e'. Jacob introduces his large family to Esau (33:1-17)
d'. *Arrival back in Canaan from Paddan Aram* (33:18 – 34:31)
c'. Stop at Bethel (35:1-29)
b'. *Esau's family* (36:1-43)
a'. Jacob's exile ends (37:1)

God is doing two things in Section D.

First, he's changing a man. Not that Jacob suddenly becomes a saint: but through the events described here he meets God and slowly becomes a little more the man God wants him to be. And God changes his name: from Jacob to Israel.

And second, he's building a nation. By the end of the section Jacob is married, with a large family. The twelve sons born to him are the foundation of what will become the people of God. Otherwise known as the nation of Israel.

A major emphasis in Section D is the blessing of God: Jacob clearly longs for it. The account answers the question *How can we receive God's blessing?* But he needs to learn that blessing doesn't come because of what *he* does, but from what *God* does.

And Jacob does something new here. At times of blessing, he sets up a memorial stone. These stones serve as a visual reminder of God's grace touching Jacob's life: he will remember what God has done for him. The memorial stone is Section D's symbol.

Before continuing to read *this* book, it would be good to spend time reading through Genesis 28:5 – 37:1. Look out for Jacob's memorial stones, and watch God blessing him.

You will see God at work, changing a man and building a nation.

And please use the opportunity to worship and pray.

Unpacking the Content

a. – Jacob's exile begins (28:5)

This verse serves as the introduction to the whole of Section D. Isaac *sent Jacob on his way, and he went to Paddan Aram* (5a).

That's not a random destination. He's going to *Laban son of Bethuel the Aramean,* and we're reminded who Laban is: he's *the brother of Rebekah, who was the mother of Jacob and Esau* (5).

So Jacob is going to safety, and to relatives.

It's worth noting, too, that the account puts the brothers' names in the reverse order: they are *Jacob and Esau* (5c). That's a reminder that it's Jacob who has received the blessing from his father Isaac, and that it's Jacob through whom God's promises are going to be fulfilled.

So Jacob's exile has begun.

b. – Esau's family (28:6-9)

Now we hear something about Esau's side of the story. He knows that his father Isaac had *blessed Jacob and had sent him to Paddan Aram to take a wife from there* (6a).

And he learns that Isaac had told Jacob *Do not marry a Canaanite woman* (6b). So Esau realises *how displeasing the Canaanite women were to his father Isaac* (8).

The result is that he marries into Abraham's family a different way. Esau goes to Ishmael's clan *and married Mahalath, the sister of Nebaioth and daughter of Ishmael son of Abraham, in addition to the wives he already had* (9).

At the end of Section C we saw how desperate Esau was for God's blessing (see chapter 27:34 and 36).

He's still hoping.

c. – Stop at Bethel (28:10-22)

So Jacob starts his journey. Something is going to happen when he reaches *a certain place* (11a): we must wait for the climax of the story to discover its name. There's a reason for that.

One way of looking at this incident is to see it in three stages.

1. What Jacob sees (10-12). At the end of the day, Jacob takes *one of the stones there, he put it under his head and lay down to sleep* (11).

He has a dream. He sees *a stairway resting on the earth, with its top reaching to heaven* (12a), and *the angels of God were ascending and descending on it* (12b). Jacob is not cut off from heaven and heaven's blessings: it's like the door is open.

2. What Jacob hears (13-15). At the top of the stairway *stood the LORD* (13a). It's unmistakeable: he tells Jacob that he's *the LORD, the God of your father Abraham and the God of Isaac* (13a).

Jacob knows that he's having an encounter with God. And God gives Jacob, this deceitful, *grabbing* individual, three promises.

The promises to Abraham are being repeated: they are for Jacob too.

+ First, God promises him the land (13b). Jacob and his descendants will receive *the land on which you are lying* (13b). This doesn't just apply to where Jacob has slept: it's land *to the west and to the east, to the north and to the south* (14a, and see chapter 13:14-15).

+ Second, God promises him descendants (14). Jacob's descendants will be *like the dust of the earth* (14a, and see chapter 13:16).

And part of this is a restating of the messianic promise: God tells Jacob that *all peoples on earth will be blessed through you and your offspring* (14b, and see chapter 12:3b and 22:18).

But there's another promise to come.

+ Third, God promises him his presence (15). These are astonishing words: *I am with you and will watch over you wherever you go* (15a). Jacob may have lived much of the time without reference to God, but God is committing himself to being with him.

God's presence will also give Jacob direction: he tells him that *I will bring you back to this land* (15).

So important are these promises that God says *I will not leave you until I have done what I have promised you* (15b).

This is what Jacob hears. So how is he going to respond?

3. What Jacob does (16-22). On waking, Jacob thinks *Surely the LORD is in this place, and I was not aware of it* (16).

He knows he's had an encounter with God: *he was afraid* (17a). Jacob never wants to forget this experience and these promises: this place is *the house of God* and *the gate of heaven* (17b).

So Jacob takes his stone pillow, sets it up *as a pillar and poured oil on top of it* to consecrate it (18). For the first time, he's setting up a memorial stone: and he's worshipping Yahweh.

And he calls the place *Bethel,* which means *house of God* (19a). The account tells us that *the city used to be called Luz* (19b). But now it has a new name, because Jacob is on the way to becoming a new man.

The proof of that is that *Jacob made a vow* (20a): it's the longest in the Old Testament.

When Jacob begins *If God will be with me and will watch over me on this journey I am taking* (20), his *If* is not expressing doubt. It's the opposite.

Because Jacob is convinced that God will fulfil his promises, he makes a promise himself: *The LORD will be my God* (21b) and the memorial stone will be *God's house* (22a).

And the decison reached at the end of our passage shows how serious Jacob is: he promises God that *of all that you give me I will give you a tenth* (22b).

This stop at Bethel has been a supernatural event. And the change in Jacob has begun.

d. – Departure from Canaan and arrival in Paddan Aram (29:1-30)

This incident is going to tell the story of how Jacob meets Rachel, who he will marry. But we also see how the one who had deceived his father Isaac is deceived himself by his uncle Laban.

1. Jacob meets Rachel (1-14a). After a long journey Jacob arrives at *a well in the open country, with three flocks of sheep lying near it because the flocks were watered from that well* (2).

As we'll see in a moment, this well is important, so the account tells us that *the stone over the mouth of the well was large* (2b). So large, in fact, that the shepherds would wait until all the flocks had arrived: then, together, they would *roll the stone away from the well's mouth and water the sheep* (3a).

In conversation with the shepherds, Jacob discovers that he has reached Harran and that his uncle Laban is known to them (see 4-5). The shepherds tell him that *here comes his daughter Rachel with the sheep* (6b).

Does Jacob want to speak to Rachel without an audience? In any case he suggests that the shepherds get on with watering their flocks and *take them back to pasture* (7b).

They explain that they can't do anything *until all the flocks are gathered* (8a); only then will the stone be *rolled away from the mouth of the well* (8b).

It looks like Jacob is inspired by Rachel's arrival: he *rolled the stone away from the mouth of the well and watered his uncle's sheep* (10b). And he does it single-handed.

Having told Rachel that they are related (see 12), Jacob kisses her because she's family, and *began to weep aloud* (11). Are these tears of joy because he's completed his journey successfully?

Rachel has gone off to tell Laban about all this (see 12b). He comes to the well and sees Jacob, *embraced him and kissed him and brought him to his home* (13).

After a short conversation, Laban is convinced: Jacob is *my own flesh and blood* (14a).

God has so arranged things that Jacob has got to his destination and met Rachel. But although Jacob is moved (see 11), there's no mention of him thanking God for his help or worshipping him for his blessing.

Jacob still has some learning to do.

But now we come to the next stage in the story.

2. Jacob loves Rachel (14b-24). After a whole month, Laban tells Jacob that he shouldn't *work for me for nothing* (15). He suggests that Jacob should *tell me what your wages should be* (15b).

Now the account stops for a moment to tell us something about Rachel, and something about her older sister Leah. Leah has *weak eyes* (17a): is this simply saying that Jacob found her uninteresting?

But Rachel seems to have everything: she *had a lovely figure and was beautiful* (17b). So now we're told that *Jacob was in love with Rachel* (18a).

The deceiver is in love, so he tells Laban he'll *work for you seven years in return for your younger daughter Rachel* (18b). And Laban is happy with this arrangement (see 19).

So Jacob works the seven years for Rachel, *but they seemed like only a few days to him because of his love for her* (20).

When the seven years are up, Jacob asks for Rachel, as agreed (see 21). Laban organises a public celebration, as befits a wedding, but then *when evening came, he took his daughter Leah and brought her to Jacob* (23).

And *Jacob made love to her* (23b).

Why does Jacob not realise that he's making love to the wrong woman? Leah is probably wearing a veil, and of course it's dark in the tent.

Because Jacob doesn't yet know Laban well, he's assumed that his uncle will keep his side of the bargain: it doesn't occur to him that Laban might be a deceiver.

But we've seen it clearly: Jacob loves Rachel. And so there's a third stage to the story.

3. Jacob wins Rachel (25-30). The account tells us that *when morning came, there was Leah!* (25a).

And so Jacob marches off to Laban and asks him *Why have you deceived me?* (25b). He is outraged that he's been deceived: the irony is clear.

But cunning, greedy and heartless Laban replies as if Jacob should have known that the older daughter must marry first (see 26). After Leah's *bridal week,* he promises, *we will give you the younger one also* (27).

But of course there's a condition attached: Jacob will get Rachel *in return for another seven years of work* (27b).

And Jacob did so (28a). After the honeymoon week with Leah, Jacob is given Rachel as a second wife, after which *he worked for Laban another seven years* (30b). And he does all this because *his love for Rachel was greater than his love for Leah* (30).

Jacob has got a taste of his own medicine: he has been humbled by the deceit of his uncle Laban. In the end he works fourteen years in order to have Rachel as his wife.

It's worth noting that Leah is given Zilpah *as her attendant* by her father (24), and that Rachel gets Bilhah as hers (see 29): this is important information for what we will read in incident e.

But for now we're asking ourselves the question: How much has Jacob been changed by what he's going through?

e. – Jacob's family becomes large (29:31 – 30:24)

Even through this very human story, we see Yahweh at work: he's beginning to fulfil the promise of a great nation given to Abraham (see chapter 12:2).

The context here is the rivalry between the two sisters Leah and Rachel. Each wife wants what the other has: while Leah longs to experience her husband Jacob really loving her, Rachel wants to have children.

One way of looking at this part of the story is to see it in four stages: the text seems to invite us to do this.

1. What Yahweh sees (29:31-35). When *the LORD saw that Leah was not loved* (31a), he *enabled her to conceive* (31b). Leah has four sons: the names she gives them are significant.

+ **Reuben** sounds similar to the Hebrew *he has seen my misery*. God has had compassion on her, which makes Leah optimistic: *Surely my husband will love me now* (32). She's going to be disappointed.

+ **Simeon** means *heard.* Leah says she's had this boy *because the LORD heard that I am not loved* (33).

+ **Levi** is a play on the Hebrew word *attached.* Leah chooses this name because *now at last my husband will become attached to me, because I have borne him three sons* (34).

+ **Judah** is derived from the Hebrew word for *praise.* Has Leah given up trying to win Jacob's love? In any case her fourth son gets so named because *this time I will praise the LORD* (35).

There is a significant note at the end of this paragraph: we're told that Leah *stopped having children* (35b).

Which brings us to stage two of our story.

2. What Rachel sees (30:1-8). Rachel *saw that she was not bearing Jacob any children*, so she's *jealous of her sister* (1a).

She expresses her desperation to her husband (see 1b), but instead of praying for her (as Isaac had prayed for Rebekah, see chapter 25:21), he simply reminds her of who is in control of such things: it is God *who has kept you from having children* (2).

Rachel's Plan B is to give her servant Bilhah to Jacob as his third wife (see 4): Bilhah can *bear children for me and I too can build a family through her* (3). The result is two more sons for Jacob.

But it's Rachel who gives them their names and, once again, they mean something.

+ **Dan** is derived from the same root as the Hebrew word *vindicate.* Rachel rejoices that *God has vindicated me; he has listened to my plea and given me a son* (6).

+ **Naphtali** is linked to the Hebrew word *struggle.* Rachel is saying that she has had *a great struggle with my sister, and I have won* (8).

Bilhah is the mother of Dan and Naphtali, but Rachel calls them her own sons.

But Leah is not to be outdone.

3. What Leah sees (30:9-21). Leah *saw that she had stopped having children*, so she *took her servant Zilpah and gave her to Jacob as a wife* (9). She's simply following Rachel's example.

Zilpah has two sons by Jacob, and of course they count as Leah's.

+ **Gad**: Leah exclaims that this is *good fortune!* (11), which is what Gad means.

+ **Asher** means *happy*. Leah's sure that *the women will call me happy* (13), though presumably she doesn't include Rachel: the sibling rivalry continues throughout incident e.

Now, in verses 14-16, we have the only recorded conversation of Leah and Rachel. It's about some mandrake plants which Reuben has found and *brought to his mother Leah* (14). So Rachel asks her sister to *give me some of your son's mandrakes* (14b).

There was a superstitious belief that mandrakes stimulate female fertility: Rachel seems to be thinking that they may be the answer to her childlessness.

When Leah refuses to play along with this (see 15a), Rachel srikes a bargain with her: Jacob *can sleep with you tonight in return for your son's mandrakes* (15b). It looks like Jacob had stopped having sex with Leah when she stopped having children.

So that's what happens. Leah tells Jacob *You must sleep with me* because *I have hired you with my son's mandrakes* (16).

But this story with its sex-for-hire element doesn't provide either woman with what she wants. Leah still doesn't experience deep love from Jacob, and the mandrakes don't result in Rachel becoming fertile.

But what *does* happen is that God *listened to Leah and she became pregnant* (17). She has two more sons.

+ **Issachar** sounds like the Hebrew word for *reward*. Leah says that *God has rewarded me for giving my servant to my husband* (18).

+ **Zebulun** is the *sixth son* that Leah bears Jacob (19). The name has the same consonants as the Hebrew word for *honour*: she calls the child *a precious gift* and concludes that *this time my husband will treat me with honour* (20).

And now the narrative informs us that *some time later she gave birth to a daughter and named her Dinah* (21): this is important because of what we'll read about in chapter 34.

There's a brief fourth stage in the account of Jacob's family becoming large.

4. Then God remembers (30:22-24). Rachel must have been praying, because God *listened to her and enabled her to conceive* (22), which is exactly what he'd done for Leah years earlier (see chapter 29:31).

When she becomes pregnant, Rachel feels that *God has taken away my disgrace* (23). Once again, the name the child receives is significant.

+ **Joseph** means *May he add*: she's hoping that God will *add to me another son* (24).

The relationships in this family are a tragedy: Leah and Rachel are rivals, and Jacob loves one wife and not the other. God, in his grace, is choosing unpromising material to achieve his purposes.

And Jacob's family is becoming large.

f. – Jacob keeps scheming (30:25-43)

In the previous incident Jacob was passive, pretty much doing whatever Leah and Rachel require of him. But now he takes the initiative himself: he's leading his family so that they can leave Laban and travel to the land of Canaan.

In incident f we see Jacob scheming again. But as he manipulates the mating of the sheep and the goats, it is God who is giving blessing: he is fulfilling his purposes for Jacob and his family.

Jacob tells Laban to *send me on my way back to my own homeland* (25). This is what he deserves: Laban knows *how much work I've done for you* (26b).

Laban doesn't want this to happen: he acknowledges to Jacob that *the LORD has blessed me because of you* (27b).

But Jacob is insistent. He tells Laban that *the little you had before I came has increased greatly*, and this has happened because *the LORD has blessed you wherever I have been* (30).

But it's time for Jacob to think of his own family. He asks Laban *When may I do something for my own household?* (30b).

And now the scheming begins again.

1. What Jacob suggests (31-33). Jacob asks Laban to let him *go through all your flocks today and remove from them every speckled or spotted sheep, every dark-coloured lamb and every spotted or speckled goat* (32).

These animals, says Jacob, *will be my wages* (32b).

Sheep are normally white, while goats are black or dark brown. So Jacob is asking that a small percentage of Laban's flocks will be his.

2. How Laban reacts (34-36). Laban is happy with Jacob's suggestion: *Let it be as you have said* (34).

But Laban has a method of ensuring that Jacob comes out really badly from this arrangement: *That same day he removed all the male goats that were streaked or spotted, and all the speckled or spotted female goats (all that had white on them) and all the dark-coloured lambs, and he placed them in the care of his sons* (35).

Then he puts *a three-day journey between himself and Jacob* (36).

So it looks like the cards are well and truly stacked against Jacob.

3. What Jacob does (37-43). Jacob takes *fresh-cut branches* from some trees and makes *white stripes on them by peeling the bark and exposing the white inner wood of the branches* (37).

Then he places these branches *in all the watering troughs, so that they would be directly in front of the flocks when they came to drink* (38).

When the flocks *were in heat and came to drink, they mated in front of the branches* (38b-39a). The account tells us that *they bore young that were streaked or speckled or spotted* (39).

Is this just a superstitious folk custom? Do prenatal impressions really affect the unborn? In recent years some have suggested that prenatal nutrition can affect gene expression: with the stripping of the bark a nutrient will have been released into the drinking water.

In any case Jacob's scheming seems to have worked. Whatever the explanation for this, God is at work here, fulfilling his purposes.

And Jacob practises selective breeding. Whenever *the stronger females were in heat, Jacob would place the branches in the troughs in front of the animals* (41), but *if the animals were weak, he would not place them there* (42a).

The result is that *the weak animals went to Laban and the strong ones to Jacob* (42b). Jacob's flock remains healthy and strong, while Laban's becomes weak.

Through all of this, Jacob *grew exceedingly prosperous* (43a): he is so rich that he can afford slaves and pack animals (see 43b). He has built up this wealth over a period of six years (see chapter 31:41).

Yes, Jacob has been scheming, and has out-schemed Laban. And yet he knows that in the end it has been God who has been blessing him (see 30). We will see more of this in incident g.

And now we come to the centre of the Jacob story.

g. – CENTRE: Jacob escapes and departs for home (31:1-55)

Throughout this chapter we are witnessing a Jacob who is changing: he clearly has a relationship with God. And he attributes his wealth not to his own scheming, but to the God who has been changing him.

1. Jacob's escape (1-21). This is a key moment in the Jacob story: he stops being passive and starts showing spiritual leadership.

+ the starting point (1-3). Jacob's decision to leave comes as a response to news that Laban and his sons are complaining about him (see 1-2).

But ultimately Jacob's escape is prompted by a direct intervention from God, who tells him to *go to the land of your fathers and to your relatives* (3). This is a reminder that Paddan Aram isn't home: Canaan is.

And God repeats the promise he gave Jacob at Bethel: *I will be with you* (3b, and see chapter 28:15).

For Jacob, that decides it. He's on the move.

+ the conversation (4-16). Jacob takes the initiative: he's had enough of being passive. He wants to meet up with *Rachel and Leah* (4): is Rachel mentioned first because she's the favourite? And this happens in *the fields* (4): it's important that this conversation doesn't get overheard.

Jacob is going to explain the whole situation to Rachel and Leah, and through it all he's clear that God is the main mover in his story. We get to see how Jacob has been changing.

Laban has been against him, but *the God of my father has been with me* (5); Laban has cheated him, but *God has not allowed him to harm me* (6-7); Laban has changed his wages, but *God has taken away your father's livestock and has given them to me* (8-9).

Jacob is openly proclaiming his faith to his wives. He's experienced blessing and he's giving all the credit to God.

He goes on to tell Rachel and Leah that his success with the mating of the speckled sheep and goats which we read about in incident f was down to God: *the angel of God* had said to him in a dream that he had *seen all that Laban has been doing to you* (11a and 12b).

God had reminded him that he was *the God of Bethel, where you anointed a pillar and where you made a vow to me* (13a). And God had told him (see 3) to *leave this land at once and go back to your native land* (13b).

So how will Rachel and Leah respond to what they've heard?

For the first time, they follow Jacob's lead: he meets with wholehearted agreement. Laban has mistreated his daughters, treating them like *foreigners* (15); they see themselves no longer as Laban's daughters but as Jacob's wives.

They agree that *all the wealth that God took away from our father belongs to us and our children* (16a). And they finish by telling Jacob to *do whatever God has told you* (16b).

How must Jacob be feeling as he hears Rachel and Leah's reponse to what he's told them? It's so clear that God is at work.

So we know what comes next.

+ the escape (17-21). So Jacob *puts his children and his wives on camels* (17) and makes his escape. He's taking *his livestock,* too (18a), and *all the goods he had accumulated in Paddan Aram* (18).

And the destination is clear: he's going *to his father Isaac in the land of Canaan* (18b).

Before they leave, Rachel *stole her father's household gods* (19): this may be because they were made of costly metal.

So the escape happens. And there's deceit involved: Jacob *deceived Laban the Aramean by not telling him he was running away* (20).

It's worth noting that Laban is described here as *the Aramean.* And Jacob is on his way home.

But because we know Laban, we know that that is not the end of the story.

2. Jacob's defence (22-54). When Laban gets news of the escape, *he pursued Jacob for seven days* (23): he may well have violence in mind.

+ the accusation (22-35). Now it's Laban who has a supernatural encounter in a dream. God tells him not *to say anything to Jacob, either* *good or bad* (24). Laban is to say nothing to Jacob that *sounds* positive but ultimately leads to his disadvantage.

But when he catches up with Jacob, he does have plenty to say.

Laban says that Jacob has *deceived me* (26), which is what Laban has been doing to Jacob for many years. He asks why Jacob has *run off secretly* (27a), without giving him the opportunity to arrange a proper send-off (see 27b).

Laban is threatening Jacob, reminding him that he has *the power to harm you* (29a), but he then admits that God has told him not to use deception (see 29b and my comments on verse 24).

And there's another thing: *Why did you steal my gods?* (30b).

Jacob tells Laban that he was afraid that *you would take your daughters away from me by force* (31). This is righteous indignation: if Laban finds his household gods, whoever has taken them *shall not live* (32a).

And the account tells us that *Jacob did not know that Rachel had stolen the gods* (32b).

So Laban starts a systematic search. He looks in Jacob's tent, Leah's tent, and the tent shared by Bilhah and Zilpah, but *he found nothing* (33).

Last of all he comes to Rachel's tent: once again, he *found nothing* (34b).

Having put Laban's household gods *inside her camel's saddle* (34), Rachel is sitting on them. She explains to her father why she can't get down from the camel: *I'm having my period* (35).

And the ruse works: Laban *could not find the household gods* (35b). The master of deceit is deceived by his own daughter.

+ the defence (36-42). Jacob is clearly incensed at Laban's behaviour: *What is my crime?* he asks (36).

He goes on to tell Laban what he knows already: he has worked hard *for twenty years now* (38a). He hasn't stolen from Laban, and when sheep were *torn by wild beasts* he *bore the loss myself* (39).

Jacob adds that *I worked for you fourteen years for your daughters and six years for your flocks* (41).

And now he speaks openly about his faith: *If the God of my father, the God of Abraham and the Fear of Isaac, had not been with me, you would surely have sent me away empty-handed* (42a). Does he call God *the Fear of Isaac* to remind Laban that this is not a God to be trifled with? He certainly reminds him that in the dream the previous night *he rebuked you* (42b).

The foundation of Jacob's defence is his commitment to the God of his fathers.

+ the pact (43-54). Laban must know that everything Jacob has accused him of is true: he doesn't have a leg to stand on. He knows he's defeated.

So Laban asks that he and Jacob *make a covenant* (44).

This is a non-aggression pact, entered into with a heap of stones and a covenant meal. The pile of stones is given a name meaning *witness heap* (47). Laban wants Jacob to know this: *If you ill-treat my daughters* [...], *remember that God is a witness between you and me* (50).

This is another example of the importance of the memorial stone: remember that it's Section D's symbol.

Laban is used to getting his own way. But now he's got to settle for a verbal agreement.

But he has a warning for Jacob: *May the God of Abraham and the God of Nahor, the God of their father, judge between us* (53a).

So Jacob *took an oath in the name of the Fear of his father Isaac* (53b). He *offered a sacrifice there in the hill country* (54). Once again we see that Jacob is a changed man: he is living consciously in the presence of the God of his fathers.

And the story is done. *Early the next morning Laban kissed his grandchildren and his daughters and blessed them* (55). Then *he left and returned home* (55b).

Which is what Jacob is going to do. He's escaped from Laban's clutches and has started for his home in Canaan.

And he knows that God has done this. God has been faithful to the vow that Jacob had made at Bethel (see chapter 28:20-22).

f'. – Jacob stops scheming (32:1-32)

Now the narrative focuses on Jacob's return to the Promised Land. And he is changing: in incident f he was still relying on his own scheming, but now in incident f' he learns to trust in God instead.

Two of Jacob's relationships need to be sorted out.

The first, which is in the forefront of Jacob's mind, is with his brother Esau. The last time they were together Esau had good reason for wanting Jacob dead: he had stolen his birthright and his blessing.

But the second relationship is much more important. All his life Jacob has been keeping God at arm's length, fighting against God and trusting in his own abilities as a deceiver.

But God has been at work, changing Jacob, turning him into the man God wants.

These two relationships are the focus of this incident.

1. Jacob's relationship with Esau (1-21). Jacob is *on his way, and the angels of God met him* (1). Presumably this means that he can actually see the angels.

This is an extraordinary moment. Just as he is nervous about meeting Esau again, Jacob has a supernatural experience: this is giving him strength for what is to come.

So Jacob says *This is the camp of God!* (2). And he names the place *Mahanaim* (2), which means *Two Camps*. One camp is Jacob's, the other is God's.

Now Jacob turns his attention to his relationship with Esau. He makes plans and he prays, but through it all he's trusting God.

+ Jacob plans (3-8). He sends messengers ahead of him to meet his brother. They are to refer to Jacob as *your servant Jacob* (4), and to make it clear that he is calling Esau *my lord* (5). And they are to tell Esau that Jacob is hoping to *find favour in your eyes* (5b).

In other words Jacob is showing humility, and seeing Esau as his superior. It should be obvious to Esau, and to us, that he is a changed man.

The messengers return with the news that Esau is *coming to meet you, and four hundred men are with him* (6). Is this entourage an army or a welcoming committee?

Understandably, Jacob is *in great fear and distress* (7a). He divides everything he has into two groups, reasoning that *If Esau comes and attacks one group, the group that is left may escape* (8).

So Jacob plans. But he does something else too.

+ Jacob prays (9-12). This is Jacob's first recorded prayer; it's a prayer prompted by fear but full of faith. It's a prayer prayed by someone who is not trusting in his own planning, but in God's power to save him.

Jacob addresses God as *God of my father Abraham, God of my father Isaac, LORD* (9), and reminds God of God's promise to him: *I will make you prosper* (9b).

He knows that he doesn't deserve God's blessings: he is *unworthy of all the kindness and faithfulness you have shown your servant* (10).

And now he asks for more grace. He begs God to *save me, I pray, from the hand of my brother Esau, for I am afraid he will come and attack me, and also the mothers with their children* (11).

At the end of his prayer Jacob reminds God of his promise to his grandfather Abraham: *I will surely make you prosper and will make your descendants like the sand of the sea, which cannot be counted* (12, and see chapter 22:17).

Jacob is sure that God is reliable: he keeps his promises. And so he prays.

But this doesn't rule out planning.

+ Jacob plans (13-21). The following morning Jacob prepares *a gift for his brother Esau* (13): a total of five hundred and fifty animals.

The gift is *huge*: it shows how great Jacob's fear is, but also how much he's changed.

He sends this gift in the care of three waves of his servants. When they are asked who all these animals belong to, they are to reply that *they belong to your servant Jacob* (18 and 20), and that they are *a gift sent to my lord Esau* (18).

Jacob is expressing real regret for having stolen Esau's blessing: the message couldn't be clearer.

So the gifts go on ahead. Jacob, meanwhile, *spent the night in the camp* (21). He has done what he can to repair his relationship with Esau: he's planned and he's prayed.

But there is another relationship that needs to be mended.

2. Jacob's relationship with God (22-32). Jacob is in a situation which is totally beyond him: does this make him open for an encounter with God?

This mysterious passage shows us God at work, doing something deep in this man. There are three things to notice about Jacob.

+ What Jacob does (22-25). First, he makes sure that his family and his possessions are in safety: he sends them *across the stream* Jabbok (23).

So Jacob *was left alone* (24a). Does he sense that something awe-inspiring is going to happen to him?

And then immediately we read that *a man wrestled with him till daybreak* (24b). We're not told who the man is, but we do know that this is a wrestling match that goes on for hours.

This man sees *that he could not overpower* Jacob (25a), so he does something unexpected: *he touched the socket of Jacob's hip so that his hip was wrenched* (25).

Is this something that helps Jacob understand who he has been wrestling with? The dislocation of a hip joint normally requires a high-energy impact, but this man has done no more than *touch* Jacob's hip.

+ **What Jacob says (26-29).** When the man asks Jacob to *let me go* (26a), Jacob replies with this extraordinary sentence: *I will not let you go unless you bless me* (26b).

It looks like he recognises that he has been wrestling with God himself: God has humbled himself and assumed human form in order to meet Jacob.

And to change him.

So Jacob's asking for blessing from God. He knows he can't earn it or deserve it; he's *asking*.

Now the man asks Jacob *What is your name?* (27). This is not a request for information; rather this is God wanting Jacob to admit who he is and what he's like. By saying his name, Jacob is saying (in as many words) *I'm a deceiver, I'm a fraud, I'm a supplanter*.

He's confessing his sin.

Now the man reveals his identity by telling Jacob that he has *struggled with God* (28). And he tells him that *your name will no longer be Jacob, but Israel* (28). *Israel* means *he struggles with God*.

At last Jacob realises that he has not really been struggling against Esau and Laban, but against God. He's been refusing to let God be God in his life and has tried to make his own way through deceit and scheming.

The name *Israel* can also mean *God struggles*. God had initiated this wrestling match (see 24), and God has been struggling with Jacob all his life, trying to turn Jacob into a man who is godly and who trusts him.

With the wrestling match between God and Jacob over, we're told that God *blessed him there* (29b).

But there is one last part to this story.

+ What Jacob knows (30-31). Jacob calls the place Peniel, which means *face of God*, because he knows what's happened: *I saw God face to face, and yet my life was spared* (30).

This has been a life-changing encounter with God. Jacob moves on: at sunrise he was *limping because of his hip* (31). He will always be reminded of what God has done in his life.

Jacob's relationship with God has been sorted. He emerges broken, but blessed.

e'. – Jacob introduces his large family to Esau (33:1-17)

There are two parts to the chapter as we look at Jacob and Esau: first, they reconcile, and second, they disengage.

1. The brothers reconcile (1-11). This is a wonderful meeting of reconciliation. Jacob's conscience won't allow him to side-step an attempt at reconciliation with his brother.

+ Esau embraces Jacob and meets his family (1-7). Jacob looks up and *there was Esau, coming with his four hundred men* (1, and see chapter 32:6).

So he separates the family into three groups: he puts *the female servants and their children in front, Leah and her children next, and Rachel and Joseph in the rear* (2).

But, very significantly, *Jacob himself went on ahead* (3a): he's acting according to his new name. This is not the old Jacob: he's a leader, not a coward. He's approaching Esau humbly but confidently.

As he approaches, Jacob *bowed down seven times* (3b). When Isaac had blessed him, he had prayed that *peoples bow down to you* (chapter 27:29); now here is Jacob bowing down before Esau.

How will Esau react?

Five verbs tell us the answer to that: Esau *ran to meet Jacob, embraced him*, hugged him, *kissed him*, and the two brothers *wept* together (4). Esau's attitude to his brother has changed completely.

When Esau asks *Who are these with you?* (5a), Jacob replies that *they are the children God has graciously given your servant* (5b). The three family groupings approach *and bowed down* (6-7).

This is an extraordinary moment. Was Jesus thinking of Esau's reaction to Jacob when describing the father's reaction to the return of his lost son (see Luke 15:20)?

+ Esau accepts Jacob and receives his gifts (8-11). When Esau asks about all the flocks and herds, Jacob explains that they're a gift *to find favour in your eyes, my lord* (8). He's still treating his brother as a superior: he is Jacob's lord.

Esau refuses the gift with the words *I already have plenty* (9): he doesn't want to be paid for accepting Jacob.

But Jacob is insistent: he wants Esau to accept the gifts, because *God has been gracious to me and I have all I need* (11). He's no longer trying to buy Esau's acceptance; rather the gifts demonstrate his gratitude for being accepted again as Esau's brother.

So *because Jacob insisted, Esau accepted it* (11b). The fact that he doesn't give Jacob a gift in return underlines that this isn't simply an exchange of civilities: the old score has been settled.

So the brothers have reconciled.

2. The brothers disengage (12-17). Jacob is being cautious here.

+ Esau offers to accompany Jacob to Seir (12-14). Esau is anxious to get moving. But Jacob is not keen: as a loving father and a good shepherd he doesn't want them to be put under pressure. If they are, then *all the animals will die* (13b).

So Jacob suggests that Esau and his people go on ahead, while Jacob will follow along behind, *at the pace of the flocks and the herds* and *the pace of the children* (14).

But he still gives the impression that he is going to *come to my lord in Seir* (14b). Is this Jacob resorting to deceit again?

+ Esau returns home without Jacob (15-17). Esau suggests leaving *some of my men with you,* probably for protection (15a): he still wants the two brothers to live side by side in peace.

But Jacob replies *Just let me find favour in the eyes of my lord* (15b). Esau probably knows that this is Jacob's polite way of turning down his proposal: he doesn't need to go to Seir to have a renewed relationship with his brother.

So Esau accepts Jacob's position: while he *started on his way back to Seir,* Jacob *went to Sukkoth* (16-17a). He spends some time there: *he built a place for himself and made shelters for his livestock* (16).

Why does Jacob not go along with Esau's plan? Is it because, despite this wonderful reconciliation, it's important to him to keep the promised line separate from the rejected line?

Jacob doesn't need protection from Esau because he has protection from God.

And Esau doesn't bear a grudge. The next time we meet him, the two brothers will be at peace with one another as they bury their father (see chapter 35:29).

d'. – Arrival back in Canaan from Paddan Aram (33:18 – 34:31)

This is an extraordinary moment: *After Jacob came from Paddan Aram, he arrived safely at the city of Shechem in Canaan* (33:18). He has reached his goal: he has arrived back in the Promised Land.

But where is Jacob as far as his relationship with God is concerned? Now that he's crossed the border and is in Canaan, does he drop his guard? He sets up camp *within sight of the city* of Shechem (18): it's enough to remind us of Lot (see chapter 13:12).

This is an unnecessary decision: Bethel, which is the place Jacob should be aiming for, is only twenty miles away. Yes, he gives honour to God by building an altar and even gives it a great name: *El Elohe Israel,* which means *El is the God of Israel* (20, and see chapter 28:21).

But Jacob is building his altar in the wrong place. Because of his decision to stay near Shechem instead of travelling straight to Bethel, appalling evil is going to be unleashed. Chapter 34 begins with a rape and ends with a massacre.

One way of seeing how that works out is to look at the chapter in five stages.

1. The rape (1-4). This is the most disturbing event in the book of Genesis. But equally disturbing is Jacob's reaction to it.

We're told that *Dinah, the daughter Leah had borne to Jacob, went out to visit the women of the land* (1). Dinah is probably around sixteen years old, and there's no way she should be going out unaccompanied.

And now it happens: *When Shechem son of Hamor the Hivite, the ruler of that area, saw her, he took her and raped her* (2). He likes what he sees, and he takes it.

Weirdly, it now looks like he falls in love with the girl he's raped: *his heart was drawn to Dinah* and *he loved the young woman* (3). Maybe he's used to getting his own way: in any case he tells his father to *get me this girl as my wife* (4).

2. The reaction (5-7). When Jacob *heard that his daughter Dinah had been defiled, his sons were in the fields with his livestock* (5a). However, instead of being outraged, *he did nothing about it until they came home* (5b).

Is Jacob paralysed by shock, or simply indifferent? Is he afraid because he's outnumbered by the Hivites? And where's the moral indignation of a man of God?

We know that *Shechem's father Hamor went out to talk with Jacob* (6), presumably to arrange his son's marriage to Jacob's daughter. Does Jacob raise his voice to Hamor? Is he demanding an apology for his daughter's rape? The fact that we read nothing about the conversation suggests that the answer is No.

So Jacob's not standing up for his daughter, and he's not standing up for his God, either.

His sons, however, react differently. They have *come in from the fields as soon as they heard what has happened* (7a). They are *shocked and furious, because Shechem had done an outrageous thing in Israel* (7b).

It's worth noting in passing that this is the first time that the name *Israel* is used to refer not to an individual (Jacob), but to the people (Jacob's family). Dinah has been demeaned, but Israel has been demeaned, too.

And the brothers are right: the narrator tells us that what Shechem has done is *a thing that should not be done* (7c).

So Jacob reacts to his daughter's rape with passivity and apathy, while his sons react with moral indignation and fury.

3. The proposal (8-12). Hamor explains that his son *has his heart set on your daughter*; he wants Jacob to *give her to him as his wife* (8). There's no apology for what Shechem has done, but rather an appeal to the brothers' self-interest to get them to agree to the marriage.

Hamor invites them to *intermarry with us* (9): doubtless he doesn't know about Abraham forbidding Isaac, and Isaac forbidding Jacob, to marry Canaanite women (see chapter 24:2-4 and 28:1-2).

And then Hamor invites Jacob and his family to *settle among us* (10a). The land, he says *is open to you. Live in it, trade in it, and acquire property in it* (10b).

And Shechem joins in: the bride-price for Dinah can be *as great as you like, and I'll pay whatever you ask me* (12).

It doesn't look like Hamor or Shechem find anything offensive about the rape: their focus is on persuading Jacob's sons to go along with their proposal.

How will they react?

4. The plot (13-24). The account tells us that *Jacob's sons replied deceitfully* (13), which means we're to see their behaviour here as shameful. The narrator approves of their moral indignation, but he doesn't approve of their tactics.

The brothers explain that giving their sister to an uncircumcised man would be *a disgrace to us* (14b). So they will only accept this marriage if *you become like us by circumcising all your males* (15). If that happens, then they are happy to intermarry with these Canaanites, to settle among them and *become one people with you* (16).

If, on the other hand, Hamor and Shechem say No to the circumcision plan, *we'll take our sister and go* (17).

The brothers' plan *seemed good to Hamor and his son Shechem* (18). They meet up with *the men of their city* (20), explaining that circumcision is a small price to pay: *Won't their livestock, their property and all their other animals become ours?* (23).

The result is that *all the men who went out of the city gate agreed* and *every male in the city was circumcised* (24). The brother's plot is working.

And so now we reach the climax of the story.

5. The massacre (25-29). Three days later, when all the men of the city are *still in pain* after their circumcision, *two of Jacob's sons, Simeon and Levi, Dinah's brothers, took their swords and attacked the unsuspecting city* (25). That word *unsuspecting* underlines for us again that the brothers have been acting *deceitfully* (13).

They finish by *killing every male* (25b). That should stop us in our tracks: they're engaging in holy war without any prompting from God.

And now the rest of the brothers sweep in and *looted the city* (27): they seize the animals and *all their women and children, taking as plunder everything in the houses* (29).

The scene is shocking: this is God's people involved in a massacre, led by Simeon and Levi.

But where is Jacob in all this? He tells Simeon and Levi that they *have brought trouble on me by making me obnoxious to the Canaanites and Perizzites, the people living in this land* (30a). There's no mention of Dinah: it's like he's only thinking of himself.

If the Canaanites *join forces against me and attack me, I and my household will be destroyed* (30b). Where is the man of faith, trusting in the promises of the God he has come to know?

Jacob's sons are incredulous. They ask him about Shechem's behaviour at the beginning of the chapter, probably because of their father's silence and non-involvement: *Should he have treated our sister like a prostitute?* (31).

It's like they're blaming Jacob: it was his refusal to get involved that forced them to act as they did.

The contrast is striking. Jacob, the appeaser, reacts to the rape with fear, while his sons, the avengers, react with fury.

Incident d' is tragic. It begins so well, with Jacob's arrival back in Canaan. But he seems no longer to be walking with God and counting on divine blessing: because of his passivity and refusal to lead the family as he should, the return to Canaan is marked by a rape and a massacre.

c'. – Stop at Bethel (35:1-29)

This brings Jacob (and us) back to Bethel, where God had revealed himself to him (see incident c, chapter 28:10-22).

There was no mention of God at all in chapter 34 (incident d'): everything there happened without reference to him. But now in chapter 35, God is everywhere.

There are two halves to the chapter, related to each other by the significance of Bethel.

1. Return to Bethel (1-15). God takes the initiative here: he speaks to Jacob.

+ Yahweh brings Jacob back to Bethel (1-7). He tells him to *go up to Bethel* (1): this is important because Jacob has a vow to fulfil (see chapter 28:20-22).

Jacob is told to *build an altar there to God* (1): this is the only time God commands one of the patriarchs to do such a thing. It's almost like God is saying *Jacob, you need to get back to worshipping me.*

So Jacob prepares his family for the journey: they are to *get rid of the foreign gods you have with you* (2). He explains that he's going to build at Bethel an altar to *God,* […] *who has been with me wherever I have gone* (3).

Jacob remembers what had happened at Bethel: is his return there signalling a return to God?

So Jacob buries *all the foreign gods they had,* including any charms, *under the oak at Shechem* (4). That done, he and his family can start the journey to Bethel.

Jacob had been afraid of what the Canaanites and Perizzites might do to him after the massacre at Shechem (see chapter 34:30), but as his family leave, *the terror of God fell on the towns all around them so that no one pursued them* (5).

This protection is divine and undeserved.

Jacob and his family come to Bethel: we're reminded that that's *in the land of Canaan* (6). There, in obedience to God's command, Jacob *built an altar* (7a). And he renames the place *El-Bethel* (7a): it looks like Jacob is recommitting himself to God.

And we're reminded why this is so important for Jacob: at Bethel *God revealed himself to him when he was fleeing from his brother* (7b).

+ **The death of Deborah, Rebekah's nurse (8).** Deborah had come to Canaan with Rebekah (see chapter 24:59); had she then been sent back to Paddan Aram to tell Jacob of his mother's death?

As a small boy Jacob may well have been close to Deborah: in any case he buries her under an oak tree he calls *Allon Bakuth* (8; it means *Oak of Weeping*).

+ **Yahweh blesses Jacob at Bethel (9-15).** This paragraph begins with a reminder that Jacob has *returned from Paddan Aram* (9): Jacob should have come here instead of settling in Shechem.

And so we read that *God appeared to him again and blessed him* (9).

The blessing involves a confirmation of three things. First, Jacob's new name: God *named him Israel* (10). Does God do this because it's almost like Jacob's memory needs jogging?

Second, God's character: he is *El-Shaddai,* which means *God Almighty* (11a). This is the name he had used when renaming Abraham (see chapter 17:1-8).

And third, the promises are confirmed to Jacob: there will be fruitfulness, a nation and kings (see 11). And Canaan figures prominently too: *The land I gave to Abraham and Isaac I also give to you, and I will give this land to your descendants after you* (12).

El-Shaddai is the God who fulfils every promise.

Jacob sets up a stone pillar and pours oil on it, but this time pours out a drink offering too (compare chapter 28:18). This is an act of worship: if Jacob has drifted spiritually since his arrival back in Canaan, this is him coming back to God.

With his memorial stone, Jacob is responding to God's blessing. He's not going to forget it.

2. After Bethel (16-29). Jacob and his family *moved on from Bethel* (16), presumably because he wants to reach Isaac in Hebron.

We're told of three important post-Bethel events.

+ The death of Rachel (and the birth of a son). Rachel is dying in childbirth. Told by the midwife that she has *another son* (17), she names him *Ben-Oni* (18; the name means *Son of my trouble*).

Jacob, however, renames the boy: perhaps he doesn't want constant reminders of the tragic circumstances of the birth. So his twelfth son is named *Benjamin* (18b; this means *Son of my right hand*). Jacob may have chosen the name because this is the son of Rachel, the unchallenged love of his life.

This leads naturally to what follows.

+ The completion of Jacob's family (21-26). Before the twelve sons of Jacob are listed, we learn that *Reuben went in and slept with his father's concubine Bilhah* (22).

It looks like Reuben is positioning himself as successor to his father: he wants to take Jacob's place as leader of the family. This incest is sinful and shocking.

And *Israel heard of it* (22). Despite his new name Israel, Jacob does nothing: once again, he opts for passivity. But Reuben's sin won't be forgotten: later he will be passed over for his father's blessing (see chapter 49:3-4).

So now we read it: *Jacob had twelve sons* (22b): his family is complete. They are listed in the order that Jacob had acquired his wives: the sons of Leah, Rachel, Bilhah and Zilpah (see 23-26).

The list ends with the summary that *these were the sons of Jacob, who were born to him in Paddan Aram* (26b). Except that's not true: Benjamin was the only son born in the promised land of Canaan (see 17-18).

There is one more event which needs to be mentioned.

+ The death of Isaac (27-29). It looks like Jacob lives in Hebron for about fourteen years before his father Isaac dies: he *breathed his last and died and was gathered to his people, old and full of years* (29a; he was one hundred and eighty years old).

And then we read that *his sons Esau and Jacob buried him* (29b). With this we're reminded that the two brothers have reconciled.

God has been at work: bringing Esau and Jacob together, completing Jacob's family and making him more and more into a man who trusts him.

Jacob is a man who's been changed by what's happened at Bethel.

b'. – Esau's family (36:1-43)

This chapter, which forms a mirror link with incident b, doesn't make interesting reading for most of us, but it's important: it shows that Esau, despite his unbelief, is not excluded from the benefits of the covenant.

There are two genealogies to look at briefly here: each begins with the words *This is the account of...* (1 and 9).

1. The short genealogy (1-8). This is a one-generation genealogy of Esau's sons born in the land of Canaan. It's *the family line of Esau (that is, Edom)* (1). Just as Jacob has a new name (Israel), which is the name of the nation of which he's the father, Esau gets a new name (Edom), which is the name of a nation too.

+ Esau marries Canaanite women (1-5). Esau *took his wives from the women of Canaan* (2a): these marriages violate the conventions of his family. Marriage to Canaanites was strictly forbidden (see, for example, chapter 24:1-9 and 26:35).

But Esau goes ahead regardless. The *sons of Esau* are listed, sons *who were born to him in Canaan* (5).

+ Esau leaves Canaan and settles in Seir (6-8). He moves *to a land some distance from his brother Jacob* (6b).

His reason for doing so is that *their possessions were too great for them to remain together* (7): history is repeating itself (see chapter 13:6-9).

So *Esau (that is, Edom) settled in the hill country of Seir* (8): this will be the national territory for the nation of Edom.

With the migration of Esau from the Promised Land, the stage is now set for God to fulfil his promises to Israel.

2. The long genealogy (9-43). At the beginning and at the end of this genealogy we are told that Esau is *the father of the Edomites* (9 and 43b).

Some names here appear in more than one list: for details, see the commentaries.

+ Esau's sons and the chiefs of the Edomite clans (9-19). The sons (and the grandsons) are listed first (see 9-14), followed by a list of those who became chiefs among the people (see 15-19).

The paragraph ends by telling us that these were *the sons of Esau (that is, Edom) and these were their chiefs* (19).

+ Seir's sons and the chiefs of the Horite clans (20-30). The sons are listed first (see 20-28), followed by *the Horite chiefs* (29-30).

+ The kings of Edom and the chiefs of the Edomite clans (31-43). The men listed here are *the kings who reigned in Edom before any Israelite king reigned* (31).

This is a fulfilment of God's promise to Abraham: God had promised him *I will make nations of you, and kings will come from you* (chapter 17:6).

This is followed by a brief list of *the chiefs descended from Esau* (43).

So this is *the family line of Esau, the father of the Edomites* (43b).

Esau cuts himself off from the covenant line of blessing by doing two things: he marries Canaanite women and he leaves the Promised Land.

But although he's not the covenant-bearer, he and his descendants still have a future (see Deut 23:7).

a'. – Jacob's exile ends (37:1)

This is a fitting conclusion to Section D: *Jacob lived in the land where his father had stayed* (1).

And we're reminded that it's called *the land of Canaan* (1b).

At the beginning of the section we read about Jacob's exile beginning (see incident a); now, at the end, Jacob comes home.

It's been a long journey and it's been a long time. Quite apart from the journey to Paddan Aram and the journey home to Canaan, Jacob spent twenty years with Laban (see chapter 31:41).

And through it all God has been working out his purposes. He's been changing Jacob, making him more and more the man he wants him to be. And he's been working out his plan for the nations, too.

With the birth of Jacob's twelve sons, the people of Israel have come into being.

Learning Genesis+

Begin by saying the titles of incidents a, b and c aloud several times, until you can say them without looking at *The Genesis+ Experiment*. Then do the same with incidents d, e and f, before saying all six incident titles. If you use your fingers, that makes everything easier.

Now say the title of incident g several times: *Jacob escapes and departs for home.*

Then do the same with the second half of the section: this will be easier because the mirror links will help you. First learn incidents f', e' and d'; and then incidents c', b' and a'.

It will help you to do this if you do it with a friend: it's fun and you can support each other.

As more and more of the content of the section gets into your memory, it will *change* you. There is power in the word of God!

Section D: The Jacob Story
and the Birth of the Nation

a.   Jacob's exile begins
b.   *Esau's family*
c.   Stop at Bethel
d.   *Departure from Canaan and arrival in Paddan Aram*
e.   Jacob's family becomes large
f.   *Jacob keeps scheming*
g.   CENTRE: Jacob escapes and departs for home
f'.   *Jacob stops scheming*
e'.   Jacob introduces his large family to Esau
d'.   *Arrival back in Canaan from Paddan Aram*
c'.   Stop at Bethel
b'.   *Esau's family*
a'.   Jacob's exile ends

Meeting God

Please remember that the book of Genesis is not only there so we can have information: it is also there so we can meet God. You can do this on your own or with a friend.

Begin by recounting the first few incidents in Jacob's story and, as you do so, start talking to God about what he is doing in Jacob's life. Ask him to be at work in you by his Spirit.

Then do the same with the next few incidents. You won't remember all the details, but talk to God about what you *do* remember. Ask him to help you to trust in him rather than in your own ability to manipulate or deceive others.

As you do this, remember the memorial stone markers: they're designed to remind Jacob of God's blessings to him. Maybe you can think of objects that remind you of important things that God has done in your life: some people use dried leaves, or pebbles.

Remember that it may help to look at the study questions about the Jacob story in Appendix 3.

And worship God: just as he never gives up on Jacob, he's not about to give up on you, either.

If you re-tell some (or all) of Section D to yourself every day, and turn it into prayer as you do, the Holy Spirit will use his word in your life to give you new joy and peace: you will be getting to know God better.

Which is what *The Genesis+ Experiment* is all about.

Section C'
The Joseph Story (Genesis 37:2 – 50:26)

This section deals with the relationship between Joseph and his brothers, and Judah in particular: next to Joseph and Jacob, Judah is the most important character in the story. In Section C' Jacob's broken family is restored, but we see much more than that: God uses a member of that family to bring blessing to many peoples. As we look at the Joseph story we will witness the grace of God in action, still fulfilling his purposes for Israel and for the world.

Then he threw his arms around his brother Benjamin
and wept,
and Benjamin embraced him, weeping.
And he kissed all his brothers and wept over them.

Genesis 45:14-15a

Enjoying the View

a. Trouble between Joseph and his brothers (37:2-11)
a'. More trouble between Joseph and his brothers (37:12-36)
b. *Sexual temptation involving Judah* (38:1-30)
b'. *Sexual temptation involving Joseph* (39:1-23)
c. Joseph interprets two dreams for fellow-prisoners (40:1-23)
c'. Joseph interprets two dreams for Pharaoh (41:1-57)
d. *Joseph's brothers come to Egypt for food* (42:1-38)
d'. *Joseph's brothers again come to Egypt for food* (43:1 – 44:3)
e. Joseph has some of his family come to Egypt (44:4 – 45:15)
e'. Joseph has all of his family come to Egypt (45:16 – 47:12)
f. *Prospering in Egypt: Joseph's ascendancy* (47:13-26)
f'. *Prospering in Egypt: Blessings for Jacob's sons* (47:27 – 49:32)
g. Death of a patriarch: Jacob (49:33 – 50:14)
g'. Death of a patriarch: Joseph (50:15-26)

You will notice that the structure of Section C' is different from that of the last few sections. David Dorsey suggests that the Joseph story is written with a number of different structures in mind (see Appendix 1 for more on his work).

For simplicity's sake I have made the decision to choose the structure that I find the most learnable: the incidents are in pairs. I have found Section C' one of the easiest to learn.

Section B had its altars, Section C its wells, and Section D its memorial stones. In Section C' it's *clothes* that are mentioned again and again.

As we look at Joseph's life, we'll see God blessing him and *making him a blessing* to the wider world. He is *being* God's blessing to others. The pointer to this is Joseph's clothes. In the Bible clothes are often an outward manifestation of the actions of the wearer (see, for example, Matthew 22:11-12, Colossians 3:12-14, 1 Peter 5:5b and Revelation 7:13-14).

Please take time to read through the whole story in your Bible. Notice how often clothes are mentioned, and see how God makes Joseph's actions a blessing to those around him.

As you read the Joseph story, please stop from time to time to talk to God. This is a key part of *The Genesis+ Experiment*.

Unpacking the Content

The section begins with the announcement that *this is the account of Jacob's family line* (2a). Jacob has an important role of course, but the key figure we're invited to focus on is Joseph.

a. – Trouble between Joseph and his brothers (37:2-11)

This incident sets the scene for the whole of what is to follow.

1. The broken family (2-4). Joseph is *a young man of seventeen* (2a): we're going to see that he has a lot of maturing to do.

He's been *tending the flocks with his brothers,* and he brings their father Jacob *a bad report about them* (2b). They may well have misbehaved in some way, but the expression means news slanted to damage the victim.

Joseph is not making himself popular. But Jacob is making things worse: he *loved Joseph more than any of his other sons*: this is because he was *born to him in his old age* (3).

Jacob rubs it in by giving Joseph *an ornate robe* (3b). This is probably not a coat of many colours, but rather a long, flowing robe reaching the wrists and the ankles. Does Joseph enjoy parading around in his lordly attire?

This is the first mention of clothes in the Joseph story. This robe will show us the heights from which Joseph will fall.

The brothers see that Joseph is the favourite, so *they hated him and could not speak a kind word to him* (4).

This is family breakdown big time. The division among the brothers is caused by Jacob's behaviour, and made worse by Joseph's.

And now Joseph starts having dreams.

2. The first dream (5-8). When Joseph tells his dream to his older brothers, *they hated him all the more* (5).

In his dream Joseph sees himself and his brothers *binding sheaves of corn out in the field* (7a). Then two things happen: *Suddenly my sheaf rose and stood upright* and *your sheaves gathered round mine and bowed down to it* (7).

This is the first dream in the Bible in which God doesn't speak. There is no need: the explanation is clear for all to see.

The brothers ask Joseph if he intends to *reign over us* (8a). And, not surprisingly, *they hated him all the more* (8b).

But soon Joseph is dreaming again.

3. The second dream (9-11). Joseph tells his brothers that *this time the sun and moon and eleven stars were bowing down to me* (9).

There's no need for an interpretation: there is no room for doubt as to the dream's meaning. The two dreams have the same message, except that this time Joseph's parents are involved, too (represented by the sun and the moon).

Joseph even goes so far as to tell the dream to his father. Jacob reacts in two ways.

First, he *rebuked him* (10a) and asks Joseph *Will your mother and I and your brothers actually come and bow down to the ground before you?* (10b). (In talking about Joseph's mother he means Leah, who had taken on mothering responsibilities on Rachel's death.)

But second, Jacob *kept the matter in mind* (11). Joseph's brothers are *jealous of him* (11), but their father is pondering all of this. He's mystified, but he's taking the dream seriously: is he thinking that this may well be from God?

So we have met Joseph. He's immature: he brags about his dreams. And he's naïve, too: does he really think this is going to endear him to his family?

Joseph has a lot of maturing to do, if he is to play his part in God's plan for him.

But there is more trouble to come.

a'. – More trouble between Joseph and his brothers (37:2-11)

The brokenness in this family will only get worse: we will see that as we watch what happens to Joseph.

1. He's sent to his brothers (12-17). Joseph's brothers are *grazing the flocks near Shechem* (13), so Jacob tells Joseph that *I am going to send you to them* (13b).

It's worth noting that at this point Jacob is referred to as *Israel* (see 13a). It's like we're being reminded that this family is the beginning of the people of God.

So Joseph travels the fifty miles from Hebron to Shechem, where he tells someone *I'm looking for my brothers* (16). The man tells Joseph that he had heard the brothers say *Let's go to Dothan* (17).

So Joseph covers thirteen more miles, in order to check on the wellbeing of his brothers.

But in Dothan something else happens to Joseph.

2. He's thrown into a cistern (18-24). Joseph's brothers spot him from a distance: do they recognise his coat? They move fast: *before he reached them, they plotted to kill him* (18).

Here comes that dreamer! they say (19): they plan to kill Joseph and *throw him into one of these cisterns* (20). The cisterns were large, bottle-shaped pits dug out for the purpose of retaining water: they could be anything up to twenty feet deep.

And the brothers plan to cover up what they've done by saying that *a ferocious animal devoured him* (20).

At this point there's an intervention from Reuben. Twice we're told that he's on Joseph's side: *he tried to rescue him* (21, and see 22b). He urges his brothers not to *shed any blood* and not to *lay a hand on him* (22). Instead, they should take Joseph and *throw him into this cistern* (22).

Reuben's plan is to come back to the cistern at some point, rescue Joseph and *take him back to his father* (22b).

Reuben is doing what the oldest brother *should* do: he's standing up to his siblings and doing what is right.

The brothers go along with him, but the assault on Joseph is brutal: they *stripped him of his robe* and they *took him and threw him into the cistern* (23-24a). Their plan is to starve Joseph to death: he has no food and no water (see 24b).

Joseph is bruised, bleeding and naked: he could die of thirst and hunger (if Reuben doesn't manage to rescue him).

But instead of a rescue, and instead of his death, something else happens to Joseph.

3. He's taken to Egypt (25-28). In their callousness, the brothers have *sat down to eat their meal* (25a), but they're interrupted by the arrival of a camel *caravan of Ishmaelites* (25a).

The narrative tells us that they were *on their way* [...] *to Egypt* (25b).

And now we get an intervention from another of the brothers. Judah, cynically opportunistic, says that instead of leaving Joseph in the cistern to die, they should *sell him to the Ishmaelites* (27a). After all, he says, *he is our brother, our own flesh and blood* (27b).

That way, the brothers will get rid of Joseph and also make money out of it.

The deal goes ahead. They sell Joseph *for twenty shekels of silver* (28), which at that time was the going rate for a male slave. And the Ishmaelites *took him to Egypt* (28b).

This all looks very random, doesn't it? But although God is never mentioned in this chapter, we're to see that he is at work, accomplishing his purposes.

There is one more thing we need to know about Joseph.

4. He's mourned by his father (29-36). It looks like Reuben has been off with one of the flocks when the camel caravan had passed by. Now he comes back and *saw that Joseph was not there* and *tore his clothes* (29).

He is distraught. He asks his brothers *Where can I turn now?* (30). Reuben can't possibly face going back to Jacob with news like this. He's showing that he does care for Joseph, and for his father too.

But there's no alternative. The brothers get *Joseph's robe, slaughtered a goat and dipped the robe in the blood* (31). They bring it home and say to Jacob *We found this. Examine it to see whether it is your son's robe* (32).

It's ironic. Their plot to deceive Jacob mirrors Jacob's plot to deceive Isaac: they use their brother's clothing and a goat (see chapter 27:15-16). And, once again, we see how important clothes are in Section C'.

Jacob is convinced by their story: he's sure that Joseph has been *torn to pieces,* because *some ferocious animal has devoured him* (32, and see 20).

And Jacob is inconsolable: he *tore his clothes, put on sackcloth and mourned for his son many days* (34). And the brothers, in their cynical ruthlessness, *came to comfort him, but he refused to be comforted* (35).

This family is broken and dysfunctional. But God is at work: he is the main character in the drama. God is using the brothers' sinful behaviour and he's getting Joseph to Egypt.

He's going to repair this messed-up family and keep his promise to bless all nations through Abraham's offspring.

The account ends with a cliffhanger. The Ishmaelites *sold Joseph in Egypt to Potiphar, one of Pharaoh's officials, the captain of the guard* (36).

But we're going to have to wait before we learn what happens to Joseph there.

b. – Sexual temptation involving Judah (38:1-30)

Chapter 38 is here partly to create suspense: we won't learn what happens to Joseph in Egypt until chapter 39.

But we're also going to see something of a transformation in Judah. He begins the chapter cold and selfish, but ends it humbled and compassionate.

1. Judah's sins (1-11). The events of these verses cover a time-span of about twenty years, but they are all recounted here so as not to interrupt the Joseph story any further.

+ the father's sins (1-5). Judah *left his brothers* (1), perhaps just in order to graze the flocks in his charge elsewhere. He meets *the daughter of a Canaanite man named Shua* (2a). Judah knows that he shouldn't marry a Canaanite, but it's apparently lust at first sight: *he married her and made love to her* (2b).

Judah's wife has three sons by him: Er, Onan and Shelah (see 3-5).

+ the sons' sins (6-10). Er gets married to Tamar (see 6). So half-Canaanite Er and his Canaanite wife Tamar are set to continue Judah's line of inheritance.

But Tamar is soon a widow: *Er, Judah's firstborn, was wicked in the LORD's sight; so the LORD put him to death* (7).

We don't know the nature of Er's wickedness, but he may well have been involved in the Canaanite abominations connected to their religious practices.

So Judah tells his second son Onan to *sleep with your brother's wife and fulfil your duty to her as a brother-in-law to raise up offspring for your brother* (8). This is an early indication of the practice of levirate marriage (see Deut 25:5-10).

But Onan doesn't want to produce offspring: that way he won't have to share any future inheritance. So *whenever he slept with his brother's wife, he spilled his semen on the ground* (9).

God *put him to death,* because *what he did was wicked in the LORD's sight* (10). His sin is not withdrawal before ejaculation, but rather his refusal to provide offspring for his brother by sleeping with Tamar.

+ the father's sin (11). Judah now tells Tamar to *live as a widow in your father's household until my son Shelah grows up* (11). It looks like Judah has decided to leave Tamar out of the picture: she will be without support if her father should die.

It may even be that Judah has no intention of ever giving Tamar to Shelah.

But Tamar has something in mind.

2. Tamar's plan (12-19). Tamar realises that she's been permanently sidelined, but her window of opportunity comes when her father-in-law Judah is widowed himself (see 12a).

+ What Tamar plans (12-14). She is determined to make her father-in-law responsible for providing for her.

When she's told that Judah *is on his way to Timnah to shear his sheep* (13), *she took off her widow's clothes, covered herself with a veil to disguise herself* and then sits by the road (14).

Here, too, clothes play an important part in the story.

Tamar's motivation is clear: *she saw that, though Shelah had now grown up, she had not been given to him as his wife* (14b).

+ What Tamar does (15-19). When Judah sees her, he assumes that she's a prostitute (see 15): he urges her to *let me sleep with you* (16b). And, of course, he has no idea that this is his daughter-in-law.

When Tamar asks what he's offering, he promises to *send you a young goat from my flock* (17a).

She's not really interested in payment: she just wants to be able to prove that Judah is the man she is going to have sex with. So she asks him to *give me something as a pledge* (17b).

She asks for *your seal and its cord* (which was probably used to hang the seal around the neck) *and the staff in your hand* (18). Judah duly *gave them to her and slept with her* (18b).

And, we're told, Tamar *became pregnant by him* (18b).

Having parted from Judah, Tamar goes home and *put on her widow's clothes again* (19).

Judah is despicable. His sexual appetite won't tolerate postponement, but he's been content to leave Tamar a childless widow.

But now there's a surprise coming.

3. Judah's repentance (20-26). Maybe that's overstating it, but certainly something is happening here that will change Judah for ever.

+ Judah keeps his promise (20-23). He tries to send the young goat, *in order to get his pledge back from the woman* (20), but she is nowhere to be found (see 21-22).

Judah has tried to keep his promise, but it has come to nothing: he still has his goat, and he doesn't have his seal, his cord and his staff.

+ Judah judges Tamar (24). *About three months later,* Judah is told that Tamar is *guilty of prostitution, and as a result she is now pregnant* (24a).

He is quick to condemn her: he decides she should be *burned to death* (24b).

+ Judah admits his sin (25-26). As Tamar is being led out to be executed, she sends a message to Judah, with his seal, his cord and his staff: she is *pregnant by the man who owns these* (25).

Judah, naturally enough, recognises his property and realises that he's been rumbled. It looks like he admits his moral failure publicly: *She is more righteous than I, since I wouldn't give her to my son Shelah* (26).

This is the first hint of a change taking place in Judah. He's recognising the consequences of manipulating people for his own ends, without consideration for their welfare.

4. Tamar's achievement (27-30). We're reaching the finale of the story.

+ the birth (27-30). *When the time came for her to give birth, there were twin boys in her womb* (27). One baby *put out his hand,* so the midwife says that *this one came out first* (28).

But then his brother comes out first: *and he was named Perez* (29). And the other twin is *named Zerah* (30). But Perez is the son of the messianic blessing.

+ the achievement. Tamar's determination to have children through the descendants of Abraham is remarkable: she single-handedly preserves the line of Judah. Tamar has secured the honour of being an ancestor of King David and of Jesus, the Saviour of the world.

Matthew includes all this in his genealogy of Jesus the Messiah (see Matt 1:2-6).

Judah has been changed. He's becoming a compassionate brother and son: later in this section the words of this new Judah will move Joseph to tears (see chapter 45:1-2).

And this change in Judah will lead to his being designated the heir of the messianic promise (see chapter 49:8-12).

This is God's grace in action.

b'. – Sexual temptation involving Joseph (39:1-23)

It looks like Joseph has been abandoned not just by his brothers but by God, too. But that's not the case: Joseph has *been taken down to Egypt* (1a), but God has travelled there with him.

And we already know what happens to him there: *Potiphar, an Egyptian who was one of Pharaoh's officials, the captain of the guard, bought him from the Ishmaelites* (1, and see chapter 37:36).

1. Joseph: blessed (2-6a). Yahweh *was with Joseph so that he prospered* (2). And that doesn't escape Potiphar's notice: he *saw that the LORD was with him* (3).

So we're told twice in two verses that God is with Joseph. God is blessing him and *gave him success* (3), so that *he prospered* (2).

The result is that Potiphar puts Joseph *in charge of his household, and he entrusted to his care everything he owned* (4). And it looks like the effect is immediate: *the LORD blessed the household of the Egyptian because of Joseph* (5).

Here is someone who's from the nations being blessed because of Joseph. The covenant God is at work to fulfil his covenant promises through this man: *the blessing of the LORD was on everything Potiphar had* (5b).

Potiphar realises that the best way of managing his affairs is to forget them: *with Joseph in charge, he did not concern himself with anything except the food he ate* (6a).

God is blessing Joseph so much that the blessing overflows to others.

2. Joseph: tempted (6b-10). Joseph, we're told, is *well-built and hand-some* (6b), so much so that Potiphar's wife wants him to *Come to bed with me!* (7).

It's tempting, but *he refused* (8a).

And Joseph explains why. Potiphar has shown trust in him: *everything he owns he has entrusted to my care,* so that *no one is greater in this house than I am* (8b-9a). So it would be wrong to abuse his master's trust.

But there's an even greater reason for Joseph's refusal to have sex with Potiphar's wife: this would be *such a wicked thing* and a *sin against God* (9b).

Joseph is open about his faith: he's not ashamed to explain his motivation.

But Potiphar's wife doesn't give up: *she spoke to Joseph day after day* (10a). Nevertheless, *he refused to go to bed with her or even to be with her* (10b).

That last phrase suggests that this is a real temptation for Joseph. So he's avoiding even being in the same room as her.

Here's a young man with so much going for him. He might have asked himself what's wrong with a bit of strategic adultery, but he remains strong. His integrity is impressive.

3. Joseph: framed (11-20a). The focus here is that Potiphar's wife is not giving up. She does three things.

+ She ambushes Joseph (11-12). One day Joseph is in the house doing his work when *none of the household servants was inside* (11). Has Potiphar's wife engineered the situation?

She *caught him by his cloak* and urges him again to *Come to bed with me!* (12a). It's an ambush.

But Joseph does exactly the right thing: *he left his cloak in her hand and ran out of the house* (12b). The loss of his cloak underlines Joseph's integrity.

+ She lies to the servants (13-15). Calling the servants, Potiphar's wife tells them that *this Hebrew has been brought to us to make sport of us!* (14), explaining that *he came in here to sleep with me, but I screamed* (14b).

And she adds that Joseph had *left his cloak beside me* (15). (And here's clothing again as a crucial ingredient in the story.)

+ She pressurizes her husband (16-19). When Potiphar comes home, she repeats the story about *that Hebrew slave you brought us* (17). It's almost like she's saying that her husband is at fault too: after all, he's the one who's responsible for Joseph working for them.

On hearing this, Potiphar *burned with anger* (19) and *put him in prison* (20a).

Is Potiphar fully convinced by his wife's story? He could have simply ordered Joseph's execution, but instead he has him locked up.

It's worth noting that we're told that this prison is *the place where the king's prisoners were confined* (20b). This is a key detail in the story: God is at work, arranging things so that Joseph will one day be working for Pharaoh himself.

Humanly speaking, incident b' ends unexpectedly.

4. Joseph: blessed (20b-23). When Joseph is in prison, *the LORD was with him* (21). God *showed him kindness and granted him favour in the eyes of the prison warder* (21).

Clearly Joseph is different from the other prisoners, so the warder puts him *in charge of all those held in the prison* (22a). More: Joseph was *made responsible for all that was done there* (22b).

This is astonishing. Just as was case when he was first working for Potiphar, the warder *paid no attention to anything under Joseph's care* (23a, and see 6).

And we're told the reason again: *the LORD was with Joseph and gave him success in whatever he did* (23b).

Joseph starts this chapter as a slave, and ends it as a slave in prison. But, through it all, God is working out his purposes. And God is *with him.*

c. – Joseph interprets two dreams for fellow-prisoners (40:1-23)

Everything in this chapter happens *some time later* (1): at this point Joseph has been in slavery and in prison for more than ten years.

One way of getting into this passage is to look at it in four stages.

1. Prisoners assigned (1-4a). Two of the prisoners have *offended their master, the king of Egypt*: they are his *cupbearer* and his *baker* (1). They had had important roles because they both had access to Pharaoh's food.

So they are both *in the same prison where Joseph was confined* (3). *The captain of the guard*, who's in overall charge, is Potiphar (3, and see chapter 39:1).

Potiphar assigns the chief cupbearer and the chief baker *to Joseph, and he attended them* (4). So Joseph is now the personal attendant of these two important men.

2. Troubling dreams (4b-8). The cupbearer and the baker have *a dream the same night* (5). These dreams are so troubling that Joseph notices the next morning that *they were dejected* (6, the Hebrew has *distraught*). So he asks them what's wrong.

The men explain that they've both had dreams, *but there is no one to interpret them* (8a): in prison they have no access to the court experts who are trained in dream analysis.

In response, Joseph asks them to tell him their dreams, because *interpretations belong to God* (8b). This is typical of Joseph: he is very quick to declare his faith in God.

So we're ready for stage three of the story.

3. Joseph's interpretation (9-19). We are about to witness Joseph's confidence in interpreting dreams.

+ the cupbearer's dream (9-15). The cupbearer tells Joseph *I saw a vine in front of me* (9). The dream relies heavily on groups of three: the vine has *three branches*, which *budded* and *blossomed* and *ripened* (10).

And the dream ends with the cupbearer seeing himself, after taking the grapes, squeezing them into Pharaoh's cup; then he *put the cup in his hand* (11).

Joseph doesn't hesitate: *the three branches are three days* (12). Within three days *Pharaoh will lift up your head and restore you to your position* (13). So the cupbearer is going to regain his dignity and honour.

But Joseph isn't finished yet. He asks the cupbearer to do four things for him on his release: to *remember me and show me kindness,* to *mention me to Pharaoh* and to *get me out of this prison* (14).

And he explains his request: Joseph had been *forcibly carried off from the land of the Hebrews,* and he has *done nothing to deserve being put in a dungeon* (15).

+ the baker's dream (16-19). The baker is willing to recount his dream because he *saw that Joseph had given a favourable interpretation* (16a). There were *three baskets of bread* on his head (16b), the top one of which contained *all kinds of baked goods for Pharaoh* (17a).

But, says the baker, *the birds were eating them out of the basket on my head* (17b).

Once again, Joseph is confident of the interpretation. The three baskets *are three days* (18). Within three days *Pharaoh will lift off your head and impale your body on a pole* (19a). And then *the birds will eat away your flesh* (19b).

4. On the third day (20-23). Now we learn that Pharaoh celebrates his birthday by giving a feast. And at that feast *he lifted up the heads of the chief cupbearer and the chief baker in the presence of his officials* (20b).

But in exactly the way that Joseph had described. Pharaoh *restored the chief cupbearer to his position* (21a), but *he impaled the chief baker* (22a).

So everything happens *just as Joseph had said to them in his interpretation* (22b). Joseph is right about the dreams: the future belongs to God and only God can reveal it.

It looks like a happy ending, doesn't it? But *the chief cupbearer, however, did not remember Joseph; he forgot him* (23). This looks to me like it may be a wilful forgetfulness.

Nothing seems to be going right for Joseph: he's experiencing disappointment after disappointment.

But God is still with him. And he's still working out his purposes.

c'. – Joseph interprets two dreams for Pharaoh (41:1-57)

Joseph is in prison for another *two full years* (1): we're feeling sympathy for him. But what is described here is going to make Joseph a blessing not only for the whole population of Egypt, but also for the surrounding nations.

1. What Pharaoh does (1-14). Events start to move fast.

+ He has two dreams (1-7). In the first he sees *seven cows, sleek and fat* (2), followed by *seven other cows, ugly and gaunt* (3). Then *the cows that were ugly and gaunt ate up the seven sleek, fat cows* (4).

In his second dream, Pharaoh sees *seven ears of corn, healthy and good* (5). Then there are *seven other ears of corn*, which are *thin and scorched by the east wind* (6). The thin ears of corn *swallowed up the seven healthy, full ears* (7).

So Pharaoh does what you'd expect.

+ He asks his experts (8). In the morning, because *his mind was troubled*, Pharaoh sends for *all the magicians and wise men of Egypt* (8a). Not just some of them, but all of them: he's frantic.

But after Pharaoh has recounted his dreams, *no one could interpret them for him* (8b).

But now something happens to cause a turn of events.

+ He sends for Joseph (9-14). It's at this point that the chief cupbearer remembers that he knows of someone who is superb at interpreting dreams. So he tells Pharaoh what had happened when he and the chief baker had been in prison.

The two men had both had dreams, which they had told to *a young Hebrew* who *was there with us, a servant of the captain of the guard* (12a). And this young man *interpreted them for us* (12b).

And, says the cupbearer, *things turned out exactly as he interpreted them to us* (13).

So of course Pharaoh sends for Joseph, and *he was quickly brought from the dungeon* (14a). They rush him to Pharaoh, stopping only for Jospeh to shave and to put on presentable clothes. (The change of clothes shows how God is blessing Joseph.)

And so Joseph *came before Pharaoh* (14b).

2. What Joseph does (15-36). Pharaoh tells Joseph that he's *heard it said of you that when you hear a dream you can interpret it* (15).

Once again, Joseph is quick to declare his faith: *I cannot do it,* he says, *but God will give Pharaoh the answer he desires* (16).

And now we see what Joseph does.

+ He hears the dreams (17-24). Pharaoh recounts both of his dreams: the dream with the two groups of seven cows (see 17-21), and the dream with the two bunches of seven ears of corn (see 22-24).

Joseph is listening. And I'm sure he's praying too.

+ He interprets the dreams (25-32). Joseph starts by telling Pharaoh that his two dreams *are one and the same* (25a): in other words both dreams have the same message.

And then, yet again, he mentions his faith: *God has revealed to Pharaoh what he is about to do* (25b).

Joseph interprets both dreams at once. *The seven good cows* and *the seven ears of corn are seven years* (26), while *the seven lean, ugly cows* and *the seven worthless ears of corn... are seven years of famine* (27).

Before completing the interpretation, Joseph goes to the trouble of repeating that *God has shown Pharaoh what he is about to do* (28): he's taking every opportunity to talk about the God he serves.

So Joseph declares that *seven years of great abundance are coming throughout the land of Egypt, but seven years of famine will follow them* (29-30a). He wants to avoid any misunderstanding: this famine will be *severe* (31b).

Joseph wants Pharaoh to know that this is absolutely certain: *the reason the dream was given to Pharaoh in two forms is that the matter has been firmly decided by God* (32).

And God, says Joseph, *will do it soon* (32b).

He has done what Pharaoh had asked him to do: he has interpreted the dreams. But Joseph has more to say: he's going to take a risk by offering unsolicited advice.

+ He applies the dreams (33-36). Pharaoh hadn't asked what he should do about the dreams, but Joseph is in full flow.

Pharaoh should *look for a discerning and wise man and put him in charge of the land of Egypt* (33). He should appoint regional *commissioners over the land to take a fifth of the harvest of Egypt during the seven years of abundance* (34): this food should be *held in reserve for the country, to be used during the seven years of famine* (36).

This is astonishing. It's not like Joseph has asked Pharaoh for a couple of days in which to work out what should be done: he knows immediately what needs to happen.

This is God at work.

3. What Pharaoh does (37-45). The plan, for that's what it is, *seemed good to Pharaoh and all his officials* (37). So Pharaoh does three things, all of them focused on Joseph.

+ He sees his wisdom (38-39). Pharaoh points at Joseph and asks his officials *Can we find anyone like this man, one in whom is the spirit of God?* (38). Egyptian culture was steeped in polytheism, so it makes sense to translate that last phrase *the spirit of the gods.*

Pharaoh's question is rhetorical. Because *God has made all this known to you,* he tells Joseph, *there is no one so discerning and wise as you* (39).

Joseph's wisdom is there for all to see. But then Pharaoh has something else for Joseph.

+ He puts him in charge (40-44). Joseph is to be *in charge of my palace,* so that *only with respect to the throne will I be greater than you* (40).

But not just the palace. Joseph is to be *in charge of the whole land of Egypt* (41): he'll be like a viceroy, second in command in the whole country (see 43a).

Pharaoh makes Joseph's new authority visible by giving him *his signet ring from his finger,* along with *robes of fine linen* and *a gold chain round his neck* (42): the beautiful clothes show how God is blessing Joseph. And whenever the people see Joseph in his chariot, they are to shout *Make way!* (43).

So Joseph's in charge. Pharaoh tells Joseph that *without your word no one will lift hand or foot in all Egypt* (44).

And then Pharaoh does something else for Joseph.

+ He gives him a wife (45). He gives him a new name, too: *Zaphenath-Paneah* (45a), which may mean *God speaks and lives.* And Joseph's wife is a priest's daughter.

With this, Joseph's integration into the Egyptian court is complete: no longer a Hebrew slave, he is now an Egyptian lord.

So we come at last to the fourth stage of the account.

4. What Joseph does (46-57). Joseph, we're told, is *thirty years old when he entered the service of Pharaoh king of Egypt* (46). His thirteen years in Egypt have brought him to the pinnacle of service in the Mediterranean world.

So what does Joseph do?

+ He stores up grain (46-49). Joseph *travelled throughout Egypt* (46b) to make sure that his plan is being carried out. During the *seven years of abundance,* Joseph *collected all the food produced* (47 and 48a).

The result is that he *stored up huge quantities of grain* (49a). This is phenomenal: Joseph *stopped keeping records because it was beyond measure* (49b).

+ He has two sons (50-52). Joseph's Egyptian wife bears two sons for Joseph.

The first he names *Manasseh* (which means *forgotten*) because *God has made me forget all my trouble and all my father's household* (51): Joseph is able to move on from any bitterness towards his brothers.

Joseph names the second boy *Ephraim* (which means *fruitful*) because *God has made me fruitful in the land of my suffering* (52): God has done amazing things through him in Egypt.

The name Manasseh celebrates the end of the old, while the name Ephraim celebrates the potential of the new.

But the really important thing to notice is that these are *Hebrew* names. Joseph may have been egyptianised and now be a fully recognised part of the Egyptian court, but he's still a Hebrew and still holding on to the promises God gave to Abraham, Isaac and Jacob.

Joseph knows who he is and he knows who he's serving. But there's something else he does.

+ He sells the grain (53-57). Because of God's intervention through Joseph, *in the whole land of Egypt there was food* during the famine (54). Joseph *opened the storehouses and sold grain to the Egyptians* (56).

But *there was famine in all the other lands* (54), with the result that *all the world came to Egypt to buy grain from Joseph, because the famine was severe everywhere* (57).

Joseph, a son of Abraham, is proving to be a blessing to the Egyptians, and to other nations too.

And, just as significantly, it's only a matter of time before Joseph's brothers come to Egypt to buy food.

Then we will see what God will do.

d. – Joseph's brothers come to Egypt for food (42:1-38)

This part of the narrative focuses on the brothers. Joseph is going to test them to see if they've changed: are they the same brothers who selfishly sold him into slavery in Egypt?

God will use these events to expose the brothers' guilt: they need to genuinely repent.

And the aim is reconciliation.

One way of looking at the chapter is to see the geographical locations.

1. Leaving Canaan (1-5). Jacob learns *that there was grain in Egypt,* so he asks his sons *Why do you just keep looking at each other?* (1).

So ten of the brothers go down *to buy grain from Egypt* (3). But only ten: Jacob doesn't allow Benjamin to go *because he was afraid that harm might come to him* (4). He still values Rachel's son over the children of his other wives.

So *Israel's sons were among those who went to buy grain* (5).

2. In Egypt (6-26). Joseph was *the governor of the land* (6a), so on arrival the brothers *bowed down to him with their faces to the ground* (6b): this is a partial fulfilment of Joseph's first dream (see chapter 37:6-7).

They have two audiences with Joseph.

+ The first audience (7-17). Joseph immediately recognises his brothers, but *he pretended to be a stranger* (7; a better translation would be *he treated them like strangers*). And Joseph *spoke harshly to them* (7).

The narrative wants us to be clear about the situation: *Although Joseph recognised his brothers, they did not recognise him* (8). They don't recognise him because he looks and sounds like an Egyptian.

And then Joseph *remembered his dreams* (9a): in other words, he realises that God is at work here.

He accuses them of being *spies* (9): this is harsh, but it's designed to elicit information from them. Which is exactly what happens.

The brothers begin by calling Joseph *my Lord* and calling themselves *your servants* (10): they've come to buy food. And they would hardly be spies, since they are *all the sons of one man* (11).

When Joseph continues with his charge of espionage, the brothers unwittingly give him more of the informatiuon he's looking for: they *were twelve brothers*; what's more, *the youngest is now with our father, and one is no more* (13).

Joseph has learnt something: Jacob and Benjamin are still alive; and they haven't forgotten Joseph, though they think he's dead.

But Joseph continues with his accusation. He tells the brothers that they *will be tested* (15a): *you will not leave this place unless your youngest brother comes here* (15b). One brother is to go back to Canaan to collect the remaining brother, while *the rest of you will be kept in prison* (16).

And Joseph *put them all in custody for three days* (17): they're tasting for three days what Joseph tasted for thirteen years.

With that, the brothers' first audience with Joseph is done.

+ The second audience (18-26). When the three days are over, Joseph has changed his plan: one brother is to stay in Egypt as a hostage, *while the rest of you go and take grain back for your starving households* (19).

This is Joseph being generous: nine brothers are going to be able to take a good amount of grain back to Canaan with them.

But, Joseph adds, *you must bring your youngest brother to me* so that *you may not die* (20). The brothers have little choice: they are willing to go along with this.

Now they talk amongst themselves, not realising *that Joseph could understand them, since he was using an interpreter* (23).

The brothers are sure that *we are being punished because of our brother* Joseph (21a): it looks like their conscience is beginning to function again. They don't mention God yet, but who else would be punishing them?

They're remembering the day they threw Joseph into the cistern and then sold him into slavery: they saw *how distressed he was when he pleaded with us for his life* (21b). And they admit that *we would not listen* (21b).

Now Reuben chimes in. He asks his brothers *Didn't I tell you not to sin against the boy?* and adds that *we must give an accounting for his blood* (22).

This is too much for Joseph: *he turned away from them and began to weep* (24a). So behind his harsh treatment of his brothers is not revenge, but deep affection.

And Joseph then *had Simeon taken from them and bound before their eyes* (24b). Maybe he does this in front of them to see if they have any affection for their brother.

And why does Joseph pick Simeon? Is it because he now knows that Reuben had tried to rescue him, so he goes for the second brother rather than the first?

The brothers' visit to Egypt is almost over. Joseph shows himself to be incredibly generous: he *gave orders to fill their bags with grain, to put each man's silver back in his sack, and to give them provisions for the journey* (25).

There's the evidence again: Joseph's actions are not motivated by revenge.

So the nine brothers *loaded their grain on their donkeys and left* (26), while Simeon sits in an Egyptian prison.

3. Returning to Canaan (27-38). The journey home will have taken them about a week. At one place where *they stopped for the night,* one of the brothers finds *his silver in the mouth of his sack* (27).

When he tells the others, *their hearts sank* (28b). And now, for the first time, they mention God, asking each other *What is this that God has done to us?* (28b). The guilt they felt earlier (see 21) they now recognise to be something God is uncovering.

The brothers know that God is doing something here.

When they come home *to their father Jacob in the land of Canaan* (29), they tell him about their encounter with *the man who is lord over the land* of Egypt (30 and 33).

Understandably, they sanitise the story a little: for example, when talking about Simeon having to stay as a hostage until Benjamin comes to Egypt, there is no mention of prison.

And now comes the shock: *As they were emptying their sacks, there in each man's sack was his pouch of silver!* (35a). At this, they and their father *were frightened* (35b).

Jacob is distraught. He tells his sons that *you have deprived me of my children*: Joseph is gone, Simeon is gone, *and now you want to take Benjamin* (36).

And he retreats into resignation: *Everything is against me!* (36b).

Reuben makes a botched offer to make clear his determination to bring Benjamin home: he tells Jacob that *you may put both of my sons to death if I do not bring him back to you* (37).

But Jacob is having none of it: *My son will not go down there with you* (38a). If he were to lose Benjamin too, *you will bring my grey head down to the grave in sorrow* (38b).

Jacob cannot know that God is behind all these events, and that this will lead to his family being reunited one day in Egypt. And he doesn't realise that God is doing something extraordinary in the lives of his sons.

However, because the famine is affecting Canaan too, it's just a matter of time before the brothers need to return to Egypt to buy more grain.

Which brings us to our next incident.

d'. – Joseph's brothers again come to Egypt for food (43:1 – 44:3)

This second trip to Egypt is going to give the brothers some surprises. But first, Jacob needs to make the decision to send his sons on their journey.

1. In Canaan (1-14). There are tensions again in the family.

+ What Jacob wants (1-2). The famine is *still severe* (1), so Jacob tells his sons to *go back and buy us a little more food* (2).

But there's a problem.

+ How Judah intervenes (3-10). Judah is not the only son involved in this conversation, but it's him taking the initiative: he's the oldest son still in good standing with Jacob.

Judah reminds his father that the governor of Egypt had told them that they *will not see my face again unless your brother is with you* (3): both of them know that this is about Benjamin.

Judah makes it very clear that there's no point in them going back to Egypt unless they take Benjamin too. He tells his father *If you will not send him, we will not go down* (5).

Jacob is frustrated (he's called *Israel* here): he asks why his sons had mentioned in Egypt that they *had another brother* (6).

The brothers explain that the governor had asked about their family: *We simply answered his questions* (7). They couldn't have known that they would be told to *bring your brother down here* (7b).

And now Judah speaks up again.

The situation is urgent: he tells his father to *send the boy along with me and we will go at once, so that we and you and our children may live and not die* (8). This is a matter of life and death: everyone needs food.

And now Judah commits himself to take responsibility for Benjamin: *I will guarantee his safety; you can hold me personally responsible for him* (9). This is a new Judah: not thinking of himself (see chapter 38) but thinking of his family by pledging himself to get Benjamin home from Egypt.

But they do really need to get moving: Judah adds that *if we had not delayed, we could have gone and returned twice* (10).

+ What Jacob decides (11-14). Jacob knows that he has no alternative: the brothers must leave for Egypt immediately, and take Benjamin with them (see 13).

They are to take gifts of *the best products of the land* (11), and also *double the amount of silver*: this is because they *must return the silver that was put back into the mouths of your sacks* (12). Jacob is hoping that this *was a mistake* (12b).

And now he prays that *God Almighty* will *grant you mercy before the man so that he will let your other brother and Benjamin come back with you* (14).

It's like Jacob has given up fighting. He's just about to say goodbye to his sons, and tells them *As for me, if I am bereaved, I am bereaved* (14b).

The decision has been made. And Judah has played a key role in helping Jacob to take it.

2. In Egypt (15-34). The ten brothers *hurried down to Egypt and presented themselves to Joseph* (15).

Except at first they are talking to Joseph's representative: his steward. Joseph has told him to *take these men to my house, slaughter an animal and prepare a meal* (16).

This is the first of the surprises.

+ Joseph's steward (16-23). The brothers are *frightened* and think they've been brought here *because of the silver that was put back into our sacks* (18): they think they are going to be overpowered and made to become slaves.

So they plead their case to Joseph's steward. They explain about the silver they found in their sacks and tell him that *we have brought it back with us* (21b). And they add that *we don't know who put our silver in our sacks* (22b).

The steward reassures them by saying *Don't be afraid* (23a). Doubtless Joseph has told him to say this: *Your God, the God of your father, has given you treasure in your sacks; I received your silver* (23).

In other words the steward is saying that God has done a miracle. The brothers must be asking themselves if they heard that right. How are they reacting?

And now the steward *brought Simeon out to them* (23b). All eleven brothers are together.

There are more surprises to come.

+ Joseph's behaviour (24-30). The steward *took the men into Joseph's house* (24a) and helps them settle in.

On Joseph's arrival they give him their gifts and *bowed down before him to the ground* (26b): his first dream is becoming reality, because all eleven brothers are here (see chapter 37:6-7).

After asking how they are doing, he asks after *your aged father you told me about*; he wants to know if he's *still living* (27). Why would this interest the governor of Egypt?

The brothers tell Joseph that their father is *alive and well,* and *bowed down, prostrating themselves before him* (28).

And when he sees Benjamin he asks if this is really him: the last time he saw his younger brother he had been little more than a toddler. And then he blesses him with the words *God be gracious to you, my son* (29b).

Joseph is *deeply moved at the sight of his brother,* so *he went into his private room and wept there* (30). The brothers don't know that this is happening, but they've heard the governor of Egypt asking God (not *the gods*) to bless Benjamin.

This is one surprise after another.

+ Joseph's hospitality (31-34). The meal is served, with Joseph eating by himself, Egyptians eating by themselves and *the brothers by themselves*, according to Egyptian custom (32).

Thousands of foreigners are coming to Egypt for food: why are Jacob's sons being singled out? Can they think of an explanation?

And the brothers find that they've been seated *in the order of their ages, from the firstborn to the youngest* (33): how do the governor and his steward know these details about them?

This is almost one surprise too many: the brothers *looked at each other in astonishment* (33b). It looks like they are utterly bewildered.

And when Benjamin is served, his portion is *five times as much as anyone else's* (34). But there's no sign of jealousy: they all *feasted and drank freely with* Joseph (34b).

The brothers who were once so callous are now a united family, full of love towards each other. At peace among themselves, they are ready to become a nation.

Joseph's testing of his brothers in not finished yet. He tells his steward to *fill the men's sacks with as much food as they can carry, and put each man's silver in the mouth of his sack* (chapter 44:1). But he is to *put my cup, the silver one, in the mouth of the youngest one's sack* (2).

Incident d' is complete: *As morning dawned, the men were sent on their way with their donkeys* (3).

e. – Joseph has some of his family come to Egypt (44:4 – 45:15)

Joseph is continuing to put his brothers to the test: have they changed, or are they still the men who sold him into slavery in Egypt?

1. Joseph tests his brothers (44:4-13). So the brothers are on their way home. But Joseph is going to test them by sending his steward to catch them up.

+ Joseph's accusation (4-6). His steward is to ask the brothers *Why have you repaid good with evil?* (4b) and *Isn't this the cup my master drinks from and also uses for divination?* (5).

So when the steward reaches the brothers *he repeated these words to them* (6). The accusation is that they have stolen his silver cup.

+ The brothers' defence (7-9). The brothers are stunned and indignant. They had brought back *the silver we found inside the mouths of our sacks* (8). So *why would we steal silver or gold from your master's house?* (8b).

They are very confident that none of them has the cup, so much so that they declare *If any of your servants is found to have it, he will die; and the rest of us will become my lord's slaves* (9).

As far as they are concerned, there is no chance of any of that happening. But they have a shock coming.

+ The cup's discovery (10-13). Joseph has prepared his steward well: he changes the punishment. The guilty brother *will become my slave; the rest of you will be free from blame* (10). In other words, only one brother will have to stay in Egypt: the others will be able to go home.

Now the steward begins the search, *beginning with the eldest and ending with the youngest* (12). So far, so good. But *the cup was found in Benjamin's sack* (12b).

At this, the brothers *tore their clothes* (13).

But what will they do? Will they abandon Benjamin to his fate and go home to Canaan? That option is on offer: will they take it?

The answer is No: *they all loaded their donkeys and returned to the city* (13).

The brothers have done well with this test. But there's more to come.

2. Joseph tests Judah (44:14-34). Now the account singles out Judah: when *Judah and his brothers* see Joseph, *they threw themselves to the ground before him* (14). This is abject, grovelling submission.

Joseph asks *What is this you have done? Don't you know that a man like me can find things out by divination?* (15).

There's no reason to believe that Joseph actually was practising divination: this is just part of his portraying himself as an Egyptian.

And now Judah speaks up.

+ He acknowledges their guilt (16). Judah is quick to describe Joseph as *my lord* and the brothers as *your servants*.

He knows that all the brothers *are now my lord's slaves*. And this is because *God has uncovered your servants' guilt*.

That sentence is extraordinary. Judah isn't talking about the theft of the silver cup, but about their guilt in heartlessly selling Joseph into slavery in Egypt all those years ago.

Judah, speaking on behalf of his brothers, is acknowledging their guilt.

And, although he thinks he's speaking to an Egyptian, he says that their guilt is something *God has uncovered.*

How must Joseph be feeling as he hears what Judah has to say? But there is one more part of the test still to come.

Joseph reminds the brothers of what his steward had told them before the cup was discovered: *Only the man who was found to have the cup will become my slave* (17; and see 10). And he adds this: *The rest of you, go back to your father in peace* (17b).

Here, once again, is their chance. The conditions are perfect for a second betrayal: the brothers can leave Benjamin to his fate and go home to Canaan. Are they tempted?

Once again, the answer is No. And Judah explains why.

+ He explains the problem (18-32). Judah reminds the governor of Egypt that, during an earlier visit, they had told him that they had *an aged father, and there is a young son born to him in his old age* (20).

He's talking about Benjamin, whose *brother is dead, and he is the only one of his mother's sons left, and his father loves him* (20b).

Judah recounts the steps in the story: Joseph had demanded that Benjamin come down to Egypt, but Jacob could not countenance any such thing. So if the brothers go back to Canaan without Benjamin, they will *bring the grey head of our father down to the grave in sorrow* (31).

Judah adds that he had *guaranteed the boy's safety to my father* (32).

So there's the problem. But Judah has a solution to suggest.

+ He makes his appeal (33-34). Here it is: *Please let your servant remain here as my lord's slave in place of the boy, and let the boy return with his brothers* (33).

This is Judah offering to substitute himself for Benjamin, and to take the punishment due to him. He's willing to sacrifice himself for Benjamin for the sake of his father.

The cost to Judah is immense. But this man is full of compassion and tenderness: he and his brothers love their father and his favourite son so much that they won't abandon Benjamin.

This is the first example of substitution in the Bible. And of course it points to the ultimate substitution of the cross: Jesus, the eternal Son of God, will one day come and take the punishment for our sins onto his shoulders.

Now the ball is in Joseph's court: how will he respond to what he has just heard?

3. Joseph reveals his identity (45:1-15). Joseph is about to lose his composure: he cries out that *everyone leave my presence* (1). This means that *there was no one with Joseph when he made himself known to his brothers* (1b).

So *he wept so loudly that the Egyptians heard him, and Pharaoh's household heard about it* (2).

Presumably the brothers have no idea what's going on here. But Joseph has three things to say to them.

+ I am Joseph! (3-4). It's impossible to imagine his brothers' shock. Joseph asks at once *Is my father still living?* (3).

The brothers are speechless: *they were terrified at his presence* (3). Is this stunned disbelief?

Joseph wants his brothers to come closer (see 4a). And now he tells them something that only their brother Joseph could know: he is *the one you sold into Egypt* (4b).

Are they convinced now?

But Joseph has something else to say.

+ God has done this (4-8). The brothers are not to *be distressed* or *be angry with yourselves for selling me here* (5a). And here's the reason: *it was to save lives that God sent me ahead of you* (5b).

Joseph isn't excusing his brothers, but he's forgiven them. He doesn't hate them, because he sees that God has been at work through his whole story, in order to save many lives through him.

He says it again: *God sent me ahead of you* (7a). And this was all *to preserve for you a remnant on earth* (7).

Joseph wants the brothers to be clear about this: in all the sin and suffering the God of their fathers has been working out his purposes for the blessing of many people.

The brothers need to know that *it was not you who sent me here, but God* (8a). And Joseph invites them to see what God has done: *He made me father to Pharaoh, lord of his entire household and ruler of all Egypt* (8b).

And so it's obvious what Joseph is going to say next.

+ Go home and get Jacob (9-13). The brothers are to go back to Canaan and give their father Joseph's message: *Come down to me; don't delay* (9).

Jacob and his family *will live in the region of Goshen and be near me* (10), and Joseph *will provide for you there* (11a). If they don't come to Egypt, they will *become destitute,* because *five years of famine are still to come* (11).

Joseph can't wait. He tells his brothers to *bring my father down here quickly* (13b).

This is a marvellous reconciliation scene. Joseph *threw his arms around his brother Benjamin and wept, and Benjamin embraced him, weeping* (14). And *he kissed all his brothers and wept over them* (15a).

And then *his brothers talked with him* (15b).

Joseph has seen that the character of his brothers has changed from selfishness to sacrifice. This is something else that God has done.

e'. – Joseph has all of his family come to Egypt (45:16 – 47:12)

Section C' began *This is the account of Jacob's family line* (chapter 37:2a). This is a reminder that Jacob is a key figure throughout all these chapters, despite the fact that Joseph is often the focus of attention.

But now we'll see how God has so arranged things that Jacob will come to Egypt.

1. Pharaoh sends for Jacob (45:16-28). When the news spreads that Joseph's brothers have come to Egypt, *Pharaoh and all his officials were pleased* (16).

+ What Pharaoh says (17-20). He tells the brothers to go home and *bring your father and your families back to me* (18a). He is going to be generous: he will *give you the best of the land of Egypt* (18b).

The brothers are to *take some carts from Egypt for your children and your wives* (19). And Pharaoh finishes by telling them *Never mind about your belongings, because the best of all Egypt will be yours* (20).

+ What Joseph does (21-24). Joseph gives his brothers the carts they need, and *provisions for their journey* (21). They get new clothes too, but Benjamin is given *three hundred shekels of silver and five sets of clothes* (22): and it looks like his brothers can cope with Joseph's favouritism.

They had stripped Joseph of *his* clothes all those years ago (see chapter 37:23); now he is supplying *them* with new clothes. Once again, clothes are showing us something.

And it's worth noting that the brothers are described here, for the first time, as *the sons of Israel* (21a): this is the embryonic nation through which blessing for the world will come.

As his brothers leave for Canaan, Joseph tells them *Don't quarrel on the way!* (24): he knows that arguing and jostling for position are not easy habits to give up.

+ How Jacob reacts (25-28). The brothers arrive home with the news that *Joseph is still alive! In fact, he is ruler of all Egypt* (26a). Jacob, understandably, is *stunned* and *did not believe them* (26b): it's too good to be true.

But two things convince him that his sons are telling the truth: first, he hears them passing on Joseph's message (see 27a); and second, he sees *the carts Joseph had sent to carry him back* (27b).

The result is that *the spirit of their father Jacob revived* (27b): he tells his sons *I'm convinced! My son Joseph is still alive* (28). And he adds that *I will go and see him before I die* (28).

Jacob will do more than that: after seeing Joseph again, he will live in Egypt for seventeen more years.

2. Jacob travels to Egypt (46:1-30). Jacob is the centre of attention in everything that happens in chapter 46. And we'll see once again that he is sometimes referred to by his new name: Israel.

+ Jacob: sent by God (1-7). So *Israel set out with all that was his* (1a). But when he reaches Beersheba, which is like the exit point from the Promised Land on the journey to Egypt, *he offered sacrifices to the God of his father Isaac* (1b).

God hasn't prompted Jacob to do this; rather it's a spontaneous act of worship. Maybe he does this because leaving Canaan is such a huge step: he knows that the destiny of his descendants will be fulfilled in Canaan and not in Egypt.

But God gives Jacob the reassurance he needs: he *spoke to Israel in a vision at night* (2). He tells him to *not be afraid to go down to Egypt,* because *I will make you into a great nation there* (3). And God promises Jacob that *I will go down to Egypt with you* (4).

But that won't be the end of the story. God says *I will surely bring you back again* (4). And Jacob's favourite son will be there at his death: *Joseph's own hand will close your eyes* (4).

So Jacob leaves Canaan because he knows that God is sending him: he *and all his offspring went to Egypt* (6). The whole family is on its way.

And Jacob is confident of God's presence and blessing.

+ Jacob: with all his family (8-27). The listing of the family members begins with the information that *these are the names of the sons of Israel,* or, in other words, *Jacob and his descendants* (8). And we're reminded that all these people *went to Egypt* (8).

The list contains the descendants of Leah (see 8b-15), the descendants of Zilpah (see 16-18), the descendants of Rachel (19-22) and the descendants of Bilhah (see 23-25). When you add in *the two sons who had been born to Joseph in Egypt, the members of Jacob's family, which went to Egypt, were seventy in all* (27).

It could be that the mention of the seventy family members is intended to remind us of the seventy nations descended from Noah (see chapter 10).

This is huge. The family of the twelve sons of Jacob which goes down to Egypt will come out of Egypt as a nation of twelve tribes.

And now we get the last piece of the jigsaw: Jacob's family finally becomes one family again.

+ Jacob: reunited with Joseph (28-30). Now, at this key moment, Judah's leadership role is emphasized again: Jacob sends *Judah ahead of him to Joseph to get directions to Goshen* (28).

Joseph goes to Goshen *to meet his father Israel* (29a). Then he *threw his arms around his father and wept for a long time* (29a).

This has been a long time coming. As the two of them weep, they must both be thanking God for his faithfulness.

Jacob tells Joseph (he's called Israel again here) that he's now *ready to die, since I have seen for myself that you are still alive* (29b).

And now it's time for him to meet Pharaoh.

3. Joseph's family before Pharaoh (46:31 – 47:12). Joseph goes about things carefully: this is going to be an important meeting.

+ Joseph prepares his family (46:31-34). Joseph explains that he will first speak to Pharaoh alone to tell him that his family, who *were living in the land of Canaan, have come to me* (31b).

Joseph will describe them as *shepherds* and will explain that *they have brought along their flocks and herds and everything they own* (32). And when Pharaoh asks the family *What is your occupation?* they are to say that they have *tended livestock from our boyhood on* (33-34a).

Joseph's careful preparation here seems to be because *all shepherds are detestable to the Egyptians* (34b), though no one seems to know why.

+ Joseph's brothers meet Pharaoh (47:1-6). After telling Pharaoh that his family has arrived (see 1), Joseph chooses *five of his brothers and presented them to Pharaoh* (2).

We don't know why he chose five, but we can be pretty sure that Judah is among them.

The brothers explain that they're shepherds and add that, because of the famine, they have *come to live here for a while* (4a). In other words, they want to live in Egypt as resident aliens: they are not planning to stay permanently.

When they ask for permission to *settle in Goshen* (4b), Pharaoh has good news for Joseph: he is to *settle your father and your brothers in the best part of the land,* that is *in Goshen* (6a). And if any of them have *special ability,* they are, says Pharaoh, to be put *in charge of my own livestock* (6b).

There is one more thing that needs to happen.

+ Jacob meets Pharaoh (47:7-10). When Joseph presents his father, *Jacob blessed Pharaoh* (7). Normally it's the greater who blesses the lesser, but that's what's happening here too: the one who's in a covenant relationship with God is greater, because the God of the covenant is greater than the gods of Egypt.

When Pharaoh asks how old Jacob is, he receives this answer: *The years of my pilgrimage are a hundred and thirty* (9a). And these years, Jacob adds, *have been few and difficult* (9b).

And, before leaving, *Jacob blessed Pharaoh* again (10).

Incident e' ends with a note that Joseph makes sure that everything is done *as Pharaoh directed* (11). He gives his family *property in the best part of the land* (11), and provides them with *food, according to the number of their children* (12).

So now all of Joseph's family are in Egypt. While they are there, they will become a nation which will one day bring blessing to all the nations: God's promises to Abraham will be fulfilled (see chapter 12:2-3 and 22:17-18).

f. – Prospering in Egypt: Joseph's ascendancy (47:13-26)

The account tells us that *the famine was severe,* and that this applies to *both Egypt and Canaan* (13). We're going to learn how Joseph deals with the situation.

He does it in two stages.

1. Stage One (14-17). Joseph is receiving a great deal of money from people *in payment for the grain they were buying* (14). He's not keeping any of this for himself: *he brought it to Pharaoh's palace* (14b).

+ What the people say (14-15). Eventually people have no money left, so they ask Joseph to *give us food* (15b). They have a question: *Why should we die before your eyes?* (15b).

It looks like they may be asking Joseph to let them have grain without having to pay for it. But he has other ideas.

+ What Joseph does (16-17). Joseph sees no wisdom in simply handing out food, so he tells the people that he *will sell you food in exchange for your livestock* (16).

So this is what happens: people bring *their horses, their sheep and goats, their cattle and donkeys* to Joseph, who gives them the grain they need (17).

This doesn't mean that they are leaving their livestock with him; rather their livestock from now on belongs to Pharaoh. And in this way Joseph *brought them through that year with food in exchange for all their livestock* (17b).

2. Stage Two (18-26). People's livestock has only provided food for one year, so a year later history pretty much repeats itself.

+ What the people say (18-19). They explain to Joseph that *our money is gone and our livestock belongs to you* (18). The only things they have left are *our bodies and our land* (18b).

So they ask Joseph to *buy us and our land in exchange for food* (19). They know that this means that *we and our land will be in bondage to Pharaoh* (19).

This is the people's suggestion: they are taking the initiative here.

+ What Joseph does (20-26). First, Joseph buys *all the land in Egypt for Pharaoh* (20). That word *all* is important: *the Egyptians, one and all, sold their fields* (20).

And so *the land became Pharaoh's* (20b), except that the priests didn't need to sell their land *because they received a fixed allowance from Pharaoh* (22).

Second, Joseph goes along with the the second half of the people's suggestion: he *reduced the people to servitude from one end of Egypt to the other* (21).

So Joseph can say that he has *bought you and your land today for Pharaoh* (23).

If we call this slavery to the crown, it's harsh. But the people are grateful to Joseph: they tell him *You have saved our lives* (25), and of course this was their suggestion in the first place (see 19a).

So Joseph is not an oppressive overlord.

Because he knows that the famine will soon be over, he gives the people seed *so you can plant the ground* (23). And when the harvest comes, they are to *give a fifth of it to Pharaoh* (24a).

This is very generous. The norm in those days would be over 30%, but the Egyptians need to give Pharaoh only 20%.

Joseph is not misusing his position; he is using his authority for the benefit of the people.

Which is another example of a son of Jacob being a blessing to others.

f'. – Prospering in Egypt: Blessings for Jacob's sons (47:27 – 49:32)

Once again, we see here how central Jacob is to the Joseph story: this is, after all, *the account of Jacob's family line* (chapter 37:2a).

In the original Hebrew, we're told that *Israel settled in Egypt* (27a): this is talking about the nation in embryo and not just about Jacob. They are *fruitful and increased greatly in number* (27b), which is fulfilling promises made to the patriarchs (see chapter 17:6; 26:4; 35:11).

At the beginning and the end of this unit, Jacob makes it clear that he wants to be buried in Canaan (see 47:29-31 and 49:29-32). This is because he knows that God's plan for his descendants includes the promise of the land of Canaan.

It's worth noting that there's a symmetry here. Jacob had spent seventeen years in Canaan with Joseph (before Joseph was sold into slavery); now he is *in Egypt seventeen years* (28).

After his death, Jacob wants Joseph to *carry me out of Egypt and bury me* in Canaan, where Abraham and Isaac are buried (30): he's thinking of the cave of Machpelah (see chapter 49:29-31).

At this, *Joseph swore to him, and Israel worshipped as he leaned on the top of his staff* (31, and see Hebrews 11:21).

The rest of this unit is full of Jacob, and it's full of blessing, too.

1. Jacob blesses Joseph's sons (48:1-22). This is about Joseph's two half-Egyptian sons, Manasseh and Ephraim. But first Jacob has some explaining to do.

+ The explanation (1-7). Joseph has been told that his father is ill, so he goes to visit him, taking *Manasseh and Ephraim along with him* (1): they are both in their early twenties. Jacob *rallied his strength and sat up on the bed* (2).

He tells Joseph that *God Almighty appeared to me at Luz* (which is Beth-el) *in the land of Canaan* (3). There *he blessed me* (3b).

This blessing includes the promises of fruitfulness, and of Canaan *as an everlasting possession to your descendants after you* (4b).

Jacob is going to pass on that blessing to *your two sons born to you in Egypt* (5): they will be *reckoned as mine* (5). He spells it out: *Ephraim and Manasseh will be mine, just as Reuben and Simeon are mine* (5b).

That sentence is important. Already Jacob is reversing the order of Joseph's sons, and Reuben and Simeon are going to be bypassed in favour of Ephraim and Manasseh.

Jacob mentions that *Rachel died in the land of Canaan* (7): because of what he is about to do, she will be credited with four sons instead of two.

+ The blessing (8-20). When he sees the two young men, Jacob asks *Who are these?* (8). Although his eyes are *failing because of old age* (10a), he knows who they are: the question is the formal start of the blessing, just as *Who gives this woman to be married to this man?* is the formal start to a wedding.

Joseph brings his sons closer to Jacob, who *kissed them and embraced them* (10b): this is the affection of a grandfather. And he says to Joseph that *I never expected to see your face again* (11a); and now *God has allowed me to see your children too* (11b).

Joseph realises that something extraordinary is about to happen: he *bowed down with his face to the ground* (12).

Now, standing up, Joseph brings his sons close to his father, with *Ephraim on his right towards Israel's left hand and Manasseh on his left towards Israel's right hand* (13). He's expecting that Manasseh, the older of the two, will receive Jacob's right-hand blessing.

But Jacob crosses his arms (see 14), so that Ephraim will receive the main blessing.

Jacob prays that God will *bless these boys* (16a): this blessing will come from the God *before whom my fathers Abraham and Isaac walked faithfully,* and *who has been my shepherd all my life to this day,* and who is *the Angel who has delivered me from all harm* (15-16a).

And he prays that Ephraim and Manasseh will be *called by my name and the names of my fathers Abraham and Isaac,* and that they'll *increase greatly on the earth* (16b).

Joseph is disconcerted (rather than *displeased,* 17): has the old man got confused? He tries to correct the mistake: indicating Manasseh, he tells Jacob that *this one is the firstborn; put your right hand on his head* (18).

But Jacob knows what he's doing: *I know, my son, I know* (19a). Manasseh will be blessed, but *his younger brother will be greater than he, and his descendants will become a group of nations* (19b).

So Jacob *blessed them that day* (20a), but *put Ephraim ahead of Manasseh* (20b).

There is one more part to chapter 48.

+ The gift (21-22). Jacob (called Israel again) tells Joseph *God will be with you and take you back to the land of your fathers* (21).

And he gives Joseph *one more ridge of land than to your brothers* (22). The word for *ridge of land* is *shechem*: it looks like Jacob had taken possession of some land near Shechem after Simeon and Levi's inexcusable massacre of the people there (see chapter 34:25-29).

But the important thing to note is that Jacob is giving Joseph part of the Promised Land. It's almost like it's a down-payment: one day all of Canaan will belong to Israel's descendants.

Jacob/Israel has blessed Ephraim and Manasseh. But he has some more blessing to do.

2. Jacob blesses his own sons (49:1-28). This is Jacob's deathbed address to his sons. He wants to tell them *what will happen to you in days to come* (1): in other words this is Jacob acting as a prophet, like Abraham before him (see chapter 20:7).

There's a real sense of history in the making here: he tells the *sons of Jacob* to *listen to your father Israel* (2). Jacob's very conscious of being the father of a nation.

In this long poetic speech the sons are not allotted equal space: it's Judah and Joseph who receive the longest blessings. So it's on them that we'll concentrate (for the details about the other brothers, see the commentaries).

+ Anti-blessings for the three eldest sons (3-7). Jacob uses majestic language as he describes Reuben as *my firstborn, my might, the first sign of my strength, excelling in honour, excelling in power* (3).

But now he calls his son *turbulent as the waters* (4): he's referring to Reuben's wanton, reckless behaviour. When he had slept with his father's concubine (see chapter 35:22) Jacob hadn't commented, but he's not holding back now: Reuben *went up onto your father's bed, onto my couch and defiled it* (4).

There's no blessing for Reuben, but rather anti-blessing: Jacob tells him that *you will no longer excel* (4).

The same applies to Simeon and Levi. Jacob can't get their unwarranted massacre at Shechem out of his mind: *they have killed men in their anger and hamstrung oxen as they pleased* (6, and see chapter 34:25-29).

So Simeon and Levi get the opposite of blessing. Jacob says *Cursed be their anger, so fierce, and their fury, so cruel!* (7a). He adds, as God's mouthpiece, that *I will scatter them in Jacob and disperse them in Israel* (7b).

The tribe of Simeon was to become absorbed into the tribe of Judah, and the Levites would be dispersed around the Promised Land.

+ Blessing for Judah (8-12). The name Judah sounds like the Hebrew word for *praise,* and Jacob tells Judah that *your brothers will praise you* (8). Although he is the fourth son, he will take on the leadership role: *your father's sons will bow down to you* (8).

The rest of the blessing for Judah looks forward to the coming of the Messiah. Judah is *like a lion* (9), and the New Testament will describe Jesus the Messiah as *the Lion of the tribe of Judah* (Revelation 5:5).

Jacob adds that *the sceptre will not depart from Judah* (10a): the sceptre is a symbol of kingship. And one day *he to whom it belongs shall come* (10).

The meaning of that phrase is disputed. Literally it reads more like *until Shiloh comes*: is Shiloh another name for the Messiah? Certainly some ancient Jewish interpreters thought so.

What all the scholars are agreed upon is that this is about the Messiah coming from the tribe of Judah; and *the obedience of the nations shall be his* (10b). It's impossible to read that phrase without remembering God's promise to Abraham (see, for example, chapter 12:2-3 and 22:18).

And Jacob describes what the Coming One will do: *He will tether his donkey to a vine* and *wash his garments in wine, his robes in the blood of grapes* (11). And *his eyes will be darker than wine* (12).

Was Jesus thinking of Jacob's words here when he turned water into wine at the wedding in Cana? (see John 2:1-11, and also Mark 2:22).

And this will all come from Judah's tribe. We first met Judah when he had sex with his daughter-in-law, thinking her to be a prostitute, but we've seen how God used that incident to change him, so that he even ended up offering himself as a substitute for his brother Benjamin in Egypt (see chapters 38 and 44).

And a descendant of Judah will one day give his life as a ransom for sinners (see Mark 10:45).

So this blessing for Judah means blessing for all the nations. It's time to worship Jesus.

+ Blessing for seven sons (13-21). Notice how brief these are: Jacob turns to Zebulun (13), Issachar (14-15), Dan (16-17), Gad (19), Asher (20) and Naphtali (21). For the most part, these are blessings, rather than anti-blessings.

And the seventh son to receive a blessing here is the youngest, Benjamin (27).

Halfway through his blessings of the six sons listed above, Jacob cries out *I look for your deliverance, LORD* (18): he's very conscious that he's speaking to his sons in the presence of the covenant God Yahweh.

Jacob knows that his descendants will meet with opposition (see 15b and 19), so he declares his trust that God will look after his people.

+ Blessing for Joseph (22-26). Joseph is like a vine *whose branches climb over a wall* (22): his life has brought overflowing blessing to others.

In the face of so much opposition and so many difficulties, Joseph has *remained steady* (24). Jacob speaks out a cascade of divine names to make it clear who was helping Joseph: God is *the Mighty One of Jacob* and *the Shepherd, the Rock of Israel*; and he's *the Almighty* (24-25).

Jacob's heart is full of praise to God as he remembers the Joseph story, and our hearts should be, too.

Jacob tells Joseph that *your father's blessings are greater than the blessings of the ancient mountains* (26a), and prays for him that all these blessings will *rest on the head of Joseph, on the brow of the prince among his brothers* (26b).

The blessings for the sons have been spoken. In what's really a narrative summary of the whole chapter, we're told that this is *what their father said to them when he blessed them, giving each the blessing appropriate to him* (28).

And, with an eye to the future, the account describes them as *the twelve tribes of Israel* (28a).

As we come to the end of incident f', it's worth remembering that it began with Jacob begging Joseph to make sure that he will be buried in Canaan (see chapter 47:27-31).

The whole unit ends in the same way. His sons are to bury him in *the cave in the field of Machpelah* (30a), where *Abraham and his wife Sarah,* and later *Isaac and his wife Rebekah were buried* (31).

This matters to Jacob not just because his ancestors are buried there. He wants to be buried *in Canaan.* Jacob knows that Egypt is not his family's final home, because he believes God's promises.

g. – Death of a patriarch: Jacob (49:33 – 50:14)

It's fitting, as we near the end of Section C', that Jacob is central: after all, the Joseph story is *the account of Jacob's family line* (chapter 37:2a).

The final pairing in this account is the death of two patriarchs: Jacob and Joseph.

1. Jacob: his death (49:33 – 50:3). Now Jacob *drew his feet up into the bed* (49:33): while blessing his sons he's been sitting on the edge of his bed.

So he *breathed his last* (49:33). At that moment Jacob is *gathered to his people,* just like Abraham, Ishmael and Isaac before him (49:33, and see chapter 25:8; 25:17; and 35:29).

Joseph *threw himself on his father and wept over him and kissed him* (1): he's there at the end, just as God had promised Jacob would be the case (see chapter 46:4).

Joseph gets *the physicians in his service to embalm his father Israel* (2): does he use his own people to avoid the pagan practices of the professional Egyptian embalmers?

And now we're told that *the Egyptians mourned for him seventy days* (3b): this shows the high regard in which they hold Joseph's father.

2. Jacob: he's taken to Canaan (50:4-11). Joseph asks Pharaoh's officials to pass on a message to their master: is this because with the grieving he no longer looks presentable?

The message is about Jacob having told Joseph to *bury me in the tomb I dug for myself in the land of Canaan* (5). He asks for permission to *go up and bury my father,* and promises *Then I will return* (5b).

So, with Pharaoh's agreement, *Joseph went up to bury his father* (7a).

This is a substantial funeral cortège, an event of state with national pomp and ceremony: *all* (not *some of*) *Pharaoh's officials accompanied* Joseph, his brothers and their households (7-8a). Only the children remain behind in Egypt, a guarantee to Pharaoh that Joseph will keep his promise and come back (see 8b and 5b).

The account is stressing that this is *a very large company* (9b): it's Egypt honouring the father of the man we call Joseph.

Once in Canaan, and specifically *the threshing-floor of Atad* (…), *they lamented loudly and bitterly* (10a). Joseph, perhaps because he's now on Canaan's soil, *observed a seven-day period of mourning* (10b): this was the usual Israelite practice.

The Canaanites living there remark that *the Egyptians are holding a solemn ceremony of mourning* (11): they probably think that everyone is an Egyptian because of the clothes they're wearing.

So Jacob's body has been brought to Canaan.

3. Jacob: his burial in the cave of Machpelah (50:12-14). So Jacob's sons *carried him to the land of Canaan,* just as he had wanted (12-13a), and they *buried him in the cave in the field of Machpelah* (13).

And now, true to his word, *Joseph returned to Egypt*, along with *all the others who had gone with him to bury his father* (14).

This is significant: Jacob has been laid to rest in Canaan, the land God has promised to his people.

g'. – Death of a patriarch: Joseph (50:15-26)

Like his father Jacob, Joseph appears in the New Testament's list of heroes of the faith (see Hebrews 11:22). His faith is still shining brightly as he approaches his death.

1. Joseph's faith: What God has done (15-21). Joseph's brothers are unsure: will he take their father's death as an opportunity to get his revenge on them? What if Joseph *pays us back for all the wrongs we did to him?* (15).

It's like they've forgotten how, after revealing his identity to them, Joseph had *kissed all his brothers and wept over them* (chapter 45:15).

The account doesn't tell us if Jacob had really sent a message to ask Joseph *to forgive your brothers the sins and the wrongs they committed in treating you so badly* (17). But surely not: after all, since Jacob arrived in Egypt, seventeen years have passed.

On receiving the message, *Joseph wept* (17b): my guess is that he's disappointed by his brothers' lack of trust.

It certainly looks like the brothers have really repented: they call themselves *the servants of the God of your father* (17). Or is it just fear in action when they *threw themselves down before him* and say *We are your slaves* (18)?

Joseph thinks it might be fear: twice he tells them *Don't be afraid* (19 and 21a).

And then he asks them a question: *Am I in the place of God?* (19). Joseph knows that vengeance belongs to God, not to human beings (see Lev 19:18; Deut 32:35; Rom 12:19).

Joseph doesn't gloss over his brothers' sin: he knows that *you intended to harm me* (20a). But he is sure that *God intended it for good to accomplish what is now being done, the saving of many lives* (20).

Through something evil done to Joseph, God has done something good for other people. God's goal in it all was the survival of many people: the Egyptians, and especially the family of Jacob.

The supreme example of God using human sin to accomplish good is found in the cross of Jesus. As Peter preached it on the day of Pentecost: *This man was handed over to you by God's deliberate plan and foreknowledge; and you, with the help of wicked men, put him to death by nailing him to the cross* (Acts 2:23).

Joseph has faith in what God has done. He underlines this by committing himself to provide for his brothers and their families, *and he reassured them and spoke kindly to them* (21b).

2. Joseph's faith: What God will do (22-26). Joseph lives *a hundred and ten years* (22), which the Egyptians considered the ideal lifespan. Ninety-three of those years Joseph has spent in Egypt. And he gets to see his family grow (see 23).

Now Joseph tells his brothers (or those of them still alive) that *God will surely come to your aid and take you up out of this land to the land he promised on oath to Abraham, Isaac and Jacob* (24).

This is Joseph's faith in action. He is the first to mention the trio of *Abraham, Isaac and Jacob,* and he's sure that God will one day bring his people to Canaan, the land of promise.

This is huge. And so, when talking about Joseph, the Letter to the Hebrews tells us that nothing in his life is as important as this: *By faith Joseph, when his end was near, spoke about the exodus of the Israelites from Egypt* (Hebrews 11:22a).

God is going to give Israel the Promised Land.

And that's why Joseph gets his brothers to swear that they will *carry my bones up from this place* (25).

Joseph is confident of what God will do.

And now he *died at the age of a hundred and ten*; then, *after they embalmed him, he was placed in a coffin in Egypt* (26).

Learning Genesis+

It's not difficult to learn the order of the events in this section: they're all in pairs. You might do this alone, or with a friend.

Begin by saying out loud the six headings from incident a through to incident c'. Do that until you can do it without looking at *The Genesis+ Experiment.* Then do the same with the eight headings from incident d through to incident g'.

Now try to say all the headings from memory: and remember that this is easier if you do this all aloud, rather than just in your mind. As you think yourself through Section C', you'll find yourself remembering all kinds of details.

The people who find it hard to learn a section are the people who don't try! And it's a wise decision to arrange with a friend that you will both try this experiment.

Section C': The Joseph Story

a.   Trouble between Joseph and his brothers
a'. More trouble between Joseph and his brothers
b.   *Sexual temptation involving Judah*
b'. *Sexual temptation involving Joseph*
c.   Joseph interprets two dreams for fellow-prisoners
c'. Joseph interprets two dreams for Pharaoh
d.   *Joseph's brothers come to Egypt for food*
d'. *Joseph's brothers again come to Egypt for food*
e.   Joseph has some of his family come to Egypt
c'. Joseph has all of his family come to Egypt
f.   *Prospering in Egypt: Joseph's ascendancy*
f'. *Prospering in Egypt: Blessings for Jacob's sons*
g.   Death of a patriarch: Jacob
g'. Death of a patriarch: Joseph

Meeting God

As you tell yourself (or a friend) the first incident, talk to God about what he is doing.

Then do the same with the next incident. And so on through the whole section.

And why not try using the questions about Section C' in Appendix 3?

Notice that God is blessing Joseph in such a way that he's a blessing to everyone he comes into contact with: his clothes bear that out again and again. You might want to ask God to make *you* a blessing.

I am praying for you that, as you re-tell the Joseph story as part of *The Genesis+ Experiment*, you will be amazed at how God is at work. You will see how God not only blesses Joseph, but also makes him a blessing to others.

And you will meet God.

Section B'
The Exodus Story (Exodus 1:1 – 13:16)

The end of the book of Genesis has left us hanging: although God has promised the land of Canaan to the descendants of Abraham, Isaac and Jacob, they are still living in Egypt. So Section B' is going to give us the account of Israel's exodus from their slavery there. We're going to see God at work: he calls Moses and he sends the plagues, climaxing in the Passover. This event will remain at the centre of Israel's life and looks forward to a future exodus when the Lamb of God will die for sinners.

When the LORD saw that he had gone over to look,
God called to him from within the bush,
Moses! Moses!
And Moses said *Here I am*.

Exodus 3:4

Enjoying the View

a. Oppression by a Pharaoh who never knew Joseph (1:1-22)
b. *Moses comes to Pharaoh's house as a baby* (2:1-10)
c. Moses departs from Egypt (2:11-25)
d. CENTRE: The call of Moses (3:1 – 4:17)
c'. Moses returns to Egypt (4:18-31)
b'. *Moses comes to Pharaoh's house as an adult* (5:1-5)
a'. Worse oppression by a Pharaoh who never knew Joseph (5:6 – 6:12)

Narrative break: The family record of Moses and Aaron (6:13-27)

a. God promises to rescue his people from Egypt (6:28 – 7:7)
b. *God's power to create life* (7:8-13)
c. Opening cycle of three plagues (7:14 – 8:19)
d. CENTRE: Central cycle of three plagues (8:20 – 9:12)
c'. Closing cycle of three plagues (9:13 – 10:29)
b'. *God's power to terminate life* (11:1-10)
a'. God rescues his people from Egypt (12:1 – 13:16)

Section B' divides into two distinct halves: the family record of Moses and Aaron marks the break between the two. In the first half, the scene is set: God sees that his people are being mistreated in Egypt, and he chooses Moses to be the one who will lead them out of slavery and into the Promised Land.

After the narrative break, the second half focuses on the exodus itself: God sends plagues on the land of Egypt, culminating in the judgment and rescue of the Passover events.

So the section shows us God saving his people, and demonstrates how God rescues people today from a godless world. This is the theme of Section B', which, like most of the sections, has its own symbol.

Anyone reading the section will be struck by the repeated mention of a *staff*: it's used by Moses to initiate a number of the plagues. And it's sometimes even called *the staff of God* (see, for example, Exodus 4:20b).

This staff is a pointer to the fact that Moses is acting with an authority given him by God. It's God, not Moses, who's providing salvation for his people.

Please take time to read from the beginning of the book of Exodus through to chapter 13:16. As Yahweh rescues his people from slavery in Egypt, notice how Moses uses the staff.

Talk to God about what you're reading, and worship him.

This is a key part of *The Genesis+ Experiment.*

Unpacking the Content

a. – Opposition by a Pharaoh who never knew Joseph (1:1-22)

This first chapter prepares the way for what is to come.

1. God's covenant plan (1-7). These verses are a bridge between the end of Genesis and the beginning of Exodus. They tell us two things.

+ A brief reminder (1-5). This is a list of *the sons of Israel who went to Egypt with Jacob* (1): we're being reminded of what happened in Section C'.

It's worth noting that the phrase *the sons of Israel* refers to Jacob's sons. But this is the last time it will be used in this way: from now on the expression will refer to the whole nation.

As we read the list we will find ourselves remembering details about the lives of some of Jacob's sons: *Reuben, Simeon, Levi and Judah; Issachar, Zebulun and Benjamin; Dan and Naphtali; Gad and Asher* (2-4).

That adds up to eleven, because *Joseph was already in Egypt* (5).

And the end of this reminder tells us that *the descendants of Jacob numbered seventy in all* (5). It's a small collection of people.

+ Massive growth (6-7). Joseph and his brothers *and all that generation died* (6), but the Israelites are clearly incredibly prolific in childbearing.

The verbs in verse 7 paint the growth for us: the Israelites are *exceedingly fruitful* and *multiplied greatly;* they *increased in numbers* and *became so numerous that the land was filled with them* (7).

This is like a new creation, this time of a nation: Egypt is overflowing with them. And this is already fulfilling God's covenant plan for his people.

But this growth leads to oppression.

2. Pharaoh's first plan: forced labour (8-14). There is *a new king* (8), which doesn't mean that he's the successor of the one Joseph had served. The key thing to note is that this is a Pharaoh *to whom Joseph meant nothing* (8).

He says that *the Israelites have become far too numerous for us* (9); if ever Egypt is attacked by another nation, the Israelites *will join our enemies, fight against us and leave the country* (10).

The solution is simple: *they put slave masters over them to oppress them with forced labour* (11).

But the plan misfires: the more God's people are oppressed, *the more they multiplied and spread,* with the result that *the Egyptians came to dread the Israelites* (12).

This *harsh labour* is *in brick and mortar* and in *all kinds of work in the fields* (14): twice we're told that *the Egyptians worked them ruthlessly* (13 and 14b).

And now Pharaoh has another idea.

3. Pharaoh's second plan: selective genocide (15-22). Pharaoh speaks to *Shiphrah and Puah,* who are presumably in charge of all *the Hebrew midwives* (15).

He tells them what they're to do when delivering babies: *If you see that the baby is a boy, kill him; but if it is a girl, let her live* (16).

Why are only the boys to be killed? The boys could grow up to be soldiers and so pose a threat to the power of Egypt, while the girls could be assimilated into Egyptian society through intermarriage.

However, this plan fails too: this time because the midwives *feared God* and *let the boys live* (17).

When Pharaoh asks how they defend their actions, they reply that *Hebrew women are not like Egyptian women*: they *give birth before the midwives arrive* (19).

This doesn't have to be a lie: we just don't know. In any case *the people increased and became even more numerous* (20), while God blesses the midwives and gives them *families of their own* (21).

Pharaoh has had enough. A new command goes out, not just to the midwives but *to all his people*: every girl is allowed to live, but *every Hebrew boy that is born you must throw into the Nile* (22).

b. – Moses comes to Pharaoh's house as a baby (2:1-10)

Chapter 2 of Exodus narrates the birth and preparation of the deliverer of Israel.

1. What Moses' mother does (1-4). She's *a Levite woman,* who's married *a man of the tribe of Levi* (1). She becomes pregnant and *gave birth to a son* (2a).

We know what's supposed to happen to the baby, but instead of throwing him into the Nile, *she hid him for three months* because *he was a fine child* (2): that word *fine* probably means that he's healthy.

But you can't keep a baby hidden for ever. So the mother *got a papyrus basket for him and coated it with tar and pitch*: putting the baby inside, she *put it among the reeds along the bank of the Nile* (3).

Is she asking God somehow to rescue her baby? Certainly the child's *sister stood at a distance to see what would happen to him* (4).

2. What Pharaoh's daughter does (5-9). Pharaoh's daughter has gone down to the river to bathe; she *saw the basket among the reeds and sent her female slave to get it* (5).

Opening the basket, she *saw the baby* and recognises that *this is one of the Hebrew babies* (6). Her heart goes out to the child: *he was crying, and she felt sorry for him* (6).

It looks like the baby's sister realises that Pharaoh's daughter is not minded to kill the boy. So she offers to *go and get one of the Hebrew women to nurse the baby for you* (7). Granted permission, she returns with Moses' mother.

Pharaoh's daughter tells the mother to *take this baby and nurse him for me, and I will pay you* (9). Which is what happens.

3. What God does (10). We're not told how old the child is when his mother *took him to Pharaoh's daughter,* but we do know that Pharaoh's daughter adopts him: *he became her son* and *she named him Moses* (10).

This is extraordinary. She must know what her father has commanded should happen to all male Hebrew babies, but she's gone against his will.

This is God at work. Under his mother's influence, Moses will have been introduced to the history of his people and to the promises God had made to Abraham, Isaac and Jacob.

And here he is now: getting to know Egyptian culture, with its religion, its language and its traditions.

He is already being equipped by God to become, one day, the deliverer of his people.

c. – Moses departs from Egypt (2:11-25)

Some time later, things happen which result in Moses having to get out of Egypt: in his speech to the Jewish Council in the book of Acts, Stephen tells us that this happened *when Moses was forty years old* (Acts 7:23).

1. Moses in Egypt (11-15). One day, he goes out *to where his own people were* and sees them *at their hard labour* (11). And, specifically, he sees *an Egyptian beating a Hebrew* (11b): and we're reminded, once again, that this man is *one of his own people* (11b).

So Moses takes the law into his own hands: making sure that there are no witnesses, *he killed the Egyptian and hid him in the sand* (12).

The next day he tries to arbitrate between *two Hebrews fighting* (13), but one of the men asks *Who made you ruler and judge over us?* (14a): the answer to that, of course, is that no one has.

But it's the second question which is so disconcerting for Moses: he's asked if he's *thinking of killing me as you killed the Egyptian* (14). He had thought the murder had gone undetected, but he was wrong.

So *Moses was afraid* (14b): he realises that he has to get out of the country. And quickly.

Pharaoh gets wind of what's happened and so *tried to kill Moses.* The result is that *Moses fled from Pharaoh and went to live in Midian,* in the Sinai peninsula (15).

2. Moses in Midian (16-22). Now we learn that *a priest of Midian had seven daughters,* who came to a well so that they could *water their father's flock* (16). When *some shepherds came along and drove them away,* Moses *came to their rescue and watered their flock* (17).

When the daughters go home and tell their father Reuel what Moses had done at the well, they refer to him as *an Egyptian* (19), presumably because of his clothes. Reuel's response is to tell them to *invite him to have something to eat* (20).

Moses gets more than a meal: some time later Reuel *gave his daughter Zipporah to Moses in marriage* (21). When Zipporah gives birth to a son, Moses calls him Gershom, explaining that he *has become a foreigner in a foreign land* (22; *Gershom* sounds like the Hebrew for *a foreigner there*).

3. God in action (23-25). The account tells us that *during that long period, the king of Egypt died* (23a).

Meanwhile, the Israelites *groaned in their slavery and cried out* (23b): are they crying out to God? It certainly looks like it: *their cry for help because of their slavery went up to God* (23b).

Now, four verbs tell us how God responds. First, he *heard their groaning* (24); and second, he *remembered his covenant with Abraham, with Isaac and with Jacob* (24): God has covenanted himself to this nation.

Third, *God looked on the Israelites* (25); and fourth, he *was concerned about them* (25).

If we were reading this account for the first time, we would know now that God plans to do something to rescue his people from their slavery in Egypt.

And that he'll use Moses to do it.

d. – CENTRE: The call of Moses (3:1 – 4:17)

This is a lengthy account, for two reasons. First, God needs to explain to Moses that he plans to rescue his people from Egypt; and second, he will deal with Moses' questions and excuses.

1. Moses: his call (3:1-10). Moses is *tending the flock of Jethro, his father-in-law* (1), who apparently has two names (see chapter 2:18).

This is humbling for Moses, steeped as he is in an Egyptian culture that despises shepherds (see Genesis 46:34b). In Egypt he was arrogant enough to think that he could take leadership (see chapter 2:11-15).

So now here Moses is: humbled. He leads the flock *to the far side of the wilderness and came to Horeb, the mountain of God* (1b). This is the mountain also known as Sinai: it looks like the names were used pretty much interchangeably.

And there, on an ordinary working day, Moses experiences something extraordinary. Seeing a burning bush is an everyday occurrence in the desert, but this bush *did not burn up* (2b). Moses doesn't know it yet, but this is *the angel of the LORD* appearing to him *in flames of fire* (2a).

So Moses is curious: he wants to know why this burning bush *does not burn up* (3).

And now God speaks *from within the bush* by calling him by name: *Moses! Moses!* (4).

God tells him to come no closer and to *take off your sandals, for the place where you are standing is holy ground* (5): in the ancient Near East this was a sign of humility before someone greater.

And now God has three things to say to Moses.

+ This is who I am (6). This is unmistakeable: this is *the God of Abraham, the God of Isaac and the God of Jacob* (6). Moses knows from his mother's teaching what that involves.

So he *hid his face, because he was afraid to look at God* (6b).

+ This is what I'll do (7-9). God has *seen the misery of my people in Egypt* (7a), so he has *come down to rescue them from the hand of the Egyptians* (8a).

He will bring them out of Egypt *into a good and spacious land, a land flowing with milk and honey* (8). This is the first time Canaan is so described in the Old Testament.

And Moses knows that God is talking about Canaan: his mother had taught him about the promises of a land, which God describes here as *the home of the Canaanites* and other nations (8b).

So this is what God will do. Has Moses already worked out why God is telling him this? Does he sense what all this is leading up to?

So God has a third thing to say to him.

+ You're the man I'll use (10). Now Moses hears something that will change his life: God tells him that *I am sending you to Pharaoh to bring my people the Israelites out of Egypt* (10).

This is what God is going to do about Israel's predicament. He is calling Moses to lead them out of slavery and into freedom.

But Moses is not just going to say *Here I am: send me.* There are issues he needs to address.

2. Moses: his questions (3:11-22). There are two questions he wants to ask.

+ Who am I? (11-12). Moses knows firsthand about the power of Pharaoh, so he asks God *Who am I that I should go to Pharaoh and bring the Israelites out of Egypt?* (11).

He doesn't fit the job description: he's on the run, he's just a shepherd and he's eighty years old. Moses may have learnt humility in the desert, but now it looks like he can't believe that God could use him for such an impossible task.

God's reply is simple: *I will be with you* (12).

And the confirmation that it is God who has sent Moses is that, one day, *when you have brought the people out of Egypt, you will worship God on this mountain* (12).

But Moses has a second question.

+ Who are you? (13-22). If Moses tells the Israelites that *the God of your fathers has sent me to you*, they may well ask *What is his name?* (13).

So what is Moses to say?

God answers the question with the words *I AM WHO I AM* (14a): that could equally be translated *I WILL BE WHO I WILL BE*.

And God spells it out so that there's no mistake: Moses is to tell the Israelites *I AM has sent me to you* (14b).

This is about the is-ness of God. He's not dependent on anything else, and he's not in the process of becoming something else. He is self-existent, unchanging and eternal.

So Moses is to tell the Israelites that he's been sent by *the LORD, the God of your fathers* (15). This name, written as the four consonants YHWH and probably pronounced *Yahweh*, was already known in Israel: we've met it numerous times in the book of Genesis.

But now its meaning has been explained.

God has more to say to Moses in answer to his second question. Three things will happen.

+ Moses must tell the elders (16-18a). He is to go back to Egypt and *assemble the elders of Israel* (16a) and tell them that God has *appeared to me* and *seen what has been done to you in Egypt* (16b).

He is to assure them that God has *promised to bring you up out of your misery in Egypt into the land of the Canaanites* (17).

And now God reassures Moses. He tells him that *the elders of Israel will listen to you* (18a).

+ Moses and the elders must speak to Pharaoh (18b-19). They are to ask him to *let us take a three-day journey into the wilderness to offer sacrifices to the LORD our God* (18b).

God is not encouraging Moses to make up a story: this is simply the beginning of a complicated piece of ancient Near-East bargaining. If Pharaoh is so stubborn as to refuse the three-day request, that shows that he will refuse everything.

So God knows that *the king of Egypt will not let you go unless a mighty hand compels him* (19).

So there is a third stage to what will happen.

+ God's intervention will result in Pharaoh letting Israel go (20-22). He will *strike the Egyptians with all the wonders that I will perform among them* (20a).

And after that, Pharaoh *will let you go* (20b).

And this release from Egypt will be a triumph for the Israelites: when they leave, *you will not go empty-handed* (21b). The Egyptians will be *favourably disposed* towards them (21a), so that they'll give them *articles of silver and gold* and *clothing which you will put on your sons and daughters* (22).

And so, says God, *you will plunder the Egyptians* (22b).

Moses' questions have been answered, and God has told him what is going to happen.

But he is anything but enthusiastic about obeying God's command.

3. Moses: his excuses (4:1-17). He has three.

+ They won't believe me (1-9). Moses thinks that the people may well not *believe me or listen to me* (1).

In response, God gives him three signs he can use to convince Israel that this is God at work.

The first sign has to do with Moses' staff. This is very significant: the staff is going to become God's authorisation of Moses to deliver his people. Moses *threw it on the ground and it became a snake, and he ran from it* (3). Obeying God's command to *take it by the tail* (4a), Moses sees it *turned back into a staff in his hand* (4b).

And God explains the purpose of the sign: it's *so that they may believe that the LORD, the God of their fathers [...] has appeared to you* (5).

The second sign has to do with Moses' hand: when he takes it out of his cloak *the skin was leprous* (6). The word was used for a variety of skin diseases: the important thing is that Moses' hand *had become as white as snow* (6b).

But when, in obedience to God, Moses repeats what he's already done with his hand, *it was restored, like the rest of his flesh* (7).

The third sign has to do with the River Nile, and is to be used *if they do not believe these two signs* (9a). Moses is to *take some water from the Nile and pour it on the dry ground*: it will *become blood* (9b).

My guess is that Moses recognises that these signs will result in the people believing.

So he moves on to a second excuse.

+ I'm not gifted enough (10-12). Moses begins by saying *Pardon your servant, Lord* (10a) because he knows that this excuse contains an implied criticism of God.

He explains that he has *never been eloquent, neither in the past nor since you have spoken to your servant* (10). He's not a polished orator, so he's not the right man to confront Pharaoh.

God replies to Moses by asking him questions: *Who gave human beings their mouths? […] Is it not I, the LORD?* (11). And he commits himself to *help you speak* and to *teach you what to say* (12).

This is an astonishing promise, which may remind us of God's words to his servant in the prophecy of Isaiah (see Isaiah 50:4, and also John 8:28).

So Moses has a third excuse as to why God shouldn't choose him as Israel's deliverer. But it isn't really an excuse at all.

+ I don't want to (13-17). Moses blurts out his request: God should *please send someone else* (13).

And now *the LORD's anger burned against Moses* (14a). Questions are fine, but disobedience is a step too far. God isn't budging from his decision to call Moses, but he agrees to send *your brother, Aaron the Levite,* too (14).

God knows that Aaron *can speak well* (14). So God will give words to Moses, Moses will speak to Aaron and *put words in his mouth* (15), and Aaron will speak those words to Pharaoh and to the Israelites: *it will be as if he were your mouth and as if you were God to him* (16).

There are no more excuses. Moses is going to obey God's call, and he's uniquely equipped for the job he's being sent to do: he understands Egyptian culture, he knows the wilderness, he knows how to get to Mount Sinai, he has a staff with which to do miracles and he has a brother to be his mouthpiece.

This is the man God will use to set his people free.

c'. – Moses returns to Egypt (4:18-31)

In incident c (see chapter 2:11-25) Moses departed from Egypt after it became known that he had murdered an Egyptian; now, in incident c', he returns.

1. Moses: leaving Midian (18-20). Moses asks *Jethro his father-in-law* for permission to go back *to my own people in Egypt to see if any of them are still alive* (18). This is Moses' way of saying that he wants to see how the Israelites are faring: after all, he was last there forty years ago (see Acts 7:30).

After Jethro has signalled his willingness for this to happen, God reassures Moses that he can return to Egypt, because *all those who wanted to kill you are dead* (19).

This phrase is picked up by Matthew in his Gospel (see Matt 2:19-20): one day it will be safe for Joseph and his family to return *from* Egypt to Nazareth.

So Moses takes *his wife and his sons* and *started back to Egypt* (20). The older boy, Gershom, we already know about; the other son is Eliezer (see chapter 18:3-4). This is an important detail for what we'll read about soon.

And Moses makes sure that he takes *the staff of God* with him (20b): with it he is going to be able to perform miraculous signs, so much so that the staff, though his, is really *the staff of God.* God is going to use it, and him, to deliver his people.

2. Moses: travelling to Egypt (21-28). His journey is full of incident.

+ The certainty of God's plan (21-23). God tells Moses to be sure to *perform before Pharaoh all the wonders I have given you the power to do* (21).

But God has something else to say about Pharaoh: *I will harden his heart so that he will not let the people go* (21b). This will demonstrate that only the God of the Hebrews is the Lord of everything.

This is a theme that will occur several times in the rest of Section B'. Sometimes, as here, it's God who hardens Pharaoh's heart, and sometimes Pharaoh hardens his own heart (see chapter 8:15).

Both are true. The apostle Paul writes without embarrassment about God hardening Pharaoh's heart (see Rom 9:14-18), while the apostle Peter declares that the death of Jesus happened because of the actions of wicked men *and* because of God's sovereign purpose (see Acts 2:22-23).

It's part of God's plan that Pharaoh should refuse to let the Hebrews go.

Moses is to tell Pharaoh that *Israel is my firstborn son* (22). This is the only time this expression is used of Israel in the Old Testament, and it's very significant here.

Israel is due to receive the firstborn's inheritance of a country that belongs to its father; if Pharaoh refuses to let Israel leave Egypt, God will *kill your firstborn son* (23). And what happens to Pharaoh will be true of all the Egyptians.

God's plan is certain.

+ The necessity of circumcision (24-26). This is a difficult passage to understand: see the commentaries for more details.

But my guess is that this is about the sign of the covenant between God and Israel, which is circumcision (see Appendix 2 for this link between Sections B and B'). This explains why, *at a lodging place on the way, the LORD met Moses and was about to kill him* (24).

Could it be that, while Gershom had been circumcised, Moses' younger son Eliezer had not? And that this means that God is angry with Moses?

Moses can't become the leader of Israel if both his sons don't bear the sign of the covenant in their bodies, so perhaps Moses becomes ill and is in danger of death.

Zipporah, Moses' wife, correctly interprets the situation and *took a flint knife* and *cut off her son's foreskin* (25a), performing the circumcision. Perhaps Moses was in no fit state to do it himself.

Zipporah *touched Moses' feet with* her son's foreskin (25). That word *feet* is sometimes a euphemism in Hebrew thinking for the genitals, and the text here says that Zipporah *threw* the foreskin: is this her way of showing her displeasure at having to perform this ritual?

Whatever the case, God's judgment is averted and Moses doesn't die: *the LORD let him alone* (26a) and Zipporah calls her husband *a bridegroom of blood to me* (25b).

So this strange story is about the necessity of circumcision as a sign of the covenant: Eliezer must be circumcised if Moses is to lead the covenant people out of slavery in Egypt.

But something else happens before Moses reaches his destination.

+ The meeting with Aaron (27-28). God has told Aaron, who of course is in Egypt, to *go into the wilderness to meet Moses*: so they meet *at the mountain of God* (27).

Moses tells Aaron *everything the LORD had sent him to say* and about *all the signs he had commanded him to perform* (28).

Now that Aaron is fully up to speed, the two brothers are ready to meet Pharaoh. So they journey on to Egypt.

3. Moses: meeting with the elders (29-31). Moses and Aaron meet with *all the elders of the Israelites, and Aaron told them everything the LORD had said to Moses* (29-30).

And *he performed the signs too* (30b). The result is that *they believed* (31a).

But there's more. *When they heard that the LORD was concerned about them and had seen their misery, they bowed down and worshipped* (31).

The Hebrew elders believe. But will Pharaoh?

b'. – Moses comes to Pharaoh's house as an adult (5:1-5)

This is the first audience that Moses and Aaron will have with Pharaoh. They begin with the words *This is what the LORD, the God of Israel, says* (1).

This is a message from Yahweh, and, in order to make things clear, they call him *the God of Israel.*

Pharaoh is to *let my people go, so that they may hold a festival to me in the wilderness* (1b).

The king of Egypt is scornful and incredulous: he asks *Who is the LORD, that I should obey him and let Israel go?* (2a). Pharaoh has absolute authority and has no intention of sharing it with a god whose authority he doesn't recognise: *I do not know the LORD and I will not let Israel go* (2b).

Moses and Aaron are not giving up: they ask Pharaoh to *let us take a three-day journey into the wilderness to offer sacrifices to the LORD our*

God (3, and see chapter 3:18). This matters because God is real: if this doesn't happen, *he may strike us with plagues or with the sword* (3b).

We already know how Pharaoh is going to react.

Pharaoh accuses Moses and Aaron of distracting the Israelites from their work: they are *stopping them from working* (5). So his message to them and to all their people is *Get back to your work!* (4).

And now the oppression gets even worse.

a'. – Worse oppression by a Pharaoh who never knew Joseph
(5:6 – 6:12)

1. What Pharaoh does (5:6-21). The big issue here is who is Lord: Yahweh or Pharaoh? We read about three things happening.

+ A new order (6-9). Pharaoh gives this order to *the slave drivers and the overseers in charge of the people* (6): the slave drivers are Egyptians and the overseers are Israelite foremen. And he issues this order *that same day* (6).

From now on the Hebrews are not to be provided with *straw for making bricks*; they're to *gather their own straw* (7). Straw is essential in brick-making, because of its holding power.

But the slave drivers and overseers are not to *reduce the quota*: the people are to *make the same number of bricks as before* (8a).

And Pharaoh wants everyone to know that the reason the Hebrews want to *go and sacrifice to our God* is that *they are lazy* (8b).

So it's clear what this new order is going to lead to.

+ Harder work (10-18). The Israelites have to go *all over Egypt to gather stubble to use for straw* (12): their workload has increased massively.

The slave drivers *kept pressing them* and *beat the Israelite overseers* (13a and 14a). The whole purpose of the exercise is to break Israel and to extinguish their hope of freedom.

The Israelite overseers complain to Pharaoh: it's not their fault that fewer bricks are being made. They ask him *Why have you treated your servants this way?* (15).

But their protest falls on deaf ears. Pharaoh accuses the people of laziness again, and repeats the command that they must find their own straw and *produce your full quota of bricks* (18).

So it's easy to see who is going to get the blame for all of this.

+ A tough message (19-21). The Israelite overseers confront Moses and Aaron, who have *made us obnoxious to Pharaoh and his officials* (21).

And so they tell them *May the LORD look on you and judge you!* (21a).

Moses is only obeying God's instructions. But things have got worse, not better.

All of this is because of what Pharaoh does.

2. How Moses reacts (5:22-23). Moses' mind is in turmoil: all his earlier reservations are being confirmed by events. So he accuses God of bringing *trouble on this people* (22).

And, what's more, says Moses to God, *You have not rescued your people at all* (23).

Moses is disappointed by God: probably he's even regretting agreeing to be sent back to Egypt.

But God has something for him.

3. What God will do (6:1-12). God makes it very clear that he is very aware of the oppression of his people. And he's going to act.

+ God's message to Moses (1-5). God repeats his promise: Pharaoh will let Israel go *because of my mighty hand* (1).

And God reminds Moses of his promises *to Abraham, to Isaac and to Jacob* (3). He identifies himself again as *the LORD* (2), explaining that *by my name the LORD I did not make myself known to them* (3).

This doesn't mean that the patriarchs had never heard the name Yahweh: the name the LORD appears many times in the book of Genesis. Rather it means that they knew the name *but not its significance*: that was a revelation given to Moses at the burning bush (see chapter 3:13-14).

God reminds Moses that he had promised to give his people *the land of Canaan, where they resided as foreigners* (4).

This is a message Moses needs to hear.

+ God's message to his people (6-9). The message Moses is to pass on begins and ends with the statement *I am the LORD* (6a and 8b).

God promises to *free you from being slaves* and to *bring you to the land I swore with uplifted hand to give to Abraham, to Isaac and to Jacob* (6 and 8).

And he promises them this: *I will take you as my own people, and I will be your God* (7a). This is the heart of the covenant relationship between Yahweh and Israel.

Moses passes the message on to the people, *but they did not listen to him,* and for two reasons: *their discouragement and hard labour* (9).

This will have been another huge disappointment to Moses. So God is going to tell him not to give up.

+ God's message to Moses (10-12). Moses is to go and *tell Pharaoh king of Egypt to let the Israelites go out of his country* (11).

But Moses is dispirited. If the Israelites will not listen to him, *why would Pharaoh listen to me, since I speak with faltering lips?* (12).

Things are not looking good. Moses is to continue obeying God, despite his own feelings of inadequacy, despite the resignation of the people and despite the hatred of the Egyptians.

So we will see what God will do to fulfil his plan and to set his people free. But before that there's a genealogy for us to look at.

Narrative break: The family record of Moses and Aaron (6:13-27)

A limited genealogy makes clear the division between the two halves of Section B'. It's limited because it only deals with the first three sons of Jacob.

The reason is clear: Moses and Aaron are from the line of Levi, the third son.

The break begins by reminding us that *the LORD spoke to Moses and Aaron about the Israelites and Pharaoh king of Egypt,* and that *he commanded them to bring the Israelites out of Egypt* (13).

But who are these two men? The genealogy gives us the answer.

After a brief mention of *the sons of Reuben* and *the sons of Simeon* (14-15), the focus is on *the sons of Levi* (16): we're going to look at the descent of Moses and Aaron, the leaders of the Israelite community.

The family record here traces Levi's family line to the fifth generation. At one point we read that *Amram married his father's sister Jochebed, who bore him Aaron and Moses* (20). Aaron is mentioned first because he's the firstborn.

At the end of the family record we're told why this listing of the family line matters: *It was this Aaron and Moses to whom the LORD spoke* (26).

There is to be no mistake: the Aaron and Moses we've met in the family record are the same people we've been hearing about in the first half of Section B'.

The account underlines this by telling us that *they were the ones who spoke to Pharaoh king of Egypt about bringing the Israelites out of Egypt – this same Moses and Aaron* (27, and see 13).

And now the order of the names is reversed: by God's choice it's Moses who will be taking the lead as we approach the exodus.

So now we turn to the second half of Section B'.

a. – God promises to rescue his people from Egypt (6:28 – 7:7)

Now the narrative starts up again exactly where it left off: verses 28-30 of chapter 6 are almost identical to verses 10-12. Moses needs to understand that even Pharaoh's refusal to allow the Israelites to leave Egypt is part of God's plan.

God tells Moses that *I have made you like God to Pharaoh, and your brother Aaron will be your prophet* (1). Pharaoh was considered to be a deity by the Egyptians, so Yahweh is setting up a confrontation between two gods, with Moses as his representative.

And Moses is given no choice as to the message he brings: he must *say everything I have commanded you* (2). Pharaoh, however, *will not listen to you* (4a).

This is because God *will harden Pharaoh's heart* (3). This is not God making the king of Egypt evil: he's simply giving Pharaoh over to his sin (as in Romans 1:24-26). God is not hardening a good person here: Pharaoh has made his own decision to commit to doing evil.

But that won't be the end of the story: God *will lay my hand on Egypt* with *mighty acts of judgment* (4a). The result will be that God *will bring out my divisions, my people the Israelites* (4b).

That word *divisions* (see also chapter 6:26) has military overtones: the people will not leave Egypt simply as slaves, but as a force ready to enter the land of Canaan.

And, when they see all this happening, even *the Egyptians will know that I am the LORD* (5): they will acknowledge that there really is a deity named Yahweh.

So this is God's promise. He is going to rescue his people from Egypt. And the reaction is faith: *Moses and Aaron did just as the LORD commanded them* (6).

And now we're told that all of this happens when *Moses was eighty years old and Aaron eighty-three* (7).

b. – God's power to create life (7:8-13)

This is Moses and Aaron's second audience with Pharaoh: it will be a confrontation between the God of the Hebrews and the deities of Egypt.

God knows that Pharaoh will tell them to *perform a miracle* (9): Aaron is then to take his staff and *throw it down before Pharaoh*. Then, God says, *it will become a snake* (9).

And this is what happens. But Pharaoh is sure that he can beat that: when he summons *the wise men and sorcerers* (11), each of them *threw down his staff and it became a snake* (12a).

Was this an illusion, like a conjuror's sleight of hand? It seems to me more likely that they're acting with the help of occult powers.

But now *Aaron's staff swallowed up their staffs* (12b): his snake swallowed up their snakes.

Just imagine it: Aaron's snake is devouring all the snakes conjured up by the Egyptian magicians. This is Yahweh's authority devouring the authority of the Egyptian gods, and he's demonstrating it though his staff.

True sovereignty belongs to Yahweh: he has the power to create life.

c. – Opening cycle of three plagues (7:14 – 8:19)

You can say two things about the plagues. On the one hand, they are God's judgment in action, punishing sin; while on the other hand they mean salvation for God's people.

This is a principle that is seen most clearly at the cross of Jesus.

In parts c, d and c' we will look at all the plagues except for the final one: the Passover. We will look at each of these nine plagues in three steps. First, we will hear God's instructions to Moses and Aaron; second, we will see the plague itself and its effects; and third, we will learn Pharaoh's response to what's happened.

And through it all we are seeing God working out his purposes. All the plagues are designed to bring home to Pharaoh (and to Israel) that *the LORD is God* (see chapter 7:17; 8:10 and 23; 9:16 and 10:2).

With the plagues of this first cycle, each time the Egyptian magicians vie with Moses as they try to replicate what God is doing. And each time, a staff has a key role.

1. Number One: the plague of blood (7:14-24). The Egyptians looked on the Nile as the source of their existence, so this is a very powerful beginning to the first cycle of plagues.

+ The instructions from God (14-19). God tells Moses in advance that *Pharaoh's heart is unyielding* (14): literally it's *heavy*, weighed down with corruption and injustice. And so *he refuses to let the people go* (14).

Moses is to meet Pharaoh *in the morning as he goes out to the river* and to *take in your hand the staff that was changed into a snake* (15).

He is to give Pharaoh a message from *the LORD, the God of the Hebrews*: he is to *let my people go so that they may worship me in the wilderness* (16).

Using his staff he will *strike the water of the Nile, and it will be changed into blood* (17). There will be three results: *the fish in the Nile will die, and the river will stink; the Egyptians will not be able to drink its water* (18).

So God tells Moses to have Aaron use his staff in this way *over the waters of Egypt* (19): *the streams and canals*, and *the ponds and all the reservoirs*. These will all *turn to blood* (19). And this will even happen to water kept in wood or stone storage vessels (see 19b).

+ The plague of blood (20-21). So *Moses and Aaron did just as the LORD had commanded* (20a). *All the water was changed into blood* (20b), with the result that *blood was everywhere in Egypt* (21b).

Dead fish, a bad smell and undrinkable water: this is God in action.

+ The response from Pharaoh (22-24). The Egyptian magicians *did the same things by their secret arts* (22), but of course they're not counteracting the plague but intensifying it.

And *Pharaoh's heart became hard* (22). Instead of listening to Moses and Aaron, *he turned and went into his palace, and did not take even this to heart* (23).

His heart is stubborn and hard.

2. Number Two: the plague of frogs (7:25 – 8:15). We're told that *seven days passed after the LORD struck the Nile* (7:25). And then the process starts again.

+ The instructions from God (1-5). Moses is to go to Pharaoh again, with the same message to *let my people go, so that they may worship me* (1).

If Pharaoh doesn't go along with this, God will *send a plague of frogs on your whole country* (2). Moses is to warn Pharaoh that *the Nile will teem with frogs* (3a), so much so that *they will come up into your palace and your bedroom and onto your bed* (3).

Moses is to tell Aaron to *stretch out your hand with the staff* and *make frogs come up on the land of Egypt* (5). The staff points to God being the one who's at work here.

+ The plague of frogs (6-7). When Aaron uses his staff in this way, *the frogs came up and covered the land* (6).

The magicians do *the same thing by their secret arts* (7), which, once again, is counterproductive: they are simply making the problem worse.

So how is Pharaoh going to react?

+ The response from Pharaoh (8-15). He's already becoming desperate: he asks Moses and Aaron to *pray to the LORD to take the frogs away from me and my people* (8a).

Then, says Pharaoh, he will *let your people go to offer sacrifices to the LORD* (8b).

In response to a question from Moses, Pharaoh asks that this happen the next day. Moses replies that *the frogs will leave you and your houses,* as Pharaoh is asking (11). The purpose of all this is that Pharaoh *may know there is no one like the LORD our God* (10).

The very next day, in answer to Moses' prayer, *the frogs died in the houses, in the courtyards and in the fields* (13). There are piles of dead frogs (the Hebrew says *They heaped them up, heaps, heaps*) and *the land reeked of them* (14).

What do you expect with piles of dead frogs in tropical sunshine?

But when Pharaoh sees that the frogs are dead, *he hardened his heart and would not listen to Moses and Aaron, just as the LORD had said* (15).

3. Number Three: the plague of gnats (8:16-19). God will continue to act in judgment if Pharaoh refuses to let his people go.

+ The instructions from God (16). This time there is to be no request for an audience with Pharaoh: there's no need for it. The king of Egypt deserves what's coming to him because he's lied and hardened his heart.

God tells Moses to *stretch out your staff and strike the dust of the ground*: throughout Egypt *the dust will become gnats* (16). This is about *gnats* or *lice.*

+ The plague of gnats (17). And this is what happens when Aaron *stretched out his hand with the staff and struck the dust of the ground: gnats came on people and animals* (17).

There are gnats everywhere.

+ The response from Pharaoh (18-19). When the magicians try to replicate this miracle, *they could not* (18): they can neither imitate nor mitigate the plague. And, of course, they themselves are covered with insects.

This prompts them to tell Pharaoh that *this is the finger of God* (19a): there is clearly something supernatural happening here.

But *Pharaoh's heart was hard and he would not listen, just as the LORD had said* (19b).

And with that, the first cycle of three plagues is complete.

d. – CENTRE: Central cycle of three plagues (8:20 – 9:12)

In this central cycle, Moses and Aaron don't make use of their staffs. And God makes a point of making sure that the Israelites aren't touched by any plague.

1. Number Four: the plague of flies (8:20-32). It looks like God has arranged another rendezvous with Pharaoh on the banks of the Nile.

+ The instructions from God (20-23). Once again Moses is to tell the king to *let my people go, so that they may worship me* (20). If Pharaoh refuses to budge, God will *send swarms of flies,* so that *the houses of the Egyptians will be full of flies* (21)

And *even the ground will be covered with them* (21b). This is about some kind of stinging fly, possibly a mosquito. So even walking will be a struggle.

Now, for the first time, we're told that God is going to protect his people from this plague: he will *deal differently with the land of Goshen* (22a). Goshen is the part of Egypt where the Israelites are living (see Genesis 45:10 and 46:28).

God is making this *distinction between my people and your people* (23), so that *you will know that I, the LORD, am in this land* (22b).

So these are God's instructions to Moses.

+ The plague of flies (24). There is no use of the staff and no human hand outstretched, but simply *And the LORD did this* (24a).

The effect is appalling: *dense swarms of flies poured into Pharaoh's palace and into the houses of his officials* (24). The country is in the process of being destroyed: *the land was ruined by the flies* (24b).

+ The response from Pharaoh (25-32). He decides to be halfway obedient: he tells Moses and Aaron to *go, sacrifice to your God here in the land* (25). He's saying Yes to a festival of sacrifice, but No to their leaving Egypt.

Moses can't agree: he knows that some of the animals the Israelites will sacrifice are regarded as sacred by the Egyptians, so this would be *detestable in their eyes* (26). He insists that they need to travel *into the wilderness* (27).

It looks like Pharaoh agrees to this (see 28), and now he asks Moses and Aaron, for the second time, to *pray for me* (28b, and see chapter 8:8).

Moses promises to pray and is confident that *tomorrow the flies will leave Pharaoh and his officials and his people* (29a).

But Moses has a warning for Pharaoh, because he sees through him: the king needs to make sure *that he does not act deceitfully again by not letting the people go to offer sacrifices to the LORD* (29b).

What's required is honest talk and immediate action.

So Moses leaves, and prays: and *the flies left Pharaoh and his officials and his people,* so that *not a fly remained* (31).

But here it comes again, like a weary refrain: *this time also Pharaoh hardened his heart and would not let the people go* (32).

So there's going to be another plague.

2. Number Five: the plague on livestock (9:1-7). This one, like all the others, is going to hurt.

+ The instructions from God (1-5). Moses is to return to Pharaoh with the same message as before.

If Pharaoh refuses to *let my people go* (1), *the hand of the LORD will bring a terrible plague on your livestock* (3a): this includes *your horses, donkeys and camels and on your cattle, sheep and goats* (3b).

The animals visited by this plague are the ones that provide food, milk, transportation and clothing.

Once again, Moses is to make clear to Pharaoh that *the LORD will make a distinction between the livestock of Israel and that of Egypt,* with the result that *no animal belonging to the Israelites will die* (4).

This protection of the Hebrews is a sign of God's love for them as his people; but it will also make it impossible for Pharaoh to believe that this plague is a random event and nothing to do with Yahweh.

And, what's more, God sets a precise time for the plague's arrival: *Tomorrow the LORD will do this in the land* (5).

+ The plague on livestock (6). The next day *the LORD did it: all the livestock of the Egyptians died, but not one animal belonging to the Israelites died* (6).

Does this mean that every single animal belonging to an Egyptian died? Or does it simply mean that every type of domestic animal was struck by the plague?

Whatever the case, this is going to destroy life in Egypt. When the previous plagues were over, life could go on; but when the livestock are dead, they're dead.

+ The response from Pharaoh (7). When Pharaoh finds out that *not even one of the animals of the Israelites had died,* it's clear what he should do.

But instead *his heart was unyielding and he would not let the people go* (7).

So now we come to the third plague in this central cycle.

3. Number Six: the plague of boils (9:8-12). Once again, this will be a plague which begins without Moses or Aaron using a staff.

+ The instructions from God (8-9). Just as with the third plague in the opening cycle, God isn't calling Moses and Aaron to appear before Pharaoh right from the start (see chapter 8:16-19). They will say nothing to Pharaoh at all.

Instead they are to *take handfuls of soot from a furnace* (8a). There is irony here: this will be one of the furnaces used by the Israelites to bake the bricks they've been making.

Moses and Aaron are to *toss* the soot *into the air in the presence of Pharaoh* (8b): it will *become fine dust over the whole land of Egypt, and festering boils will break out on people and animals throughout the land* (9).

Is this going to be smallpox? Or anthrax?

+ The plague of boils (10-11). Everything happens just as God has said: Moses takes the soot and *tossed it into the air, and festering boils broke out on people and animals* (10).

And, in the final mention of the Egyptian magicians, we're told that *they could not stand before Moses because of the boils that were on them* (11): they are more impotent than ever.

+ The response from Pharaoh (12). This time we read that *the LORD hardened Pharaoh's heart and he would not listen to Moses and Aaron* (12).

Sometimes Yahweh hardens Pharaoh's heart (see chapter 4:21 and 7:3), and sometimes Pharaoh does it himself (see chapter 8:15 and 32). Pharaoh is responsible for his own sin, but God is sovereign and has decreed what should happen.

And with that, the central cycle of plagues is over.

c'. – Closing cycle of three plagues (9:13 – 10:29)

During this cycle, Moses uses his staff (although only his hand is mentioned in chapter 10:21-22); and some of the Egyptians are going to listen to him.

1. Number Seven: the plague of hail (9:13-35). Just as with the first and fourth plagues, Moses is to go and stand before Pharaoh.

+ The instructions from God (13-22). God's message is going to come to Pharaoh again: he must *let my people go, so that they may worship me* (13).

Things are hotting up: if Pharaoh remains stubborn, Yahweh *will send the full force of my plagues against you,* so that it will be clear that *there is no one like me in all the earth* (14).

God is reminding Pharaoh of his power: he could have sent a plague *that would have wiped you off the earth* (15). But God is going to use Pharaoh so that *my name might be proclaimed in all the earth* (16).

Moses is to warn Pharaoh that *at this time tomorrow* Yahweh will send *the worst hailstorm that has ever fallen on Egypt* (18). The timing is precise. So everything must be brought *to a place of shelter,* because any person or animal still out in the fields when the hail comes *will die* (19).

Some of Pharaoh's officials *bring their slaves and livestock inside* because they *feared the word of the LORD* (20), but others leave *their slaves and livestock in the field* because they *ignored the word of the LORD* (21).

Yahweh's instructions to Moses are nearly complete. God tells him to *stretch out your hand towards the sky so that hail will fall all over Egypt* (22). And of course we know what he has in his hand.

+ The plague of hail (23-26). When Moses has passed on God's message and *stretched out his staff towards the sky, the LORD sent thunder and hail, and lightning flashed down to the ground* (23). Throughout Egypt the hail *struck everything in the fields* and *beat down everything growing in the fields and stripped every tree* (25).

This is a scene of utter devastation. But not everywhere: *the only place it did not hail was the land of Goshen, where the Israelites were* (26).

Surely Pharaoh is going to change his mind now, and let God's people go.

+ The response from Pharaoh (27-35). The king summons Moses and Aaron and tells them that *this time I have sinned* and that *the LORD is in the right, and I and my people are in the wrong* (27).

But it's a grudging admission. He has only sinned *this time*: Pharaoh is still lying and manipulating.

Nevertheless, for the third time he asks Moses and Aaron to *pray to the LORD, for we have had enough thunder and hail* (28a).

And now Pharaoh makes a promise: he will *let you go; you don't have to stay any longer* (28b).

Moses is sceptical. Yes, he will pray and the thunder and hail will stop, *so you may know that the earth is the LORD's* (29). But, far from Pharaoh having had a change of heart, Moses knows that *you and your officials still do not fear the LORD God* (30).

At this point the account tells us that not all the Egyptian crops have been destroyed by the hail: the crops which *ripen later*, such as *wheat and spelt* (32) will be able to provide food for the Egyptians. This is God's grace in action, even in judgment.

So how does Pharaoh react when Moses prays and the thunder, hail and rain stop? He *sinned again: he and his officials hardened their hearts* (34).

So *Pharaoh's heart was hard and he would not let the Israelites go.* And this is *just as the LORD had said through Moses* (35).

If we were reading this for the first time, we would be wondering if anything could change the situation. The next plague perhaps?

2. Number Eight: the plague of locusts (10:1-20). We might wonder how Moses is coping with all of this. I assume he's frustrated that none of the plagues is having the desired effect. But, at the same time, he's full of confidence that God is going to keep his promise to bring his people out of Egypt.

+ The instructions from God (1-12). God begins by reminding Moses that he's hardened Pharaoh's heart *so that I may perform these signs of mine* (1): this is all part of his plan.

And God adds that this is all happening so that *you may tell your children and grandchildren how I dealt harshly with the Egyptians and how I performed my signs among them* (2). He wants his people's descendants to know that *I am the LORD* (2b).

This applies to us, too. The account of these plagues is here to bring us to worship.

So Moses and Aaron go to Pharaoh in the name of *the LORD, the God of the Hebrews* and rebuke him by asking *How long will you refuse to humble yourself?* (3). If there is no change of policy, Yahweh will *bring locusts into your country tomorrow* (4).

The Egyptians are used to locusts, but there will be so many that they will *cover the face of the ground* and *devour what little you have left after the hail* (5). And, perhaps even worse, the locusts *will fill your houses* (6).

After Moses has left, Pharaoh's officials urge him to *let the people go,* and even ask him if he doesn't *yet realise that Egypt is ruined* (7).

So Pharaoh has Moses and Aaron brought back, and tells them to *go, worship the LORD your God* (8).

However, it looks like Pharaoh is having difficulty making up his mind. He ends by telling them that he will let *only the men go and worship the LORD* (11): that way he will be holding the families hostage.

With that Moses and Aaron are ejected: they are *driven out of Pharaoh's presence* (11).

And so God gives instructions to Moses again: he is to *stretch out your hand over Egypt so that locusts swarm over the land and devour everything* (12). Once again, the staff is of crucial importance.

+ The plague of locusts (13-15). So Moses *stretched out his staff over Egypt* (13). An east wind starts to blow, so that by morning locusts have invaded all Egypt: *they covered all the ground until it was black* (14 and 15).

The locusts devour everything growing, so that *nothing green remained on tree or plant in all the land of Egypt* (15b).

Surely this must result in real repentance from Pharaoh.

+ The response from Pharaoh (16-20). He's in a hurry: he *quickly summoned Moses and Aaron* (16). He admits that he's *sinned against the LORD your God and against you* (16).

Pharaoh asks them to *forgive my sin once more and pray to the LORD your God to take this deadly plague away from me* (17).

That sounds real, doesn't it?

After leaving, Moses prays. And God brings a west wind *which caught up the locusts and carried them into the Red Sea.* The result is that *not a locust was left anywhere in Egypt* (19).

But here it comes again: *the LORD hardened Pharaoh's heart, and he would not let the Israelites go* (20).

So there's another plague.

3. Number Nine: the plague of darkness (10:21-29). After this ninth plague we'll read about what all this has been leading up to: the Passover will take place.

+ The instructions from God (21). God has nothing to say to Pharaoh, so he simply tells Moses what to do. He is to *stretch out your hand towards the sky so that darkness spreads over Egypt* (21).

And this will be *darkness that can be felt* (21b).

+ The plague of darkness (22-23). When Moses does this, *total darkness covered all Egypt for three days* (22). The result is that, during that time, *no one could see anyone else or move about* (23a).

It must have been terrifying.

But not everyone in Egypt is enveloped in darkness: *all the Israelites had light in the places where they lived* (23b).

We can more or less guess what's going to happen now.

+ The response from Pharaoh (24-29). Pharaoh summons Moses and tells him to *go, worship the LORD.* This time he says that *even your women and children may go with you* (24).

But they are to *leave your flocks and herds behind* (24b).

Moses, in reply, makes it clear that it's all or nothing. They need the livestock because they want to bring *sacrifices and burnt offerings to the*

LORD our God (25). And *until we get there we will not know what we are to use to worship the LORD* (26).

But *the LORD hardened Pharaoh's heart, and he was not willing to let them go* (27). So Pharaoh says to Moses *Get out of my sight! Make sure you do not appear before me again! The day you see my face you will die!* (28).

The plague of darkness is the last plague before the Passover lambs are slaughtered. Is it coincidence that, as Jesus hangs on a cross as the ultimate Passover Lamb, everything will be enveloped in darkness (see Matthew 27:45)?

b'. – God's power to terminate life (11:1-10)

Although the Passover event won't take place until chapter 12:29, chapter 11 contains the announcement to Pharaoh of what is to come: it retains the pattern we saw with the first nine plagues.

1. The instructions from God (1-3). This is God telling Moses what he's about to do. *One more plague* is coming: it's not a natural occurrence but something God *will bring* (1a).

And this plague is going to achieve its aim: after it, Pharaoh will *let you go from here, and when he does, he will drive you out completely* (1b).

The Israelites are to *ask their neighbours for articles of silver and gold* (2): this will be a fulfilment of what God had said to Moses in chapter 3:22 and to Abraham in Genesis 15:14.

If this surprises us, there's an explanation: *the LORD made the Egyptians favourably disposed towards the people* (3a). Did many of them realise that what their nation had been doing to the Israelites for over four centuries was wrong?

And another reason why the Egyptians will hand over material goods is that *Moses himself was highly regarded in Egypt by Pharaoh's officials and by the people* (3b). But not, one assumes, by Pharaoh himself.

God must have also described the coming tenth plague to Moses, who now tells Pharaoh what is going to happen.

2. The plague on the firstborn (4-8). God will go throughout Egypt *about midnight* (4; the Hebrew says *in the middle of the night*).

This is to be a final, horrible plague on Egypt: *every firstborn son* will die, and *all the firstborn of the cattle as well* (5). This will affect every family: *from the firstborn son of Pharaoh* all the way down to *the firstborn son of the female slave* (5).

And so *there will be loud wailing throughout Egypt* (6), as every family is bereaved that same night.

But none of this will affect God's people. In Goshen, where the Israelites live, *not a dog will bark at any person or animal* (7): in other words, no dog will disturbed in the night by any cries of despair.

We've seen this before: God treating his own people differently. So Pharaoh will *know that the LORD makes a distinction between Egypt and Israel* (7b).

And Pharaoh's own officials will stop bowing down to him; rather, says Moses, they will *come to me, bowing down before me* and begging him to lead his people out of Egypt (8).

It's Moses who has the upper hand now, as Yahweh unleashes this last, terrible plague. And now *Moses, hot with anger, left Pharaoh* (8b): he's incensed at Pharaoh's refusal to repent of his sinful stubbornness.

3. The response from Pharaoh (9-10). God had told Moses that *Pharaoh will refuse to listen to you* (9), and that's exactly what happens. Moses and Aaron *performed all these wonders before Pharaoh* (10a), but there is no change of mind: *the LORD hardened Pharaoh's heart* (10b).

So the response is the same as ever: Pharaoh *would not let the Israelites go out of his country* (10b).

a'. – God rescues his people from Egypt (12:1 – 13:16)

Now the narrative is slowing down: because these events are so significant, there's also an emphasis on their being remembered through all the generations to come.

The Passover and the Exodus are only briefly described (see chapter 12:29-42). Beforehand the people have much preparation to do, and afterwards there are even more instructions about how all this is to be remembered.

1. Passover and Exodus: the preparation (12:1-28). This preparation must begin four days before the Passover itself will take place: with the choice of the sacrificial victim.

+ God speaks to Moses (1-20). God has two main things to make clear to his servant.

First, what to do (1-13). *Each man is to take a lamb for his family, one for each household* (3). God tells Moses that the animals the people choose must be *year-old males without defect,* and they can be taken *from the sheep or the goats* (5).

So the animals must be unblemished.

On *the fourteenth day of the month* the Israelites *must slaughter them at twilight* (6): it's like this is a united act of worship. Then they are to *take some of the blood and put it on the sides and tops of the door-frames of the houses where they eat the lambs* (7).

That same night the families are to *eat the meat roasted over the fire* (8). Along with the meat, they will eat *bitter herbs, and bread made without yeast* (8). The herbs will remind them of their bitter lives in slavery (see chapter 1:14), while the bread is unleavened because the departure from Egypt is going to be quick: time is short.

And, because of this, God tells Moses that the people must all be dressed ready to leave: they are to eat *with your cloak tucked into your belt, your sandals on your feet and your staff in your hand* (11).

They are to *eat it in haste; it is the LORD's Passover* (11b).

Now Yahweh tells Moses that *on that same night I will pass through Egypt and strike down every firstborn of both people and animals*; in this way he will *bring judgment on all the gods of Egypt* (12).

And what's with the blood on the lintel and on the doorposts? This, says God, *will be a sign for you on the houses where you are* (13a). With the blood they will have signalled that they belong to God's people: they are Israelites, not Egyptians.

God promises that *no destructive plague will touch you when I strike Egypt*, because *when I see the blood, I will pass over you* (13).

All of this is what Moses and the people are to do. But there's more.

Second, how to remember (14-20). This extraordinary event must never be forgotten: *you shall celebrate it as a festival to the LORD,* and this is for *the generations to come* (14).

This feast will last seven days, during which the people are to *eat bread without yeast* and to *remove the yeast from your houses* (15). And anyone who eats anything with yeast in it *must be cut off from the community of Israel* (19).

God is telling Moses here how the people are to celebrate the Feast of Unleavened Bread, which was so close to Passover that this would all be seen as one festival (see, for example, chapter 23:15).

So God has spoken to Moses. Now Moses will speak to the people.

+ Moses speaks to Israel (21-27). And, once again, there are instructions about what to do, followed by instructions about how to remember. Moses speaks to *all the elders of Israel* (21), who will pass everything on to the people.

First, what to do (21-23). They are to *select the animals for your families and slaughter the Passover lamb* (21). They must then *take a bunch of hyssop, dip it into the blood in the basin and put some of the blood on the top and on both sides of the door-frame* (22).

And, of course, *none of you shall go out of the door of your house until morning* (22b).

This matters because, when God goes through the land to strike down the Egyptians, *he will see the blood on the top and sides of the door-frame and will pass over that doorway* (23). In other words, God *will not permit the destroyer to enter your houses and strike you down* (23b): is the destroyer an angel of judgment?

Second, how to remember (24-27). The people are to *obey these instructions as a lasting ordinance for you and your descendants* (24), and when they first enter Canaan, *the land that the LORD will give you as he promised,* they are to *observe this ceremony* (25).

Down the generations this will make children curious so that they ask *What does this ceremony mean to you?* (26). The adults will reply that *it is the Passover sacrifice to the LORD, who passed over the houses of the Israelites in Egypt and spared our homes when he struck down the Egyptians* (27).

When they learn what God has told Moses, it's no wonder that *the people bowed down and worshipped* (27b).

So everything has been prepared: *the Israelites did just what the LORD commanded Moses and Aaron* (28). They have slaughtered the animals, put the blood on the lintel and the doorposts, and they've eaten the meal.

They're ready to leave.

2. Passover and Exodus: the event (12:29-42). It's really two events, of course, but they are inextricably linked.

+ The Passover (29-36). In the middle of the night *the LORD struck down all the firstborn in Egypt*: the catastrophe is all-embracing (29).

The scene is appalling: *there was loud wailing in Egypt, for there was not a house without someone dead* (30).

So Pharaoh summons Moses and Aaron and tells them to *leave my people, you and the Israelites* (31): and they are to take their *flocks and herds,* too (32). Everyone and everything can leave. Now.

And then, strangely, Pharaoh adds *And also bless me* (32b). Is this really genuine? It won't be long before he pursues the Hebrews to destroy them.

The Egyptians are gripped by panic: they *urged the people to hurry and leave the country* because they think that otherwise *we will all die* (33).

So the Israelites leave, carrying the unleavened bread on their shoulders (see 34), and with it the *silver and gold* and *clothing* that they'd asked the Egyptians for (35).

And so *they plundered the Egyptians* (36).

The Passover has happened. And so we know what comes next.

+ The Exodus (37-42). This is a description of the beginning of the Exodus. There are *about six hundred thousand men on foot, besides women and children* (37): this is a huge number, but it does look like it's intended as a real figure.

And the Israelites are not alone: *many other people went up with them* (38). Does this include some of those mentioned in chapter 9:20?

And there's another mention of the unleavened bread: *the dough was without yeast because they had been driven out of Egypt and did not have time to prepare food for themselves* (39).

This account of how the Exodus begins ends with a note that *the Israelite people lived in Egypt* for *430 years* (40). This is the fulfilment of God's promise to Abraham (see Genesis 15:13, which has a round number of 400 years).

And this, we're reminded, must never be forgotten: *Because the LORD kept vigil that night to bring them out of Egypt, on this night all the Israelites are to keep vigil to honour the LORD for the generations to come* (42).

Which brings us to the third part of the material here.

3. Passover and Exodus: the remembering (12:43 – 13:16). We have already heard lots about remembering these events (see, for example, chapter 12:14-20); but now we get more details.

As with the first part (the preparation for the Passover and the Exodus), God first speaks to Moses, before Moses speaks to Israel.

+ God speaks to Moses (12:43 – 13:2). There are three kinds of people who are not permitted to participate in future Passover celebrations: *no foreigner may eat it* (43b), and *a temporary resident or a hired worker may not eat it* (45).

But *any slave you have bought may eat it after you have circumcised him* (44).

It's important that *the whole community of Israel must celebrate it* (47): this event is the reason the nation will be in the Promised Land.

There's a brief mention here of the fact that, when eating the celebratory meal, they are told *Do not break any of the bones* (46b). In his Gospel the apostle John tells us that, at the crucifixion, none of Jesus' bones was broken (see John 19:36): he tells us this because he sees Jesus as the perfect Passover offering and the Lamb of God (see John 1:29, and also 1 Corinthians 5:7). (And in the other three Gospels the last supper is described as a Passover meal [see Mt 26:17, Mk 14:12 and Lk 22:7-8].)

Returning to Exodus chapter 12, it's clear that *no uncircumcised male may eat* the Passover meal (48b).

There is one more thing God tells Moses. The Israelites are to *consecrate to me every firstborn male*: whether human or animal, the firstborn *belongs to me* (1).

In Egypt God had destroyed the firstborn of the Egyptians; now he redeems Israel's firstborn and they belong to him.

+ Moses speaks to Israel (13:3-16). The people are to *commemorate this day, the day you came out of Egypt, out of the land of slavery* (3). This happened because *the LORD brought you out of it with a mighty hand* (3).

They are to *observe this ceremony* when God brings them into *the land he swore to your ancestors to give you* (5). They must *eat unleavened bread* in the seven days of the *festival to the LORD* (6b and 7).

And they are to tell their children that *I do this because of what the LORD did for me when I came out of Egypt* (8). They won't only tell the story; they'll explain it too.

And this *will be for you like a sign on your hand and a reminder on your forehead that this law of the LORD is to be on your lips* (9). Later, some Jews interpreted this literally and introduced phylacteries, but there's no reason to think that they were right to do this.

Verses 11-16 is Moses passing on to the people what God had told him in chapter 13:1-2. They are to *give over to the LORD the first offspring of every womb* (12).

And when their children ask what this means, they are to tell the Passover story, about when *the LORD killed the firstborn of both people and animals in Egypt* (15).

God had spared the firstborn of the Israelites, so now they belong to him.

The Passover has happened and the Exodus has happened. In the letter to the Hebrews we read this about Moses: *By faith he kept the Passover and the application of blood, so that the destroyer of the firstborn would not touch the firstborn of Israel* (Hebrews 11:28).

All of this has revealed the justice and the grace of God. And, with the Exodus, we have reached the end of Section B' of *The Genesis+ Experiment*.

Learning Genesis+

Once again, it's easy to learn the outline of the section.

Begin with the first half, in other words everything up to the narrative break. Start by saying the headings for a, b, c and d out loud several times, until you can say them without looking at *The Genesis+ Experiment*.

Then, because of the mirror links, you will find it easy to learn the headings for c', b' and a'.

Now make sure you (or you and your friend) can say the whole of the first half from memory.

When that's done, use the same method to learn the headings for the second half of the section. Remember that this is all much easier if you say everything out loud, and if you count on your fingers.

Finally, have a go at saying all of Section B'.

The basic structure of the section can be learnt by most people in ten to fifteen minutes.

Section B': The Exodus Story

a. Oppression by a Pharaoh who never knew Joseph
b. *Moses comes to Pharaoh's house as a baby*
c. Moses departs from Egypt
d. CENTRE: The call of Moses
c'. Moses returns to Egypt
b'. *Moses comes to Pharaoh's house as an adult*
a'. Worse oppression by a Pharaoh who never knew Joseph

Narrative break: The family record of Moses and Aaron

a. God promises to rescue his people from Egypt
b. *God's power to create life*
c. Opening cycle of three plagues
d. CENTRE: Central cycle of three plagues
c'. Closing cycle of three plagues
b'. *God's power to terminate life*
a'. God rescues his people from Egypt

Meeting God

As you say the incident headings, on your own or with a friend, you will find yourself remembering all kinds of details.

In the first half of the section, thank God for preparing Moses to take on the role of Israel's human deliverer. Thank him for his patience in answering Moses' questions and dealing with his excuses.

As you think of the headings in the second half of the section, thank God for his power at work, both in bringing the plagues on Egypt and in using Pharaoh to fulfil his purposes.

And remember why the staff is important: it's a constant reminder that this is *God* bringing salvation: that's why the staff is the symbol in Section B'. Some people find it helpful to have such a reminder in their living-room: a cross, perhaps.

You might like to use the study questions about Section B', either on your own or with a friend: you'll find them in Appendix 3.

And as you thank God for the Passover, take time to thank God for Jesus, the ultimate Passover Lamb. Thank him that he didn't just rescue his people then: through the cross he's rescued you, too.

As you spend time thinking and praying through Section B', you will be getting to know God better. That's what *The Genesis+ Experiment* is all about.

Section A'
Wilderness Journey (Exodus 13:17 – 19:2)

After the drama of the Passover and the Exodus from Egypt, the Israelites are on their way to the land God promised to their ancestor Abraham. Section A' will take them all the way to Mount Sinai, where God will give the law to his covenant people. But first he will give them a final victory over the Egyptians in the dramatic events at the Red Sea.

Then Moses stretched out his hand over the sea,
and all that night
the LORD drove the sea back with a strong east wind
and turned it into dry land.
The waters were divided.

Exodus 14:21

Enjoying the View

a. Introduction: Departure from Egypt (13:17-22)
b. *Victory over the Egyptians at the Red Sea* (14:1 – 15:21)
c. God provides the Israelites with water at Marah (15:22-27)
d. CENTRE: God provides manna and quail (16:1-36)
c'. God provides the Israelites with water at Rephidim (17:1-7)
b'. *Victory over the Amalekites at Rephidim* (17:8-16)
a'. Conclusion: Arrival at Sinai (18:1 – 19:2)

Section A' is short: it has only seven parts. The same is true of *Section A: Primeval History*. We will notice some other aspects of the mirror link as we move through Section A' (and see Appendix 2 for more).

As the narrative takes us from Egypt to Sinai we will see two things: first, the Israelites' grumbling in incidents b, c, d and c'; and second, God graciously providing for his people every step of the way (see incidents a, b, c, d, c' and b').

Please take time to read through the whole section in your Bible. As you do so, stop sometimes to talk to God about what you're reading. There is power in the word of God!

Unpacking the Content

a. – Introduction: Departure from Egypt (13:17-22)

At the start of this incident the Israelites are still in the Egyptian desert. But *God did not lead them on the road through the Philistine country, though that was shorter* (17a).

This is to avoid the Israelites clashing with the Philistines: God says that *if they face war, they might change their minds and return to Egypt* (17b).

So *God led the people around by the desert road towards the Red Sea* (18a). The comment that they are *ready for battle* (18b) probably just means that the Israelites are not a rabble, but travelling in an orderly way.

There's a note here that Moses has made sure to take *the bones of Joseph with him* (19a). Joseph had never looked on Egypt as home, and had showed that with his demand for his embalmed body to be buried one day in Canaan (19b, and see Genesis 50:24 and Hebrews 11:22).

The Israelites are now at the gate of freedom: they camp *at Etham on the edge of the desert* (20).

But they are not alone. There's *a pillar of cloud* by day and *a pillar of fire* by night (21). This is *to guide them on their way.* So they know that *the LORD went ahead of them,* so that *they could travel by day or night* (21).

This is a visual reminder of Yahweh's presence with his people: *Neither the pillar of cloud by day nor the pillar of fire by night left its place in front of the people* (22).

They're on their way.

b. – Victory over the Egyptians at the Red Sea (14:1 – 15:21)

The events here will never be forgotten by Israel (see, for example, Psalm 78:13 and 106:7-12).

1. Crisis at the Red Sea (14:1-14). It may be a crisis, but God is in control of everything.

+ God's plan (1-4). Moses is to *tell the Israelites to turn back* and then to *camp by the sea* (2). This is so Pharaoh will think that they are *wandering around the land in confusion* (3), hemmed in by desert, water and mountain, not knowing which way to turn.

And Yahweh, once again, will *harden Pharaoh's heart, and he will pursue them* (4a), thinking that victory over the Israelites is going to be easy.

Why is God doing all this? It's so that *I will gain glory for myself through Pharaoh and all his army* (4b): he wants the Egyptians to *know that I am the LORD* (4b).

So this is God's plan. And *the Israelites did this* (4b).

+ Pharaoh's decision (5-9). Now that the Hebrews have left, Pharaoh and his officials have *changed their minds* (5), saying to each other *What have we done?* (5): they have lost a major source of cheap labour.

So Pharaoh assembles a substantial military force, including *six hundred of the best chariots* (7). Just as he had promised Moses, God *hardened the heart of Pharaoh king of Egypt, so that he pursued the Israelites* (8).

So the Egyptians *pursued the Israelites and overtook them as they camped by the sea* (9): in other words, they catch up with them.

Probably the greatest fighting force in the world is preparing to capture their enemy. So what chance do the Israelites have?

+ Israel's fear (10-14). Understandably, the Israelites are *terrified and cried out to the LORD* (10).

But they're crying out to Moses too: they ask him *What have you done to us by bringing us out of Egypt?* (11b). They remind Moses that they had told him to *leave us alone* and *let us serve the Egyptians* (12), and they tell him that *it would have been better for us to serve the Egyptians than to die in the desert* (12b).

They would rather serve the Egyptians than Yahweh.

But Moses knows God's plan, and so he has an answer for his people. He tells them to *not be afraid* (13a). If they *stand firm,* they will *see the deliverance the LORD will bring you today* (13).

God's going to bring them deliverance and he's going to do it *today.* And they are not going to contribute anything to this: they are simply spectators, watching what God does.

Moses tells the people that *the Egyptians you see today you will never see again* (13b), because *the LORD will fight for you* (14).

The people *need only to be still* (14).

All of which makes us want to keep reading.

2. Miracle at the Red Sea (14:15-31). Yahweh is going to reassure Moses, before saving his people and judging his enemies.

+ Yahweh announces his plan (15-18). When God asks Moses *Why are you crying out to me?* (15), he's treating him as the representative of his complaining people.

Moses is to *raise your staff and stretch out your hand over the sea*: this will *divide the water so that the Israelites can go through the sea on dry ground* (16). The Egyptians *will go in after them* (17) because God will harden their hearts.

This is God's plan: *the Egyptians will know that I am the LORD when I gain glory through Pharaoh, his chariots and his horsemen* (18).

+ Yahweh saves his people (19-22). Up to now, *the angel of God,* acting in God's name, has been *travelling in front of Israel's army* (19, and see chapter 13:22). But now the angel is *coming between the armies of Egypt and Israel* (20a).

The cloud brings *darkness to one side and light to the other* (20). And so *neither went near the other all night long* (20b).

And now it happens: *Moses stretched out his hand over the sea* (21), and we know that he's holding his staff. This is going to show that what's about to happen isn't a chance accident: it's an act of God. And now a strong east wind blows all night, which *drove the sea back* and *turned it into dry land* (21).

So the waters of the Red Sea are *divided, and the Israelites went through the sea on dry ground, with a wall of water on their right and on their left* (21b-22).

Yahweh is sovereign and omnipotent: he is saving his people.

+ Yahweh judges the Egyptians (23-28). So *all Pharaoh's horses and chariots and horsemen followed them into the sea* (23).

During *the last watch of the night* (24; this is between 2am and 6am) God looks down from the pillar of fire and cloud at the Egyptian army *and threw it into confusion* and *jammed the wheels of their chariots* (24b-25a).

The Egyptians finally get it: they know they need to get away from the Israelites, because *the LORD is fighting for them against Egypt* (25b).

And now God tells Moses, once again, to *stretch out your hand over the sea*, this time *so that the waters may flow back over the Egyptians* (26).

And this is what happens: the result is that, as the Egyptians are trying to escape, *the LORD swept them into the sea* (27b).

It's a rout: *not one of them survived* (28b).

The account gives us a summary of what has happened (see 29-30): *the LORD saved Israel* and *Israel saw the Egyptians lying dead on the shore* (30).

The Red Sea story has a number of echoes of the creation account in Section A: the pillar of the divine presence brings light into darkness (see chapter 13:21, and compare with the first day of creation); the waters are divided (see chapter 14:21, and compare with the second day of creation); and dry land emerges (see chapter 14:29, and compare with the third day of creation). For more on this, see Appendix 2.

And, when the Israelites see what God has done, *the people feared the LORD and put their trust in Moses his servant* (31).

3. Praise at the Red Sea (15:1-21). The response of God's people is to worship him: this is the first hymn of praise in the Bible.

It has three stanzas.

+ Stanza One: God's power (1-6). This is a song sung by *Moses and the Israelites* (1), and its beginning sets the tone: *I will sing to the LORD, for he is highly exalted. Both horse and driver he has hurled into the sea* (1).

There is space here to mention only some of the details.

Yahweh is *my God* and *a warrior* (2 and 3). The Egyptian armies have *drowned in the Red Sea* (4), so that they *sank to the depths like a stone* (5).

The stanza ends with the singers addressing God directly: *Your right hand, LORD, was majestic in power* (6).

God's power has saved his people and vanquished his enemies.

+ Stanza Two: God's majesty (7-11). God *threw down those who opposed you* in *the greatness of your majesty* (7).

The Egyptians had boasted: *I will pursue, I will overtake them. I will divide the spoils; I will gorge myself on them. I will draw my sword and my hand will destroy them* (9).

But God *blew with your breath, and the sea covered them* (10).

And so the Egyptian gods, and all other so-called gods, are nothing compared to Yahweh. The singers ask *Who among the gods is like you, LORD? Who is like you – majestic in holiness, awesome in glory, working wonders?* (11).

God's majesty is there at the beginning and the end of the stanza (see 7 and 11).

+ Stanza Three: God's dwelling (12-18). This last part of the song is about God guiding his people to the land he's promised them.

He'll do that in his *unfailing love* (13): this is about God's covenant loyalty to his people.

Pagan nations will *hear* what God has done and *tremble* (14a). These are the nations the Israelites will meet on their journey: Philistia, Edom, Moab and Canaan (see 14-15).

And the singers praise God because he will certainly bring his people into Canaan *and plant them on the mountain of your inheritance* (17a). This is *the place, LORD, you made for your dwelling* (17b).

This is why Israel will be at home in Canaan: God will be dwelling there, with his people.

And so the song ends like this: *The LORD reigns for ever and ever* (18).

Miriam the prophet joins in too. She's *Aaron's sister* (20): she's Moses' sister too of course, but Aaron is the brother mentioned because he's older.

She takes *a tambourine in her hand, and all the women followed her, with tambourines and dancing* (20). And the song they sing begins in exactly the same way.

Are the women repeating the song the men have sung? Or are they singing the same chorus after every stanza?

> *I will sing to the LORD,*
> *for he is highly exalted.*
> *Both horse and driver*
> *he has hurled into the sea.*
> (1 and 21)

What God has done at the Red Sea has resulted in an outpouring of praise from his people.

c. – God provides the Israelites with water at Marah (15:22-27)

Moses is exercising leadership here: the statement that he *led Israel from the Red Sea* (22a) signals that this is his own initiative. After all, it's an important part of his job to bring Israel to the Promised Land.

But there are problems on the way.

1. The people grumble (22-24). *For three days they travelled in the desert without finding water* (22b): and arriving at Marah doesn't help, because *they could not drink its water because it was bitter* (23; *Marah* means *bitter*).

The result is that *the people grumbled against Moses* (24): this is the first time that the word *grumble* appears in the Old Testament. So we can imagine crowds gathering around Moses and asking *What are we to drink?* (24b).

This is the Israelites having a rebellious attitude to their leader, which only partially masks a rebellious attitude to God.

2. God intervenes (25-27). When Moses has *cried out to the LORD*, God somehow shows him *a piece of wood*. He throws it *into the water, and the water became fit to drink* (25a).

There's no mention here of the people drinking the water, though of course they do. What's more important is that *the LORD issued a ruling and instruction for them and put them to the test* (25b).

It's a principle and a promise. If God's people will *pay attention to his commands and keep all his decrees,* God won't *bring on you any of the diseases I brought on the Egyptians* (26). The diseases God mentions are the plagues of chapters 7-12.

This is the principle: God promises that obedience will bring blessing. God's blessing for Israel is dependent on the obedience of his children.

And this is a test: will the Israelites commit themselves to obey God?

Now the people arrive at Elim, where *there were twelve springs and seventy palm trees* (27): now they have plenty of food and water.

As long as they stay in Elim, that is.

d. – CENTRE: God provides manna and quail (16:1-36)

It's now about a month since the Israelites left Egypt (see 1 and chapter 12:6 and 31).

1. The problem and the solution (2-10). We might be able to guess what the problem is.

+ The people grumble (2-3). This grumbling is more widespread than the grumbling at Marah: *the whole community grumbled against Moses and Aaron* (2). Everyone is joining in, and they're aiming at Aaron too.

Moaning and unbelief are in danger of becoming a habit for God's people.

They're saying *If only we had died by the LORD's hand in Egypt!* (3), because in Egypt *we sat round pots of meat and ate all the food we wanted* (3).

Is that really how they remember their time as slaves in Egypt? Did Pharaoh really treat them so well?

But they're sure of it: Moses and Aaron have *brought us out into this desert to starve this entire community to death* (3b).

So they're grumbling. It looks like they've already forgotten what God did for them at Marah.

+ God intervenes (4-10). God promises Moses that *I will rain down bread from heaven for you* (4a). The word *bread* is probably being used here as a synonym for *food.*

And the people, says God, are to *go out each day and gather enough for that day* (4). This will be a test to see *whether they will follow my instructions* (4b; and see chapter 15:25b-26).

God now tells Moses that what the people do on the sixth day is to be different: they are to bring in *twice as much as they gather on the other days* (5).

Now Moses and Aaron pass on this information to the people: *In the evening you will know that it was the LORD who brought you out of Egypt* (6), and not just a historical accident. And *in the morning you will see the glory of the LORD* (7).

This matters because they've been *grumbling against him* (7).

Moses spells it out: God will give the people *meat to eat in the evening and all the bread you want in the morning* (8). And he warns them that *you are not grumbling against us, but against the LORD* (8b).

And now Moses urges Aaron to tell the whole community of Israel to *come before the LORD, for he has heard your grumbling* (9). While Aaron is still speaking, the people *looked towards the desert, and there was the glory of the LORD appearing in the cloud* (10).

This is the divine glory manifested. We're not told what this looked like or how the people were affected; but we know that this is Yahweh graciously revealing himself to the whole community.

2. The manna and the quail (11-30). So now we learn what this whole thing looked like in practice.

+ Every day (11-16). Moses is to tell the Israelites *At twilight you will eat meat, and in the morning you will be filled with bread* (11). This is not just so that they won't be hungry; it's so that the people will *know that I am the LORD your God* (11b).

In the evening, *quail came and covered the camp* (13a). Quail fly mostly at night, and after migration the birds are so exhausted that you can catch them with your bare hands.

In the morning *there was a layer of dew around the camp;* and, when the dew was gone, *thin flakes like frost on the ground appeared on the desert floor* (13b and 14).

The Israelites look at this and ask each other *What is it?* (15), which is why we learn later in the chapter that they call this bread *manna* (31a; the word sounds like the Hebrew for *What is it?*).

So this is what is to happen every day: everyone is *to gather as much as they need* (16). They are to *take an omer for each person you have in your tent* (16b; an omer is about 1.4 kilograms).

+ Six days (17-21). So this happens for six days. At first *the Israelites did as they were told* (17): using the omer measurement, they gathered *just as much as they needed* (18b).

Moses had said to the people that *no one is to keep any of it until morning* (19), but *some of them paid no attention to Moses* and *kept part of it until morning* (20a). But the following morning what they've kept is *full of maggots and began to smell* (20b).

The result is that Moses is *angry with them* (20b): they're failing the test and refusing to trust God (see 4, and chapter 15:25b-26).

+ The seventh day (22-30). On the sixth day the people gather *twice as much* (22), because Moses has told them that *tomorrow is to be a day of sabbath rest* (23). This is the first time the word *sabbath* appears in the Bible, but the Israelites know about the principle from the creation account (see Genesis 2:2-3).

This is a link between Section A' and Section A.

So at the end of the sixth day the people are saving food for the sabbath, and *it did not stink or get maggots in it* (24).

But despite all of this, some of the Israelites think that, when it comes to manna, they know better: they go out *on the seventh day to gather it, but they found none* (27).

So God, speaking to Moses as the covenant mediator, asks *How long will you refuse to keep my commands and my instructions?* (28). And he underlines the importance of the sabbath day: *Everyone is to stay where they are on the seventh day; no one is to go out* (29).

And so *the people rested on the seventh day* (30).

3. The conclusion (31-36). The chapter ends with a brief description of manna: it was *white like coriander seed and tasted like wafers made with honey* (31).

Moses listens to God's command to *take an omer of manna and keep it for the generations to come* (32): it's to teach future generations that God has provided for his people.

So Moses tells Aaron to *take a jar and put an omer of manna in it* (33a). In time this will be kept in the ark of the covenant (see Hebrews 9:4).

In all, *the Israelites ate manna for forty years,* in other words *until they reached the border of Canaan* (35).

We've seen how God's people have repeatedly disobeyed God's commands, but we've also seen God graciously providing for his people.

c'. – God provides the Israelites with water at Rephidim (17:1-7)

Step by step, the Israelites are moving southwards, towards Mount Sinai.

1. The people grumble (1-3). When they camp at Rephidim, they discover that there's *no water for the people to drink* (1). At Marah (see incident c) there was water, which just needed to be made drinkable; but at Rephidim there's no water at all.

So the Israelites *quarrelled with Moses,* and say *Give us water to drink* (2a). This is actually more than grumbling: they're picking a fight with him. Once again, they're deciding not to trust God.

In reply Moses asks the people two questions: *Why do you quarrel with me? Why do you put the LORD to the test?* (2b). God has been testing *them* (see chapter 16:4 and 15:25b-26), but now they are testing *him*.

2. God intervenes (4-7). Moses is at the end of his tether: he asks God *What am I to do with these people?* and adds that it feels like *they are almost ready to stone me* (4).

God tells Moses to do three things. First, he's to *go out* of the camp; second, he's to take *some of the elders of Israel* with him, presumably as witnesses; and third, he's to make sure to take *the staff with which you struck the Nile* (5).

That mention of the Nile is important. When Moses used his staff there, the Egyptians had been *deprived* of water (see chapter 7:21), but now, by that same staff, the Israelites will be *provided* with water.

Moses is to go to *the rock at Horeb* (6): is this a particular rock Moses is familiar with? *Horeb* is another name for Mount Sinai, but the people have not reached there yet (see chapter 19:1-2), so perhaps *Horeb* refers to a wider area than just the mountain.

God promises Moses that he *will stand there before you* (6): is the glory cloud going to come down on the rock? Then Moses is to *strike the rock, and water will come out of it for the people to drink* (6).

So *Moses did this in the sight of the elders of Israel* (6b).

There's no mention of the water coming out and and the Israelites being able to drink their fill, but of course that's what happens: it's an astonishing miracle.

And Moses calls the place *Massah and Meribah* (7). *Massah* means *testing*, and *Meribah* means *quarrelling*: in choosing to quarrel with Moses and therefore to not trust God, they have been putting God to the test (see 2b).

Will they learn a lesson from the two names given to the place?

b'. – Victory over the Amalekites at Rephidim (17:8-16)

This is the first battle against another nation since the Israelites left Egypt. Amalek was Esau's grandson (see Genesis 36:15-16): his descendants have become a people.

1. Preparing for battle (8-10). The Amalekites *came and attacked the Israelites at Rephidim* (8). This looks to be unprovoked: are they afraid that they might lose control of the region to these newcomers?

Moses knows what to do: he appoints Joshua as field commander and tells him to *choose some of our men* for the battle (9a). Moses, on the other hand, *will stand on top of the hill with the staff of God in my hands* (9b).

This is the first mention of Joshua in the Bible. Why does Moses decide to get him to lead the fight? One reason is, presumably, that Moses is eighty and so probably not in the best shape to head up a military attack.

A second reason is that his staff is a symbol of God's power in action: we saw that again and again in Section B'. All the Israelites have witnessed this in Egypt, at the Red Sea and when they were first at Rephidim (see chapter 17:6).

Because Moses is going to be standing *on top of the hill* (9), everyone fighting is going to be able to see Moses' staff, which is also *the staff of God* (9).

So that's the preparation done: *Joshua fought the Amalekites as Moses had ordered, and Moses, Aaron and Hur went to the top of the hill* (10).

2. Fighting the battle (11-13). When *Moses held up his hands, the Israelites were winning* (11a). But there's a problem: whenever he lowered his hands, *the Amalekites were winning* (11b).

There's no indication in the account that this has anything to do with prayer (though I'm sure that there was a lot of praying going on). Rather it's about the Israelites being able to see *the staff of God* (9).

When Moses is tired, Aaron and Hur sit him on a stone and *held his hands up* (12). This goes on for quite a few hours: *his hands remained steady till sunset* (12b).

The result is that Joshua *overcame the Amalekite army with the sword* (13). Well, he did and he didn't. The staff of God is the key: God has been acting in power to enable Israel to win the battle with the Amalekites.

There's no mention of anyone being killed here. The Amalekites have been disabled (13: *overcame* is literally *disabled*): when sunset came, did they give up and beat a retreat?

3. After the battle (14-16). When it's all over, Moses does two things.

+ First, he writes in the scroll (14). God tells him to write what's happened *on a scroll.* But the Hebrew says <u>the</u> *scroll*: this must be an existing document chronicling important events in Israel's history.

So Moses will write an account of the battle, and how it was won; he will also record Yahweh's promise to *blot out the name of Amalek from under heaven* (14). And he is to make sure *that Joshua hears it* (14).

But Moses does something else too.

+ Second, he builds an altar (15-16). Moses *built an altar and called it The LORD is my Banner* (15). The name of the altar suggests that it's for commemoration rather than sacrifice.

Yahweh's staff in Moses' hands on the hill was an object of hope for all the Israelites in the battle: it was like a banner to encourage everyone to trust in Yahweh and his power.

The altar is to remind Israel that *the LORD will be at war against the Amalekites from generation to generation* (16).

a'. – Conclusion: Arrival at Sinai (18:1 – 19:2)

Mount Sinai is sometimes described as Horeb, so in one sense the people of God have already reached their destination: Rephidim is at Horeb (see chapter 17:6). But, as we've already seen, it looks like Horeb is a wider area than just the mountain itself.

But before the Israelites arrive at the mountain, Moses has a significant encounter with his father-in-law.

1. Moses talks to Jethro (18:1-12). The last time we heard anything about Jethro, he was agreeing to Moses returning to Egypt (see chapter 4:18).

+ What Jethro does (1-6). Jethro comes to visit Moses: he sends word that he is *coming to you with your wife and her two sons* (6). The account tells us that Moses had at some point *sent away his wife Zipporah,* with *her two sons,* who are called *Gershom* and *Eliezer* (2-4).

Was this for reasons of safety, when it became clear to Moses that delivering the Israelites from Egypt would be fraught with danger?

Why does Jethro decide to come and visit Moses *where he was camped near the mountain of God*? (5). One reason may be that he's *heard of everything God had done for Moses and for his people Israel, and how the LORD had brought Israel out of Egypt* (1).

And he wants to hear more.

+ **What Jethro hears (7-8).** Moses is humble: he *went out to meet his father-in-law and bowed down and kissed him* (7a).

He must have greeted his wife and sons too, but the focus is on Jethro. Moses tells his father-in-law three things: first, about *everything the LORD had done to Pharaoh and the Egyptians for Israel's sake*; second, about *all the hardships they had met along the way*; and third, about *how the LORD had saved them* (8).

My guess is that this takes some time: Moses has a wonderful story to tell and Jethro is hungry to hear it. When we remember that Jethro is a Midianite, it looks to me like this is a gospel conversation: Moses is *declaring the praises of him who called* Israel *out of darkness* in Egypt *into his wonderful light* (see 1 Peter 2:9b).

And Moses isn't patting himself on the back: he's careful to give the glory to God. Twice in verse 8 he talks about what *the LORD* has done.

This is what Jethro hears.

+ **How Jethro reacts (9-12).** He is *delighted* (9): he says *Praise be to the LORD* (10), using the name Yahweh. God, he tells Moses, *rescued you from the hand of the Egyptians and of Pharaoh* (10).

And now comes something even more extraordinary: Jethro says that *I know that the LORD is greater than all other gods* (11). This is a Gentile acknowledging that the God of the Israelites is the saviour God and that there is none like him.

Jethro has experienced a conversion. We don't know if it's happened during his visit to Moses or if it had happened before, but this Midianite is certainly a believer in Yahweh.

One way Jethro expresses that is by bringing *a burnt offering and other sacrifices to God* (12a): his instinctive response is worship.

Now Aaron comes *with all the elders of Israel to eat a meal with Moses' father-in-law*. And this happens *in the presence of God* (12b).

2. Jethro talks to Moses (18:13-27). Now Jethro has something to say to Moses.

+ The problem he outlines (13-16). The next day *Moses took his seat to serve as judge for the people,* who *stood round him from morning till evening* (13).

So Jethro asks his son-in-law a question: *Why do you alone sit as judge, while all these people stand round you from morning till evening?* (14). Crowds of people are coming to Moses to get their cases heard: they need a decision.

But Moses is doing all this single-handedly, and the result is that the people spend hours waiting for their turn.

Moses replies that *the people come to me to seek God's will* (15): they do this *whenever they have a dispute* (16). And Moses' job is to *decide between the parties and inform them of God's decrees and instructions* (16).

It's almost like Moses doesn't see the problem.

+ The solution he suggests (17-23). Jethro doesn't mince his words: what Moses is doing is *not good* (17).

If they go on like this, Moses and the people *will only wear yourselves out* (18a). And Jethro is concerned for Moses: *The work is too heavy for you; you cannot handle it alone* (18b).

So it's not like Jethro thinks the work of judging doesn't matter; rather it's not being dealt with wisely. Jethro absolutely sees that Moses is *the people's representative before God,* and must *teach them his decrees and instructions* (19 and 20).

But, says Jethro to Moses, *I will give you some advice* (19).

Moses should appoint a team of judges. They are to be *capable men,* men who *fear God,* who are *trustworthy* and who *hate dishonest gain* (21). The judges will decide *the simple cases,* but *bring every difficult case to you* (22).

This solution makes sense, says Jethro, because *it will make your load lighter* (22b).

And this won't just benefit Moses: *If you do this and God so commands, you will be able to stand the strain, and all these people will go home satisfied* (23).

So Jethro has given Moses his advice. What will Moses do?

+ The reaction he gets (24-26). Moses decides to follow Jethro's advice. He chooses *capable men from all Israel and made them leaders of the people* (25): they serve *as judges for the people at all times* (26a).

Which means that Moses only needs to hear *the difficult cases* (26b).

This is an interesting situation. Before the battle with the Amalekites, Moses delegated leadership to Joshua (see chapter 17:9): this was probably because he knew that he was physically not able to do it.

But with the job of deciding cases and settling disputes among the Israelites, Moses may have thought, as he was mentally in good shape, that he should do this work on his own.

God has used Jethro to help Moses discover a better way.

3. Israel arrives at Mount Sinai (19:1-2). This crucial moment comes *on the first day of the third month after the Israelites left Egypt* (1): they *entered the Desert of Sinai* (2).

They've arrived at the place where Yahweh will give his covenant people his law: *Israel camped there in the desert in front of the mountain* (2).

So much has happened since God called the world into being. He has called Abraham, Isaac and Jacob and promised them that they will become a nation and receive a land: he's promised them, too, that all the nations will be blessed through them.

And if we are believers in Jesus, we are part of the fulfilment of the promises to the patriarchs. Our response should be like Jethro's: to worship.

Learning Genesis+

Section A' is easy to learn because it's short.

First, say the headings for incidents a, b, c and d out loud several times, until you can do it without looking at *The Genesis+ Experiment*. Then do the same with incidents c', b' and a'.

Then say the headings for the whole section out loud.

Knowing that a friend is also learning the order of the events will help you to commit yourself to doing it too. And using your fingers will be a help.

Now, as you say the incident headings, you'll get a surprise: all kinds of details will occur to you.

I hope you will give it a try. It's worth it!

Section A': Wilderness Journey

a.   Introduction: Departure from Egypt
b.   *Victory over the Egyptians at the Red Sea*
c.   God provides the Israelites with water at Marah
d.   CENTRE: God provides manna and quail
c'. God provides the Israelites with water at Rephidim
b'. *Victory over the Amalekites at Rephidim*
a'. Conclusion: Arrival at Sinai

Meeting God

It is absolutely worthwhile to run through this material in your head. Or you could meet up with a friend and do this together. And feel free to use the study questions in Appendix 3.

As you tell yourself the story of the victory at the Red Sea, you may find yourself stopping to worship God: he's *majestic in holiness, awesome in glory, working wonders* (see chapter 15:11). And as you see God providing food and water for his people in the wilderness, take time to thank him for the way he provides for you.

As you go through this material in your mind, or with a friend, you will be meeting God. And the Holy Spirit will be using his word to help you know him better.

My Conclusion:
The Experiment goes on

I hope you have used your time in *The Genesis+ Experiment* to learn the structure. You may have just read one or two of the sections, or you may have read all seven.

If you've read through the whole book, you have witnessed God creating the world and then re-creating it after the flood; you've seen him call Abraham and give him astonishing promises of a nation and a land; you've watched God protecting Isaac, Abraham's son, and giving him two sons of his own: Esau and Jacob.

You've seen him take Jacob, such unpromising material, and give him the new name of Israel: he is the father of what would become a nation; you've witnessed Joseph suffering greatly and being used by God to bring blessing to Egypt, to the surrounding nations and to his own family.

You've seen God call Moses to be the deliverer of Israel, and use him, through the events of the Passover, to bring his people out of slavery in Egypt; and you've watched God rescuing Israel from the Egyptians by bringing them through the Red Sea and then to Mount Sinai.

I hope you've been amazed by the wisdom, the love and the power of God.

But that process doesn't need to stop because you've reached the end of this book. I want to suggest a few ways in which you can keep using Genesis+ to get to know God better.

1. Using Genesis+ for worship and prayer

Take one section of Genesis+. As you begin to run through it in your mind (without your Bible), don't just remember the order of the events: talk to God about what he's doing in human history. Enjoy spending time with him. Worship him for his power and his love. And pray for yourself as you think your way through the section: after all, you are part of the fulfilment of the promises to Abraham.

You can do this at home in your room, or while you're sitting on the bus. You might decide to use Section A this way for a week; the following week you could move on to Section B.

Or you could just pick out one section and start there.

2. Using Genesis+ to help you pray for others

Sometimes you want to pray for a friend or for a member of your family, but you're not sure how. Why not take one section of Genesis+ and pray through it, praying the whole time for this special person?

With some incidents you will be praying that she will hear God's call and decide to trust him; sometimes you will be praying that she will be encouraged as she sees God working in awful situations to fulfil his purposes; sometimes you will pray that she will be moved by the love of God and by how he changes those who trust him.

Genesis+ can help you pray for others, whether these people are already Christians or not.

3. Using Genesis+ for a Genesis+ Walk

Go for a walk (without a Bible) with a friend who has learnt the same section(s) of Genesis+ as you have. Take turns to tell each other the incidents, including as many details as you can remember. This is not a competition: you can help one another as you re-tell Genesis+.

When you get home you might take some time to thank God and worship him together. (You might also want to turn to the Bible to remind yourselves of details neither of you could remember.)

The Genesis+ Walk works well with a group too. But however you do it, it's so healthy to be using Genesis+ to help you talk about God!

4. Using Genesis+ in a teaching programme

Your youth group or student group might decide to use the structure of Genesis+ in its term programme. At your first meeting you could look at Section A, at your second meeting Section B, and so on.

Different small groups could look at different parts of the section and then share with everyone what they've learnt. And some of the group might decide to learn the structure of the week's section for themselves, so that they can get to know God better.

This could work well, too, in a church's Sunday teaching programme. You could have two or three sermons on each of the seven sections.

5. Using Genesis+ in a home group

It is possible to study the whole of Genesis+, and to learn it too, in a home group context. There are suggested outlines for such a series in Appendix 3.

Finally…

Thank you for reading *The Genesis+ Experiment*.

Being a Christian is about much more than just believing a message: it's about trusting the God of the Bible, who sent his Son Jesus as a fulfilment of the promises to the patriarchs. The Holy Spirit is living inside every Christian, and he loves to use his word to *change* us.

The greatest commandment is that we love God with all our heart, our soul, our mind and our strength (see Deuteronomy 6:5 and Mark 12:30).

Please pray for yourself, and for others trying the Genesis+ experiment, that all of us will find ourselves loving God more.

As we do that, we'll bring glory to him and experience his joy.

Appendix 1:
Questions about Genesis+

Below are some of the questions I have most often been asked as I've been writing *The Genesis+ Experiment*. I can only comment briefly here: to learn more, please go to the commentaries. And, of course, I am still learning.

1. Who says Genesis+ has a structure at all?

I can't prove that it has, but it seems to me to make sense.

In a culture in which you couldn't print off copies of books, it strikes me that writing a book with a memorable structure is the obvious thing to do. It makes sense to believe that the people of God are to talk about what God has done in history: if they could learn the order of the events off by heart, that's exactly what they could do.

2. Who says this structure of Genesis+ is the right one?

There are lots of suggested structures of Genesis and of Exodus, and it's a brave Bible scholar who claims they have found *the* right one.

Professor David Dorsey was a Professor of Old Testament in the United States. He wasn't much interested in learnability, but he held that it was common in the ancient world to write with a clear structure.

So he wrote a book to suggest a structure, or sometimes multiple structures, for each Old Testament book. For me, one of the most convincing is the structure of Genesis 1:1 to Exodus 19:2.

If Dorsey's structure of what I call Genesis+ is not the correct one, that doesn't bother me. I am not using this structure to teach some weird and wonderful new doctrine: if you've read the book (or parts of it) you will see that what I have been trying to do is simply teach through the material.

But in such a way that you can commit it to memory.

I find Dorsey's book fascinating.

David A. Dorsey, *The Literary Structure of the Old Testament*, Baker Academic 1999 and 2004.

3. Why am I writing on Genesis 1:1 to Exodus 19:2?

Dorsey maintains that the first books of our Bible were not originally individual books, but were known together as, for example, the Book of Moses: indeed, Jesus uses just that expression in Mark 12:26.

Dorsey suggests that Exodus 19:3 through to Numbers 10:10 is God's great treaty with Israel: he gives his Law to his people. Everything before that is like a historical prologue: after a record of creation, the Fall and the flood, there's an account of his dealings with the patriarchs, leading to the creation of the nation of Israel.

This prologue, according to Dorsey, has been divided into seven literary units; each unit has its own structure and its own focus.

Because the structure of the whole is so learnable (see above), I decided to write a book teaching through the whole of this historical prologue, from Genesis 1:1 to Exodus 19:2.

And I called it *The Genesis+ Experiment.*

4. Which is my favourite commentary on Genesis+?

I have learnt from many commentaries on Genesis and Exodus.

On Genesis I have studied works by Kidner and by Hughes. Bruce Waltke's commentary is the only one I've discovered that even acknowledges the existence of David Dorsey's book (see Question 2, above). Richard Belcher's commentary was very helpful, and contains a quite brilliant introduction to Genesis.

But the Genesis commentary I am most impressed by and have used most is IVP's Tyndale Old Testament Commentary by Andrew Steinmann. Of course we will all find different books on Genesis helpful, but for my money this one wins easily. (An added bonus is that, from chapter 12 onwards, Steinmann estimates *the date* of every incident.)

Andrew E. Steinmann, *Genesis: An Introduction and Commentary*, Inter-Varsity Press 2019.

On Exodus I have profited from works by Harman and by Cole. But the one I have used most is by John Currid: it's thorough and it's clear.

John D. Currid, *A Study Commentary on Exodus* (Volume 1: Chapters 1-18), Evangelical Press 2000.

Appendix 2:
The Section Mirror Links in Genesis+

The seven sections in Genesis+ have the following titles:

Section A	Primeval History	Genesis 1:1 – 11:32
Section B	*The Abraham Story*	*Genesis 12:1 – 21:7*
Section C	The Isaac Story	Genesis 21:8 – 28:4
Section D	*The Jacob Story*	*Genesis 28:5 – 37:1*
Section C'	The Joseph Story	Genesis 37:2 – 50:26
Section B'	*The Exodus Story*	*Exodus 1:1 – 13:16*
Section A'	Wilderness Journey	Exodus 13:17 – 19:2

You will notice that there are mirror links between the sections, in other words between Section A and Section A', between Section B and Section B', and between Section C and Section C'.

Section D, which records the birth of the nation through the sons of Jacob, is, for obvious reasons, the central section.

Dorsey's book (see Appendix 1, Question 2) points to a number of mirror links between the sections. Here are a few of them:

Section A and Section A'
1. The creation story and the Red Sea story have a number of things in common:
+ both demonstrate Yahweh's power over the sea;
+ both stories begin with the wind of God (see Gen 1:2 and Ex 14:21);
+ in both stories God divides the waters (see Gen 1:6-8 and Ex 14:22);
+ in both God creates dry land in the midst of the sea (see Gen 1:9-10 and
    Ex 14:16 and 22).

2. The Sabbath occurs only in these two sections (see Gen 2:1-3 and
    Ex 16:21-30).

Section B and Section B'
1. There are a number of links between the exodus story and the account of Abraham leaving Egypt (see Gen 12:10-20):
+ Abram, like Israel, travels from Canaan to Egypt because of a famine;
+ God brings great plagues on Pharaoh's house so that Sarai will be released (see Gen 12:17, the Hebrew has *great plagues*);
+ Pharaoh summons Abram in order to get relief from the plagues (see Gen 12:17-18). In the Exodus story, Pharaoh keeps summoning Moses;

+ Pharaoh tells Abram to *Go!* (see Gen 12:19). A later Pharaoh says exactly the same thing to Moses: *Go!* (see Ex 8:25; 10:8 and 24);
+ Abram is made richer by the Egyptians (see Gen 12:16, 13:2), as are the Israelites as they leave Egypt (see Ex 12:35-36).

2. God tells Abram *Know for certain that for four hundred years your descendants will be strangers in a country not their own, and that they will be enslaved and ill-treated there. But I will punish the nation they serve as slaves, and afterwards they will come out with great possessions* (Genesis 15:13-14). This is all fulfilled in the Exodus story.

3. Central to the Abraham account is God's promise to make Abraham into *a great nation* (Gen 12:2; see also 13:16 and 15:5). The Exodus story begins and ends with the fulfilment of that promise (see Ex 1:7 and 12:37).

4. Both sections mention circumcision (but none of the other sections does): see Gen 17:10-14 and Ex 4:24-26.

Section C and Section C'

1. The Isaac story and the Joseph story are both dominated by strife between older and younger brothers. And in each case God chooses the younger brother (Jacob, not Esau; Joseph, not his older brothers).

2. Both sections feature stories about a father's deep love for his son (Abraham's for Isaac; Isaac's for Esau; Jacob's for Joseph).

3. In both sections the patriarchal blessing is important. And the greater blessing goes to the younger son (Jacob, not Esau; Joseph, not Judah; Ephraim, not Manasseh).

4. Both sections feature burials in the cave of Machpelah in Hebron (see Gen 23:19 and 25:8-9; and Gen 50:12-13).

Appendix 3:
Genesis+ in a Small Group

The following series of studies has 7 sessions and is designed for group use; but of course you could also use these questions for your own study or one-to-one with a friend.

These questions are designed for people who have already read the relevant section in *The Genesis+ Experiment*. In a home group everyone will have to read the evening's section before coming to the meeting.

And, of course, a group might decide, at first, just to study one section, rather than all seven.

It is up to you whether you combine answering the questions with learning the order of the events!

Seven Weeks in Genesis+

Week One
Section A: Primeval History
Genesis 1:1 – 11:32

Look at chapter 1:1 – 2:3

1. What does this chapter tell us about God? Can we make a list of words to describe him?

2. How does the account make clear that the creation of humankind is special? How might we sum up what God is calling human beings to be?

Look at chapter 2:4 – 4:26

3. Why is there such a contrast between chapter 2 and chapter 3? In the account of the Fall in chapter 3, where do we see God punishing and where do we see him acting in grace?

4. In chapter 3 verse 15 God promises to send a saviour one day. How do we know that this is talking about Jesus? And how do we react to this?

Look at chapter 6:9 – 9:29

5. Where does the account explain why God decided to flood the earth? And why do we think he decided to save Noah and his family?

6. After the flood God makes a covenant with Noah. What promises does Noah receive?

Look at chapter 10:1 – 11:9

7. What was wrong with humankind's decision to build a tower? Why did God decide to intervene? And where do we see the results of that today?

8. As we look back on the first eleven chapters of Genesis, what does each of us find most striking? Why?

Do any of us know the order of the events in Section A? Or would any of us like to?

Week Two
Section B: The Abraham Story
             Genesis 12:1 – 21:7

Look at chapter 12:1 – 14:24

1. What is there to show that the call of Abram is all God's initiative? Why does this matter? What are the main promises to Abram, and which do we think is the most important?

2. What are Abram's strengths in these three chapters, and what are his weaknesses? And why do we think he sometimes builds an altar?

Look at chapter 15:1 – 18:15

3. How does God make a covenant with Abraham in chapters 15 and 17? Is God repeating promises already made, or are they more specific? Are there some which stand out to us?

4. Can we make a list of what God does in these chapters to help Abraham and Sarah to believe the promises?

Look at chapter 18:16 – 21:7

5. What does the destruction of Sodom and Gomorrah tell us about God? In what ways do we see God acting in grace here? And do we think God wouldn't have done this if Abraham hadn't interceded for Lot and for Sodom?

6. What does the story of Abraham calling Sarah his sister in Gerar show us about him? Is God just a spectator in this incident? In what ways is he actively at work here?

Let's look at the whole of Section A

7. What do we think are the three most important things that happen to Abraham in this section? In what ways is Abraham like us?

8. Let's take a few minutes for each of us to choose one part of the Abraham story which we find particularly important. And then let's share our answers.

Do any of us know the order of the events in Section B? Or would any of us like to?

Week Three
Section C: The Isaac Story
               Genesis 21:8 – 28:4

Look at chapter 21:8 – 22:19

1. Let's focus on Abraham's sacrifice of Isaac (22:1-19). What does this incident tell us about God? And about Abraham? And why do we think God chooses to repeat the promises in verses 15-18?

2. How many links can we see between this incident and God the Father's sacrifice of his Son Jesus? What does this tell us about God?

Look at chapter 22:20 – 25:18

3. Why do we think the account gives so much space to the finding of Rebekah as a wife for Isaac? What's so important about it? And what does the account emphasize?

4. Abraham's death is recorded in chapter 25:8. How might we sum up his life? What would we say are the four highlights of his life?

Look at chapter 25:19 – 28:4

5. Let's look at chapter 25:21-34. How might we describe Rebekah's relationship with God? And can we find one word that sums up Jacob, and one that sums up Esau? Why do we think God decides to work with this messed-up family?

6. Let's look at chapter 27. Why do we think the account is so long: is it just because it's a great story? What are we meant to learn from it?

7. Looking at the whole of Section C, what kind of a man do we think Isaac is? What are his strengths and his weaknesses?

8. Let's each of us choose one incident from the section that impacts us the most. Then let's share our answers and explain our decision.

Do any of us know the order of the events in Section C? Or would any of us like to?

Week Four
## Section D:	The Jacob Story and the Birth of the Nation
Genesis 28:5 – 37:1

Look at chapter 28:5-22

1. In his dream at Bethel Jacob sees something and hears something. Which is more important? Why would one without the other be incomplete? What does God want to communicate to Jacob, and how does he want to change him?

2. What do we make of Jacob's vow after his dream? Is this a new Jacob, or still the old one?

Look at chapter 29:1 – 32:32

3. What does Jacob's willingness to work fourteen years for Laban in order to be able to marry Rachel tell us about him? How does this change him?

4. In these four chapters, do we think Jacob is trusting God or his own scheming? Are we sorry for Jacob, or do we admire him?

5. What do we make of the account of Jacob wrestling (see chapter 32:22-32)? How do we know he's wrestling with God? Who wins? In what way does this experience change Jacob for the better?

Look at chapter 33:1 – 34:31

6. What steps does Jacob take before meeting Esau again? Is he just wanting to avoid danger, or is he wanting reconciliation? How could we describe him here?

7. Why is the story of the massacre at Shechem important? Does Jacob react in the right way?

Look at chapter 35:1 – 37:1

8. Why do we think God gives Jacob a new name? Does it say something about who Jacob is or about what he's going to become? What impact do we think God's promises to him in chapter 35:11-13 have on Jacob?

Do any of us know the order of the events in Section D? Or would any of us like to?

Week Five
Section C': The Joseph Story
Genesis 37:2 – 50:26

Look at chapter 37:2 – 39:23

1. How might we describe Joseph in the first half of chapter 37? Does he deserve what he gets in the second half of the chapter?

2. Why is Judah's story in chapter 38 important? Why do we think he and Joseph deal so differently with sexual temptation? How might we describe Joseph in chapter 39?

Look at chapter 40:1 – 44:3

3. Why do we think Joseph doesn't give up on God when he's left in prison for another two years because the chief cupbearer has forgotten him?

4. Joseph doesn't just interpret Pharaoh's dreams: he explains what action Pharaoh needs to take. What does this tell us about Joseph?

5. Why do we think Joseph doesn't reveal his identity to his brothers as soon as he meets them? And why is he insistent on seeing Benjamin?

Look at chapter 44:4 – 47:12

6. What is there here that shows that Joseph's brothers realise that God is at work in their lives? And why is Judah's offer to become Joseph's slave so powerful?

Look at chapter 47:13 – 50:26

7. What do we think are the most significant parts of Jacob's blessings on his sons? And why does it matter where Jacob, and then Joseph, are going to be buried?

8. How might we describe God, having read Section C' and especially chapter 45:5-8 and chapter 50:20?

Do any of us know the order of the events in Section C'? Or would any of us like to?

Week Six
Section B': The Exodus Story
Exodus 1:1 – 13:16

Look at chapter 1:1 – 4:17

1. What form did Pharaoh's oppression of the Israelites take? And what is there in the first half of chapter 2 to show that God has something special in mind for Moses?

2. What are the main reasons Moses has to leave Egypt? How does this fit into God's plan for him?

3. What does Moses learn about God from his first contact with him at the burning bush? Which of his questions is the most important? And why do we think God bothers to deal with Moses' excuses?

Look at chapter 4:18 – 7:13

4. Do we think Moses expected Pharaoh to agree immediately to let the Israelites leave Egypt? What promises does God repeat to Moses?

5. How do we feel about God hardening Pharaoh's heart? Do we think this is unfair? Does it make Pharaoh less guilty than he otherwise would be?

Look at chapter 7:14 – 10:29

6. Which of these nine plagues strikes us as being the hardest for the Egyptians to experience? What is God's purpose in sending them all? Is it simply about the Israelites being released from their slavery in Egypt?

Look at chapter 11:1 – 13:16

7. What are some of the things the Israelites must be careful to do at the Passover? Why do they matter? What's the significance of the blood on the doorposts and the lintel?

8. In what ways do the events of the Passover show that God is both just and gracious? And why do we think it's important that Israel should always remember these events through all the generations?

9. What links are there between the Passover lambs and Jesus? What do we learn about God from the Passover and from the Cross?

Do any of us know the order of the events in Section B'? Or would any of us like to?

Week Seven
Section A': Wilderness Journey
Exodus 13:17 – 19:2

Look at chapter 13:17 – 15:21

1. How does the Israelites' rescue at the Red Sea show them that God is totally committed to them? Is it unfair of God to drown the Egyptian soldiers?

Look at chapter 15:22 – 17:7

2. What's the difference between God providing water for the Israelites at Marah and his doing the same thing at Rephidim? How might we describe the Israelites? Are we surprised that they're like this?

3. Why do we think God provides manna and quail for his people? What's the evidence here that they are not fully committed to following him?

Look at chapter 17:8 – 19:2

4. Why do we think the Israelites were winning the battle against the Amalekites when Moses' staff was in the air? What was it reminding God's people of?

5. What evidence is there here that Jethro is fully trusting Yahweh? How do we think he's helped by hearing Moses talk about everything God has done for the Israelites?

6. How does Moses learn from Jethro? Why do we think Moses needed someone to help him see things more clearly? And why is it so important that God's people arrive at Mount Sinai? What's going to happen to them there?

Let's look back at the whole of Genesis 1:1 – Exodus 19:2

7. Let's each think for one minute about which of the seven sections of Genesis+ is our favourite. Then let's share with each other and explain our reasons.

8. Let's each think for one minute about which one incident in the whole of Genesis+ is our favourite. Then let's share with each other and explain our reasons.

Do any of us know the order of the events in Section A'? Or would any of us like to?

Appendix 4:
The Structure of Genesis+

Section A: Primeval History
Genesis 1:1 – 11:32

a. Creation (1:1 – 2:3)
b. *Degeneration* (2:4 – 4:26)
c. Ten generations from Adam to Noah (5:1 – 6:8)

a'. The flood (6:9 – 9:29)
b'. *Degeneration* (10:1 – 11:9)
c'. Ten generations from Shem to Abram (11:10-26)

d. Conclusion: Introducing Abram (11:27-32)

Section B: The Abraham Story
Genesis 12:1 – 21:7

a. Introduction: the promise of descendants (12:1-9)
b. *Abram lies about Sarai in Egypt* (12:10-20)
c. Lot settles in Sodom (13:1-18)
d. *Abram intercedes for Lot and Sodom militarily* (14:1-24)
e. Promise of a son: from Abram himself (15:1-21)
f. *Ishmael: his birth* (16:1-16)
g. CENTRE: God's covenant with Abram/Abraham (17:1-22)
f'. *Ishmael: his circumcision* (17:23-27)
e'. Promise of a son: from Sarah herself (18:1-15)
d'. *Abraham intercedes for Lot and Sodom in prayer* (18:16-33)
c'. Lot flees Sodom, which God destroys (19:1-38)
b'. *Abraham lies about Sarah in Gerar* (20:1-18)
a'. Conclusion: the birth of Isaac (21:1-7)

Section C: The Isaac Story
Genesis 21:8 – 28:4

a.   God chooses the younger son: Isaac (21:8-19)
b.   *Marriage of nonchosen older son: Ishmael* (21:20-21)
c.   Strife with Abimelek of Gerar over Abraham's wells (21:22-34)
d.   *Abraham's sacrifice of Isaac* (22:1-19)
e.   Nonchosen genealogy: the family of Nahor (22:20-24)
f.   *The death of Sarah* (23:1-20)
g.   CENTRE: God chooses Rebekah as Isaac's wife (24:1-67)
f'.   *The death of Abraham* (25:1-11)
e'.   Nonchosen genealogy: the family of Ishmael (25:12-18)
d'.   *Esau's sacrifice of his birthright* (25:19-34)
c'.   Strife with Abimelek of Gerar over Abraham's wells (26:1-33)
b'.   *Marriage of nonchosen older son: Esau* (26:34-35)
a'.   God chooses the younger son: Jacob (27:1 – 28:4)

Section D: The Jacob Story
and the Birth of the Nation
Genesis 28:5 – 37:1

a.   Jacob's exile begins (28:5)
b.   *Esau's family* (28:6-9)
c.   Stop at Bethel (28:10-22)
d.   *Departure from Canaan and arrival in Paddan Aram* (29:1-30)
e.   Jacob's family becomes large (29:31 – 30:24)
f.   *Jacob keeps scheming* (30:25-43)
g.   CENTRE: Jacob escapes and departs for home (31:1-55)
f'.   *Jacob stops scheming* (32:1-32)
e'.   Jacob introduces his large family to Esau (33:1-17)
d'.   *Arrival back in Canaan from Paddan Aram* (33:18 – 34:31)
c'.   Stop at Bethel (35:1-29)
b'.   *Esau's family* (36:1-43)
a'.   Jacob's exile ends (37:1)

Section C': The Joseph Story
Genesis 37:2 – 50:26

a.   Trouble between Joseph and his brothers (37:2-11)
a'. More trouble between Joseph and his brothers (37:12-36)
b.   *Sexual temptation involving Judah* (38:1-30)
b'. *Sexual temptation involving Joseph* (39:1-23)
c.   Joseph interprets two dreams for fellow-prisoners (40:1-23)
c'. Joseph interprets two dreams for Pharaoh (41:1-57)
d.   *Joseph's brothers come to Egypt for food* (42:1-38)
d'. *Joseph's brothers again come to Egypt for food* (43:1 – 44:3)
e.   Joseph has some of his family come to Egypt (44:4 – 45:15)
e'. Joseph has all of his family come to Egypt (45:16 – 47:12)
f.   *Prospering in Egypt: Joseph's ascendancy* (47:13-26)
f'. *Prospering in Egypt: Blessings for Jacob's sons* (47:27 – 49:32)
g.   Death of a patriarch: Jacob (49:33 – 50:14)
g'. Death of a patriarch: Joseph (50:15-26)

Section B': The Exodus Story
Exodus 1:1 – 13:16

a.   Oppression by a Pharaoh who never knew Joseph (1:1-22)
b.   *Moses comes to Pharaoh's house as a baby* (2:1-10)
c.   Moses departs from Egypt (2:11-25)
d.   **CENTRE: The call of Moses (3:1 – 4:17)**
c'. Moses returns to Egypt (4:18-31)
b'. *Moses comes to Pharaoh's house as an adult* (5:1-5)
a'. Worse oppression by a Pharaoh who never knew Joseph (5:6 – 6:12)

Narrative break: The family record of Moses and Aaron (6:13-27)

a.   God promises to rescue his people from Egypt (6:28 – 7:7)
b.   *God's power to create life* (7:8-13)
c.   Opening cycle of three plagues (7:14 – 8:19)
d.   **CENTRE: Central cycle of three plagues (8:20 – 9:12)**
c'. Closing cycle of three plagues (9:13 – 10:29)
b'. *God's power to terminate life* (11:1-10)
a'. God rescues his people from Egypt (12:1 – 13:16)

Section A': Wilderness Journey
Exodus 13:17 – 19:2

a. Introduction: Departure from Egypt (13:17-22)
b. *Victory over the Egyptians at the Red Sea* (14:1 – 15:21)
c. God provides the Israelites with water at Marah (15:22-27)
d. CENTRE: God provides manna and quail (16:1-36)
c'. God provides the Israelites with water at Rephidim (17:1-7)
b'. *Victory over the Amalekites at Rephidim* (17:8-16)
a'. Conclusion: Arrival at Sinai (18:1 – 19:2)

Books by Andrew Page

The Matthew Experiment

How Matthew's Gospel can help you know Jesus better

Are you looking for a new way of getting to know Jesus better?

A great place to start is to get into one of the four Gospels. This book is designed to help us to do just that. After writing books about Mark's Gospel and about John's Gospel, Andrew Page has now turned his attention to the Gospel of Matthew.

The Matthew Experiment is two things. First, it's a basic commentary: Andrew unpacks the message of Matthew by teaching through the Gospel from beginning to end. And second, it's an invitation: the book explains how readers can learn the order of the incidents in Matthew, and so try the experiment of using what they have learnt to help them meditate their way through the Gospel. This stems from Andrew's conviction that Matthew wrote not only to give us information about Jesus, but also to help us to meet him.

Would you like to give it a try? If your answer is Yes, The Matthew Experiment is the book for you.

Pb. • 184 pp. • £10.00 / US$16.00 / €13.00 / CHF 16.00
ISBN 978-3-95776-069-2

The Mark Experiment

How Mark's Gospel can help you know Jesus better

If you are looking for a new way into Mark's Gospel and you long to allow the Gospel to help you worship and experience Jesus, The Mark Experiment is the book for you.

In The Mark Experiment Andrew Page shows you how to commit the Gospel to memory and explains how learning to meditate on the Gospel events has transformed his relationship with Jesus. Think what this might mean for your understanding of the life and ministry of Jesus.

One exciting result of this book has been the development of an innovative drama in which a team of 15 Christians from a church or student group acts out every incident in the Gospel of Mark as theatre-in-the-round. The Mark Drama is now being performed in many countries around Europe. ⇨ https://themarkdrama.com

Available in English, German, Dutch, French, Italian, Spanish, Hungarian, Swedish, and Swahili.

Pb. • 106 pp. • £8.00 / US$13.95 / €9.50 / CHF 12.80
ISBN 978-3-937965-21-5 (English)

The Luke Experiment

How Luke's Gospel can help you know Jesus better

Luke's Gospel is many people's favourite: they love the unfolding of the Christmas story; they are moved by the parable of the lost son and they enjoy the account of the two disciples meeting the risen Jesus on the road to Emmaus. And in his introduction, Luke tells us that he has written an orderly account.

So after writing books about Matthew's Gospel, Mark's Gospel and John's Gospel, Andrew Page has now turned his attention to the Gospel of Luke.

The Luke Experiment is two things. First, it's a basic commentary: Andrew unpacks the message of Luke by teaching through the Gospel from beginning to end. And second, it's an invitation: the book explains how readers can learn the order of the incidents in Luke, and so try the experiment of using what they have learnt to help them meditate their way through the Gospel. This stems from Andrew's conviction that Luke wrote not only to give us information about Jesus, but also to help us to meet him.

Would you like to give it a try? If your answer is Yes, The Luke Experiment is the book for you.

Pb. • 200 pp. • £11.00 / US$18.00 / €14.00 / CHF 17.00
ISBN 978-3-95776-146-0

The John Experiment

How John's Gospel can help you know Jesus better

Are you looking for a new way into the Gospels? Whether you have been a Christian for many years or are just considering the Christian faith, John's Gospel is a great place to start.

In The John Experiment Andrew Page unpacks John's Gospel and shows you how to commit it to memory. He explains how learning to meditate on the Gospel events is transforming his relationship with Jesus.

Would you like to give it a go? If your answer is Yes, then The John Experiment is the book for you.

Pb. • 146 pp. • £9.50 / US$15.00 / €12.00 / CHF 15.00
ISBN 978-3-95776-070-8

The Acts Experiment

How the Book of Acts can help you follow Jesus better

Many people find the book of Acts to be the most exciting of the whole New Testament. The reason is obvious: it tells the story of how the Holy Spirit equipped the apostles and all the believers to tell the world about Jesus.

So, after writing books about the four Gospels, Andrew Page has now turned his attention to the book of Acts.

The Acts Experiment is two things. First, it's a basic commentary: Andrew unpacks the message of Acts by teaching through the whole book from beginning to end. And second, it's an invitation. Using the markers Luke has written into his book, Andrew explains how readers can learn the order of the incidents in Acts, and so try the experiment of using what they have learnt to help them meditate their way through the book.

Would you like to give it a try? If your answer is Yes, The Acts Experiment is the book for you.

Pb. • 165 pp. • £10.00 / US$16.00 / €12.50 / CHF 15.00
ISBN 978-3-95776-147-7

How to Teach the Bible
so that People Meet God

This is unashamedly a how-to book. Andrew has trained others in this method of teaching a Bible passage in a number of countries around Europe, and now for the first time the method is available as a book.

So, 3 questions before you buy this book:

● Do you want to find out if God has given you the gift of teaching?

● Do you want to grow in the gift you believe you have?

● Do you want to help a friend to develop as a Bible teacher?

If you have said Yes to any of these questions, How to Teach the Bible so that People Meet God is a great place to start.

Pb. • 64 pp. • £7.50 / US$11.75 / €9.95 / CHF 12.50
ISBN 978-3-95776-035-7 (English)
ISBN 978-3-95776-038-8 (German)

How to Lead Group Bible Study
so that People Meet God

Are you part of a Christian small group? Does your church or CU offer training to those who lead group Bible study? Do you know people who want help in how to prepare and lead group Bible study? If you are looking for practical training in this area, How to Lead Group Bible Study so that People Meet God is the book for you. Andrew Page believes that small group Bible study can be a supernatural event.

So, 3 questions before you buy this book:

● Do you want to start leading group Bible study?

● If you already lead group Bible study, do you want to do it better?

● Do you want to help others to learn to lead group Bible study?

If you have said Yes to any of these questions, How to Lead Group Bible Study so that People Meet God is a great place to start.

Pb. • 62 pp. • £7.50 / US$11.75 / €9.50 / CHF 12.00
ISBN 978-3-95776-130-9 (English)
ISBN 978-3-95776-140-8 (German)

Read Mark in 30 Days

The Christian message claims that God came into our world in a man called Jesus.

But is it true?

Many people who ask that question have never read any of the source documents: they are the four Gospels in the New Testament. All of them were written in the first century.

If you're an honest sceptic, or just wanting to know more about Jesus, reading Mark's Gospel is a great place to start.

In Read Mark in 30 Days Andrew Page suggests a passage in Mark to read for each day, adding a few comments of his own, designed to help us understand Mark's message.

After 30 days you'll have read through the whole Gospel. And be in a much better position to answer the question Is it true?

Pb. • 34 pp. • £5.00 / US$7.50 / €5.00 / CHF 6.00
ISBN 978-3-95776-098-2 (English)
ISBN 978-3-95776-141-5 (German)

The 5 Habits of Deeply Contented People

Have you found contentment? Most people are looking for it. If you're not, it may be because you've given up…

If you are searching or want to start your search again, The 5 Habits of Deeply Contented People is the book for you.

The Bible says that everyone is made in God's image. Andrew Page says there are 5 habits which express that image of God in us. He says "If we can work out what these habits mean in practice for us as individuals, we will experience a deeper level of contentment."

Basing what he writes on the second chapter of the Bible, and making clear that these habits work even if we don't believe in God, Andrew invites his readers to try out the habits for themselves.

● Do you want to be more contented, whatever life throws at you?

● Are you curious to know what it means to be made in God's image?

● Would you like to find out if the 5 habits work?

If you have said Yes to any of these questions, The 5 Habits of Deeply Contented People is a great place to start.

Pb. • 57 pp. • £7.00 / US$11.00 / €8.00 € / CHF 10.00
ISBN 978-3-95776-009-8 (English)
ISBN 978-3-95776-008-1 (German)

VTR Publications • Gogolstr. 33 • 90475 Nürnberg • Germany
http://www.vtr-online.com